Using
the Asus
Eee PC

Bill Lawrence

 800 East 96th Street
Indianapolis, Indiana 46240

Using the Asus Eee PC

Copyright © 2009 by Que Publishing

ISBN-13: 978-0-7897-3810-3
ISBN-10: 0-7897-3810-4

Library of Congress Cataloging-in-Publication Data

Lawrence, Bill, 1953-
  Using the Asus Eee PC / Bill Lawrence. -- 1st ed.
    p. cm.
  ISBN 978-0-7897-3810-3
  1. Asus Eee PC (Computer) 2. Laptop computers. I. Title.
  QA76.8.A757L39 2008
  004.16--dc22

                                        2008034194

Printed in the United States of America
First Printing: September 2008

Trademarks

Warning and Disclaimer

Bulk Sales

Que Publishing offers excellent discounts on this book when ordered in quantity for bulk purchases or special sales. For more information, please contact

U.S. Corporate and Government Sales
1-800-382-3419
corpsales@pearsontechgroup.com

For sales outside of the U.S., please contact

International Sales
international@pearson.com

Associate Publisher
Greg Wiegand

Acquisitions Editor
Rick Kughen

Development Editor
Kevin Howard

Managing Editor
Patrick Kanouse

Senior Project Editor
San Dee Phillips

Copy Editor
Bill McManus

Indexer
Brad Herriman

Proofreader
Sheri Cain

Technical Editors
Kenneth D. Holt
Marco Chiapetta

Publishing Coordinator
Cindy Teeters

Cover and Interior Designer
Anne Jones

Composition
TnT Design, Inc.

Table of Contents

vi   **Using the Asus Eee PC**

8   Getting More Linux Applications 159

Using a Package Manager 160

Using the Easy Mode Package Manager 161

Using the Synaptic Package Manager and the apt-get Command 161

Picking Repositories That Work with the Eee PC 162

Using the Synaptic Package Manager 163

Loading Repositories 163

Finding and Loading Packages 165

Using the apt-get Command-Line Package Manager 169

Adding Packages to the KDE Menu 172

Finding a Newly Installed Application with Synaptic 173

Finding a Newly Installed Application with the which Command 173

Finding Instructions for Applications That You've Installed 174

Adding a Package to the Launch Menu 175

Installing Software the Old-Fashioned Way 177

Managing Installed Packages 179

Summary 180

9   Must-Have Utilities 181

GIMP 182

Inkscape 183

VLC Media Player 185

Tor and Privoxy 186

KompoZer 188

BitTornado 189

K3b 190

Stuff That Doesn't Work Under Xandros 192

TrueCrypt 192

Scribus 193

Summary 193

10   Introducing Google Applications 195

Setting Up an iGoogle Account 196

Setting Up Your iGoogle Home Page 198

Using Gmail as a File System 202

Installing Gspace 202

Setting Up Gspace 202

Using Gspace 203

Combining Google Docs and OpenOffice.org 204

Reasons to Use Google Docs with Open Office 206

Setting Up Google Docs 207

Working with the Google Docs File System 207

Working with Documents in Google Docs 208

Working with Presentations 209

Working with Spreadsheets 211

About the Author

Bill Lawrence is a writer, illustrator, graphic designer, and web designer with more than 30 years of experience in the field. His most recent works include *Setting Up Google Apps Standard Edition* and, as co-author, *Google in Education*. Previous works include *The Complete Desktop Publisher* (co-author), *The GEM Desktop Publisher*, and *DR. DOS 6.0 by Example*. Bill has written dozens of technical manuals and help systems, designed full-color magazine ads, authored courseware, created press releases, designed sales collateral, and created hundreds of illustrations. He's currently working as senior software engineer for Eaton Corporation. Bill is well versed in Linux and UNIX, and has been an open source evangelist for years. Bill's books, magazine articles, and technical publications have won nine regional and one international award from the Society for Technical Communication (STC). Bill has also been a speaker at meetings and conferences for STC and the International Association of Business Communicators (IABC).

Dedication

To my darling wife, Kathy. Without your help, encouragement, and patience, this would have never been possible. You are the love of my life.

To Andrew and Stephanie, who pitched in and helped while dad was pounding away on the keyboard. Thanks so much!

To Sarah, Garett, Zane, and Kira. Thanks for being so patient with "Pappy" while I wrote this.

We Want to Hear from You!

As the reader of this book, *you* are our most important critic and commentator. We value your opinion and want to know what we're doing right, what we could do better, what areas you'd like to see us publish in, and any other words of wisdom you're willing to pass our way.

As an associate publisher for Que Publishing, I welcome your comments. You can email or write me directly to let me know what you did or didn't like about this book—as well as what we can do to make our books better.

Please note that I cannot help you with technical problems related to the topic of this book. We do have a User Services group, however, where I will forward specific technical questions related to the book.

When you write, please be sure to include this book's title and author as well as your name, email address, and phone number. I will carefully review your comments and share them with the author and editors who worked on the book.

Email: feedback@quepublishing.com

Mail: Greg Wiegand
Associate Publisher
Que Publishing
800 East 96th Street
Indianapolis, IN 46240 USA

Reader Services

Visit our website and register this book at informit.com/register for convenient access to any updates, downloads, or errata that might be available for this book.

Introduction

The Asus Eee PC ultra-portable computer is more than just a capable little machine—it's a phenomenon. The Eee PC not only started the movement toward inexpensive, accessible computers, it spawned a cult following, similar to the Ford Model T in its day. Eee PC owners, devotees, and hackers have run practically every operating system, window manager, and software application imaginable on these little machines. Others have modified the hardware, adding components that Asus does not provide.

The Eee PC is a step toward selling the "next billion computers." It was partly born out of the desire to create a real, tangible, commercial offering in the spirit of the One Laptop Per Child project. It was designed to be extremely easy to use and portable. Much of Asus's early focus was to make the Eee PC an ideal, inexpensive computer for schoolchildren around the world. It's wildly popular in both developed and developing countries, and has found niche markets that Asus likely never imagined.

This book is an odyssey through the possibilities of the Eee PC. It starts out with an introduction to the machine and then covers how to connect it to the Internet. Next, you'll learn how to customize Easy Mode (and why there's nothing easy about customizing it). From there, you'll discover how to acccess the hidden KDE desktop (Full Desktop) built into the Eee PC.

The following few chapters cover Xandros Linux in detail, including how to customize and change the window manager. You'll learn how to use the various package managers to find and install hundreds of free programs for your Eee PC. You'll also find recommendations for the best software to install on your Eee PC. Finally, this section of the book finishes with a quick-and-painless introduction to the Linux command line.

Next, you'll learn about the various operating system options for your Eee PC, including several alternative Linux distributions, Sun OpenSolaris (a true UNIX operating system), and three versions of Windows. The Windows installation chapter includes instructions for reducing the size of Windows Vista before installing it on the Eee PC. You'll also learn how to configure Windows XP to run as efficiently as possible on the Eee PC.

The tiny Eee PC benefits more than most computers from cloud computing technologies, and you'll discover how set up two cloud computing suites: Google Applications and Windows Live.

Finally, the book concludes with hardware upgrades including Bluetooth and GPS, as well as how to set up both from within Xandros Linux. You'll discover what may be the defining Windows application on the Eee PC: Microsoft Streets & Trips. You'll also learn how to dissassemble your Eee PC and, if you're technically inclined, how to attach a USB hub directly to the motherboard.

If this book whets your appetite for more information, you can get involved in the Eee PC community through http://www.eeeuser.com and various other blogs, forums, and websites dedicated to the Eee PC.

How This Book Is Organized

This book provides the how-to knowledge to make your Eee PC do practically anything. Whether you have a Xandros Linux–equipped model or a machine running Window XP, you'll find a vast assortment of useful tips, information, and procedures that you can use to get the very most from your Eee PC. The book contains the following chapters:

- Chapter 1, "Getting to Know Your Eee PC," covers the basics of the Eee PC, its controls, and how to use the machine. This includes how to connect the Eee PC to the Internet.

- Chapter 2, "Adding Peripheral Devices," covers connecting the Eee PC to common peripherals, such as printers, keyboards, mice, and monitors. It covers basic operations such as using the webcam and working with the internal sound system.

■ Chapter 3, "Configuring Internet Applications," discusses how to set up email applications, chat (messenger) software, RSS feeds, and Skype.

■ Chapter 4, "Customizing Easy Mode," covers not only how to use Easy Mode, but how to configure it and get the most benefit from it. This is especially useful to folks who are setting up Easy Mode for one or more other people.

■ Chapter 5, "Working with the (Full) KDE Desktop," covers how to launch and use the KDE (Full) Desktop. Using the Eee PC in Easy Mode shows only a small part of what the machine can do. Working in the KDE Desktop opens up endless possibilities.

■ KDE isn't the only other desktop you can run on your Eee PC. Chapter 6, "Using Other Window Managers," discusses how to get, load, and configure three other popular desktops: Beryl, GNOME, and Fluxbox.

■ Chapter 7, "Looking at the Installed Software," provides a tour of the wide array of installed software in the Eee PC. This includes productivity, entertainment, and educational applications.

■ Chapter 8, "Getting More Linux Applications," shows how to use the Xandros package manager, through both the Synaptic and command-line interfaces. It discusses how to access additional software repositories, set "pinning," and download and install additional software. It also discusses how to download packages and install them with dpkg.

■ After Chapter 8 shows you how to download additional packages, Chapter 9, "Must-Have Utilities," discusses the very best and most useful packages to get.

■ An ultra-portable machine such as the Eee PC benefits quite a lot from online applications. The Eee PC has built-in connections to the Google Apps online productivity suite, and Chapter 10, "Introducing Google Applications," talks about how to use this online suite, including the unique Google Gears plug-in that allows you to run these applications while disconnected from the Internet.

■ Chapter 11, "Introduction to the Linux Command Line," provides a gentle introduction to the most commonly used Linux commands.

■ Chapter 12, "Loading Other Linux Distributions," discusses how to reinstall the Xandros Linux operating system and how to install three other Linux distributions that work especially well on the Eee PC: Mandriva, Puppeee, and Ubuntu (my personal favorite operating system for the Eee PC).

- Chapter 13, "Loading OpenSolaris," takes the tiny Eee PC to a whole new level by covering how to load and configure the Sun Microsystems version of UNIX.

- Chapter 14, "Loading Windows," covers how to load both Windows XP Home Edition and Windows XP Professional. In addition, it discusses how to "lighten up" Microsoft Windows Vista and install Vista on the Eee PC.

- Chapter 15, "Windows Configuration," covers how to configure Windows XP to reduce its footprint on the Eee PC, and provides extremely useful Windows tips for overclocking, securing your data, and running PortableApps.com applications. It also explains how to load Microsoft Office to replace the built-in Microsoft Works.

- Windows Live is Microsoft's foray into cloud computing, and XP-equipped Eee PCs have hooks into Windows Live. Chapter 16, "Windows Live," explores how to use Windows Live with various versions of Microsoft Office and Internet Explorer, and the advantages and drawbacks.

- Chapter 17, "Upgrading the Hardware," covers how to add Bluetooth and GPS to your Eee PC, and includes a survey of Linux and Windows GPS applications. This chapter gets really "hard core" by walking through a basic "hardware mod" to add an internal USB hub and Bluetooth capability to the Eee PC. This is not for the faint of heart, and includes instructions for soldering connections to the motherboard.

Conventions Used in This Book

Although this book was designed to be as simple to follow as possible, there is one convention throughout of which you should be aware.

Linux Prompts

This book talks about a number of Linux systems, some of which use the `sudo` command to run commands with administrative authority, and some of which use `su`.

For systems that use `sudo`, I simply chose the following for the prompt character, because there is no need to differentiate when you are running with root privileges:

```
>
```

For Linux system shells that do use root privileges, I use the following conventions:

If you're running as yourself (a user):

```
$
```

If you're running with root privileges:

```
#
```

Let Me Know What You Think

I'm always interested in what my readers think. If you'd like to contact me, you can reach me at bill.lawrence@mayanscribe.com.

Getting to Know Your Eee PC

Meeting the Asus Eee PC Family

Starting with the 701, the Eee PC family has grown to machines with both 7" and 8.9" monitors. Each model has its own limitations and advantages.

Eee PC 701 Series

The four models in the 701 series (2G Surf, 4G Surf, 4G, and 8G) all have the following components:

- Seven-inch display.
- Intel GMA 900 graphics processor, using a shared memory architecture. A VGA port supports monitor resolutions up to 1600×1280 dpi.
- Xandros Linux with the IceWM (Easy Mode) and KDE (Full Desktop) window managers. The machine can also be purchased with Microsoft Windows XP or, if you purchased a Linux-equipped Eee, you can load XP yourself. Some folks have reported loading various other Linux distributions, Microsoft Windows Vista, Microsoft Windows XP Professional, and even Sun OpenSolaris. We'll talk about that in Chapters 12, 13, and 14.
- Three USB ports (you'll probably want more).
- Ethernet connector.
- Wireless (802.11b and 802.11g).
- Realtek High-Definition Audio with built-in speakers and microphone.
- DC power connector.
- MMC/SD/SDHC card reader.

Table 1.1 outlines the components that differ among the 701 series models.

Table 1.1   Asus 701 Eee PC Model Comparison

Hardware	701 2G Surf	701 4G Surf	701 4G	701 8G
Memory	512MB		512MB[1]	1GB[1] (socketed)
Flash memory storage (drive)	2GB	4GB		8GB
Webcam 640×480	No		Yes	
Processor	800MHz Intel Celeron M, underclocked at 571MHz	900MHz Intel Celeron M, underclocked at 630MHz		
Battery	4-cell, lithium-ion battery, 7.4V, 4400mAh, providing 2 hr, 45 min of battery life		4-cell, lithium-ion battery, 7.4V, 5200mAh, providing 3 hr, 30 min of battery life (typical maximum)	
Weight	1lb 15.5oz (895g)	2lb 0.5oz (920g)		
Color	Pure White, Galaxy Black, Blush Pink, Sky Blue, Lush Green		Pearl White, Galaxy Black, Blush Pink, Sky Blue, Lush Green	

[1] You can upgrade memory, even if your unit has the "warranty is void..." sticker. This will not void the warranty.

The primary differences to keep in mind follow:

- The Surf models don't have a webcam.
- The 2G Surf doesn't have expandable memory, runs a little slower, and has a bit shorter battery life. Some 4G units may also have the lighteer.

All four models have a solid-state drive (SSD), which is a fancy way of saying that, for storage, they use flash memory instead of a hard drive. This allows the unit to be smaller, nearly immune to bumps and jolts, and use less power, but using flash memory does have its limitations (namely, capacity and life expectancy).

Eee PC 900

The 900 is similar to the 701 series, with a few changes:

- The 900MHz Intel Celeron M processor is clocked at a full 900MHz.
- 1GB of memory is standard.
- The screen is 8.9 inches, with the speakers located on the bottom of the machine.
- The resolution of the webcam is 1.3 megapixels (MP).
- The unit weighs 990g.
- The storage is 12GB (Windows version) or 20GB (Xandros version).

Eee PC 901

The 901 is similar to the 900, but substitutes an Intel Atom processor for the Celeron M. Its differences include:

- 1.6 GHz Intel Atom processor.
- Intel 950 graphics processor.
- 7.4V, 6600 mAh battery proving 4.2h+ hours of battery life.
- The unit weighs 1140g.

Eee PCs Yet To Come

The Eee PC 1000, with a 10 inch screen, 40 or 80 GB SSD, and an Intel Atom processor will soon be available. Other machines that should hit the market in 2008 include the Eee Box, a Mac Mini-like Eee PC designed as a desktop machine, and the Eee TV, which will be a combination TV, computer, and video game machine.

A Guided Tour of the Eee PC

This section gives you a tour of the exterior of my Eee PC 4G, a Pearl White model that I have named Stelios. Because the Eee PC manual also provides an introduction to the outside of the Eee PC, I'll try to make this tour a little more interesting by pointing out some tidbits of information that aren't covered in the manual. Note that the exterior of the 900 series is slightly different from the 701 series, so the figures presented in this section might not depict exactly what you see if you have an Eee PC 900.

Front View

Figure 1.1 shows an image of the front of the Eee PC 4G. The features identified in Figure 1.1 are described next.

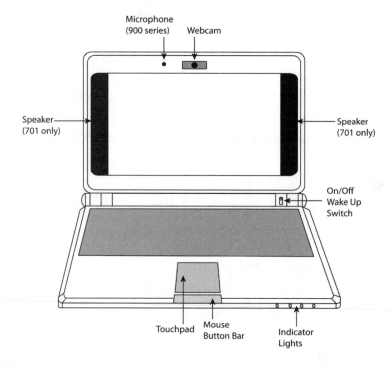

FIGURE 1.1

Front view of the Eee PC 4G.

Webcam: If your 701 Eee PC model has a webcam, it has up to 640×480-pixel resolution. If you have an Eee PC 900, you have 1.3MP to play with. The Eee PC can handle a frame rate of 30 frames per second (fps), regardless of model.

Display: The Eee PC sports a thin-film transistor (TFT) display. The display has excellent contrast, making it not only quite readable but also useful as an e-book display device. When we discuss how to set up the video in Chapter 2, I'll explain how to make your Eee PC into something akin to an Amazon Kindle.

On/Off/Wake Up switch: Press to turn on the Eee PC, and press and hold for 5 seconds to turn it off. Although this is not the normal way to turn off the Eee PC, it does shut down gracefully by closing and saving files (unless the system was locked up, in which case it might not). When the Eee PC hibernates, you can press this switch to wake it up.

Touchpad and mouse button bar: You can control it by

- Sliding your finger in the direction you want the mouse pointer to move
- Tapping the pad to simulate a mouse click
- Clicking the left side of the mouse button bar to simulate a left-click
- Clicking the right side of the bar to simulate a right-click
- Sliding along the extreme right edge to perform vertical scrolling. There's a line on the right side of the touchpad that marks the area you can user for vertical scrolling. If you have wide fingers, place only half your finger on the touchpad.

The 900 and later units have some more advanced scrolling and zooming gestures. You can scroll vertically or horizontally by placing two fingers on the touchpad and moving them in the direction you wish to scroll. A limited number of applications, such as Open Office and Adobe Acrobat Reader, also support zooming in and out on the touchpad. To zoom out, place two fingers on the touchpad and spread them out. To zoom in, do the opposite and draw your fingertips together.

Indicator lights: The Eee PC has an array of four lights, listed here from left to right:

- **Power (yellow):** Lit when the Eee PC is on.
- **Battery (red):** Lit when the Eee PC is charging and unlit when it is fully charged. If it blinks, 10% or less of the battery power remains, which means you should shut down as quickly as possible, without losing any data, or plug your power supply into the Eee PC.
- **Disk indicator (yellow):** Flashes when data is being written to or read from the solid-state disk (flash disk), similar to a drive indicator light on any other computer.
- **Wireless (blue):** Lit when the wireless network transceiver is active.

Speakers: The speakers, which actually sound reasonably good, are to the left and right of the display on the 701 series. On the 900 series, they are on the bottom of the Eee PC (and therefore slightly muffled). Thus, the 900 series sacrifices sound quality in favor of a wider display.

Microphone: Having the microphone mounted downward pointing is suboptimal, but it is functional. If you plan to use your Eee PC often for video conferencing or phone conversations, consider getting a headset.

Bottom View

Figure 1.2 shows an image of the bottom of the Eee PC 4G. The features identified in Figure 1.2 are described next.

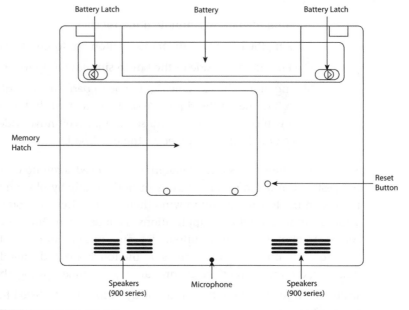

FIGURE 1.2

Bottom view of the Eee PC 4G.

Battery panel latches: The latch on the left is spring loaded and the latch on the right latches. Here's how you remove the battery:

1. Slide the latch on the right to the right (it will stay in position; if you see the red dot, then the latch is unlocked).
2. Slide the latch on the left to the left.
3. Remove the battery while holding the left latch at its leftmost position. The battery slides straight out the back, not up or down.

Reset button: You access the Reset button through a small hole next to the bottom-right corner of the memory hatch. This is the all-else-has-failed button that you press when the computer is frozen and won't respond to any controls. It's similar to the emergency latch on a CD or DVD drive. To use it, bend the end of a paper clip straight and gently insert it into the small hole until you feel the button depress and the system resets. Should this fail (and it shouldn't), unplug the unit and remove the battery.

> **tip** To reinstall the battery, just slide it along until the latches drop into place (feel free to help them a little if they're hanging up). Then slide the right-side latch to the left to ensure that the battery is secured.

Warning! Do this at risk to your data and your solid-state drive (SSD). The reset switch will stop the machine in the middle of writing data, so check the disk indicator and make sure that it isn't flashing. This is especially risky if you install another Linux distribution and decide not to use a journaling file system to reduce writes to the SSD.

Memory hatch: Open this hatch to access the memory module. On the Eee PC 2G Surf model, the memory module is soldered onto the board, so you can't upgrade the memory. For all other models, this is where you plug in a bigger memory module, as covered in detail in Chapter 17.

> **note** The reason you would want to upgrade to as much memory as possible under Xandros is that swapping is disabled. This makes sense, given the limited space for storage on the Eee PC and the fact that every read and write shortens the life of the SSD.

Good news Windows XP fans: you don't need to do anything special to access 2GB of RAM. Also, other Eee PC Linux distributions can access the additional RAM.

So why not just chuck Xandros in favor of another operating system? Well, Xandros does have its endearing qualities, including the nifty Easy Mode. If you get the urge to change the version of Linux, take a look at Chapter 12.

Right-Side View

Figure 1.3 shows an image of the right side of the Eee PC 4G, which has the following slots and ports:

Kensington slot: The little slot toward the rear is for a Kensington locking device. This is a widget for fastening the Eee PC to something sturdy and difficult to move, such as a desk. The drawback here is that although the cable may be very tough, the Eee PC's case is not. A vigorous yank and the thief has your Eee PC, albeit with a ruptured case.

VGA port: The VGA port is a typical 15-pin connector. Resolutions up to 1600×1200 are possible and not hard to set up, although sometimes anything over 1024×768 DPI requires a bit of tinkering, which is covered in Chapter 2.

note The Kensington slot and VGP port are located so close together that they cannot be used at the same time.

USB ports: The two USB ports on this side are both USB 1.1 and USB 2.0 compatible.

MMC-SD slot: The slot will accept any MultiMediaCard or Secure Digital format flash memory, including the newer

tip Many USB devices draw their power from the Eee PC, so running a USB device while the Eee PC is running on battery shortens the battery life.

SD High Capacity (SDHC) cards. This is the best and least expensive way to provide extra storage, although USB flash drives work quite handily as well.

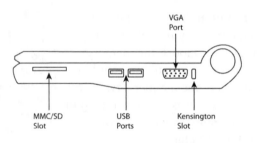

VGA
Port

MMC/SD
Slot

USB
Ports

Kensington
Slot

FIGURE 1.3

The right-side connectors.

Left-Side View

Figure 1.4 shows an image of the left side of the Eee PC 4G, which has the following ports:

Network port: This is an Ethernet 10/100Mbps port for a standard Cat5 or Cat6 cable. If you purchase a cross-over cable (or build your own), you can connect your Eee PC directly to another computer. I've used such as cable to set up and configure industrial equipment with Ethernet ports. You could also do this with two "straight" Ethernet cables and an ethernet hub or switch in between.

Modem port: The presence of this port is a tease. There is no hardware in the Eee PC to support a modem, so this port is plugged up. It is a useful access hole into the case for controls for any hardware modifications (mods) that you may install.

USB port: Like the two USB ports on the right side, this third and final port of entry for peripheral devices is USB 1.1 and USB 2.0 compatible.

Microphone port: This port takes any standard PC microphone.

Headphones port: You can plug in headphones or powered speakers here. Okay, you can plug in unpowered speakers as well, but remember that they draw their power from the Eee PC.

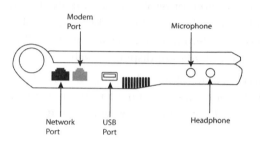

FIGURE 1.4

The left-side connectors.

Back View

Finally, our tour ends at the back of the unit, where we find the DC power port. There's nothing else back there.

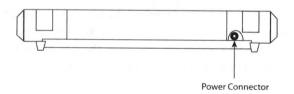

FIGURE 1.5

The lonely power connect on the back.

Using the Special Keyboard Functions

Use the following key combinations:

- **Fn+F1:** Enter Sleep Mode. Have care with this as you can lose your external monitor resolution setting on wakeup. This can occur if you're using dual monitors and the Eee PC enters sleep mode. Press the power button to wake the computer.

- **Fn+F2:** Toggle the Wireless Transceiver on and off.

ourselves, because we haven't touched on switching from Easy Mode to Full Desktop. If you don't know how to do this, consult the "Getting to the Full Desktop" section near the end of this chapter.

Establishing a Wireless Connection

Connecting through wireless on the Eee PC is also actually quite easy, and almost sets itself. When in Easy Mode and with wireless active, the Eee PC pops up a little box showing that you are in range of a wireless network. When you click the pop-up box, a window opens with a list of any wireless networks in range.

The first step in getting wireless to work is to enable it. In Easy Mode, click either the Wireless Network icon on the Internet tab or the wireless icon (which looks like a fan with a wrench) in the system tray (properly called the panel in the Linux world). In Full Desktop, click the wireless icon in the panel and select Wireless Networks in the shortcut menu.

The next step is to connect to a wireless network, which is easy enough if it's broadcasting its ESSID. The Wireless Networks dialog box shows the available wireless networks. To connect to one, double-click it. If it has security (you'll see a lock icon beside the name), a dialog box will appear prompting you to enter the key or passphrase. If a connection point isn't broadcasting its ESSID, you must go back the Network icon and enter all of the information for that wireless connection.

There are two types of protected access, both of which require you to enter a key or passphrase:

- **Wired Equivalent Privacy (WEP):** You need to know the network key, which may be either 40 or 128 bits. These keys are usually pairs of numbers and letters (actually, hexadecimal characters). You also need to know the key index, although this is almost always 1. The use of WEP is diminishing, except in home networks, because it isn't secure against a concerted attack. It's really just a polite way of saying "stay out."

- **Wi-Fi Protected Access (WPA):** You need to know the passphrase. You'll likely encounter WPA at public hotspots.

After you double-click the network name of a security-enabled connection point, you enter the key or passphrase and then click Connect to connect. If you want to reconnect to this network in the future, you simply click the Network icon on the Internet tab, select the wireless network, and select Connect under Connection.

If you want to connect automatically to a network, such as your home network, when you start the Eee PC, you can also set that up:

note If you want to get a little fancier than that, you can set up a fallback network by using the Fallback drop-down list box in the Properties dialog box (see Figure 1.6). For example, if you have multiple network connections (say wired and wireless), you can try to connect to the wired network first and then, if that doesn't work, connect to a wireless network.

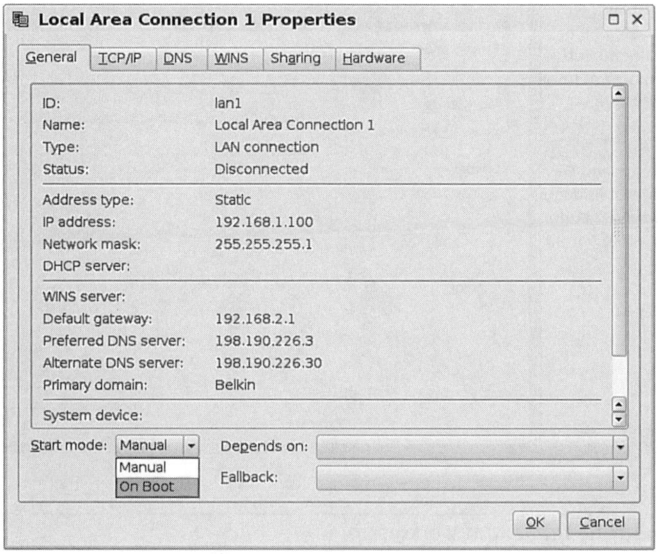

1. Click the Network icon.

2. Select the network to which you wish to autoconnect on bootup.

3. Click the Properties button to open the Properties dialog box, shown in Figure 1.6.

4. In the Start Mode drop-down list box in the lower-left corner, choose On Boot. Click OK, and then click OK again.

5. Allow the Eee PC to restart the network connection, after which your system should attempt to join that connection on bootup.

FIGURE 1.6
Setting a network to start on bootup.

Joining a Windows Network

If you have a Windows network at home (that is, you have set up Windows networking with workgroups and so forth), the Eee PC dives right into that arrangement with absolute ease. You first need to set up the Windows workgroup that you want to join, and you'll need to do this from the Full Desktop. Start the Control Center (choose Launch, Control Center, Control Center), expand Network, and then select Windows Networking, as shown in Figure 1.7. Changing this sort of thing requires administrative access, so click the Administrator button.

In Easy Mode, you can share through the File Manager. Right-click the directory (or partition) you wish to share, then click Sharing. Select Windows sharing in the shortcut menu and then select Share this item and its contents. You can now select the share name, sharing permissions, etc.

Enter the machine name you'd like to use on the Windows network (yes, you can change it from the default) and the name of the Windows workgroup you'd like to join. You can also check the box to enable file and printer sharing. Click the Apply button when you're finished.

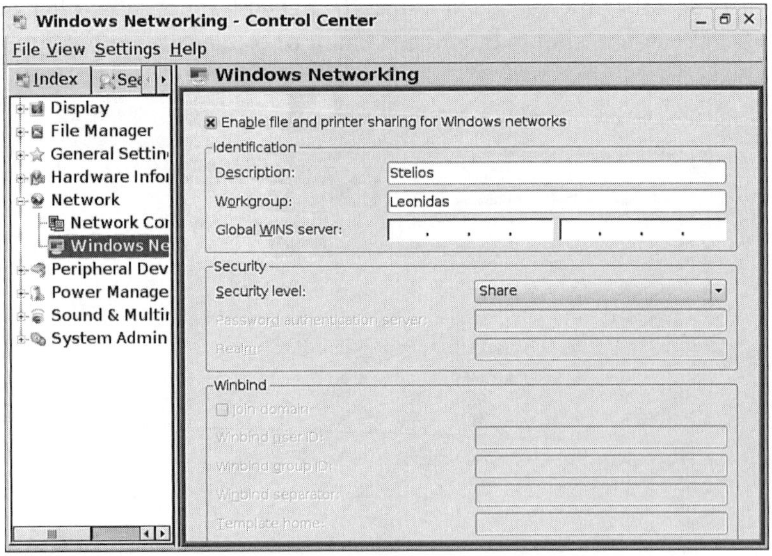

FIGURE 1.7
Setting the machine name and workgroup.

When that's done, in the File Manager, simply click on the Windows network in the tree, and you'll see the other computers in the workgroup. You'll need to set this up before you can tap into any shared printers on a Windows network.

Introducing the Video and Sound Features

The following is simply and introduction to the video and sound capabilities of the Eee PC. Actual detailed use is covered in Chapters 2 and 3.

With the combination of built-in webcam, microphone, and speakers, the Eee PC is just about the most portable video-conferencing device around.

> **tip** If you want a little more privacy, invest in a microphone/headphones combination or a headset.

Webcam

Both the non-Surf 701 models and the Eee PC 900 and 901sport nifty webcams that you can use for video conferencing and so forth. You can use the webcam in video conferencing with a number of applications, such as Skype. You can also build your own YouTube videos by using the built-in webcam application, ucview. This is available in Easy Mode on the Play tab, or by choosing Launch, Applications, Multimedia, ucview in Full Desktop.

Regardless of how you run it, ucview is a very competent package. You can record in low (300kbps), medium (800kbps), and high-quality (8000kbps) formats, or you can define the bitrate, encoding, quality, and frames per second yourself (choose the Custom compression quality under Tools, Video). Videos are stored in Ogg Theora video format, which is a good thing. Theora is an open standard from the Xiph.org Foundation, which is dedicated to making high-quality video and audio tools for the patent-free, open source world.

YouTube, unfortunately, is not Theora-friendly. There is an Ogg sort of YouTube environment called Theora Sea (http://en.theorasea.org/), but don't get too excited, because there's hardly any content on it. However, VLC (one of the applications covered in Chapter 9, "Must-Have Utilities") can convert Theora format to MPEG, which YouTube does like.

Microphone

The Eee PC has a tiny microphone mounted below the mouse pad area. Actually, despite its diminutive size, it has reasonable sound quality. Sound pickup is a little less than optimal, but not terrible. As shown in Figure 1.8, the Sound Recorder application has a number of quality options and can record in mono or stereo. To do stereo, you need a stereo input (which the single built-in mic isn't). You can launch the Sound Recorder from the Multimedia tab in Easy Mode or by choosing Launch, Applications, Multimedia, Sound Recorder in Full Desktop.

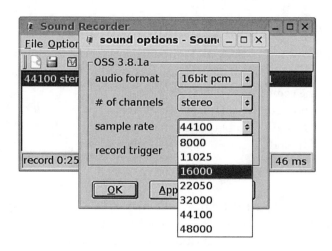

FIGURE 1.8

Recording quality options in the Sound Recorder.

The Sound Recorder saves in standard .wav file format, so the files it creates are very compatible with most other applications. If you want to edit sound files that you record, refer to Chapter 9, which discusses Audacity, a very powerful and yet simple-to-use sound editor.

Speakers

The really surprising thing about the Eee PC 701 is its speakers. PCs sound tinny at best, but the 701 speakers, mounted on either side of the screen, actually sound somewhat reasonable. This is especially true if your media player supports an audio equalizer so that you can pump up the base a bit. The sound quality isn't as good with the Eee PC 900, with its speakers on the bottom.

> **note** Check out the "Sound Mixer" section in Chapter 2 for information about how to set the balance and volume of the various inputs and outputs.

Setting the Clock in Full Desktop

In Full Desktop, right-click the time display in the system tray and select Configure Clock from the shortcut menu, as shown in Figure 1.9.

In Full Desktop, you can set the style of the clock, and change the foreground and background colors and the font for both the time and the date. The digital clock looks just like you might imagine. The analog clock is far too small for the system tray (well, at least it is for my eyes) and, oddly, displays the time in words rather than numbers. Otherwise, the settings are quite straightforward.

FIGURE 1.9

Configuring the clock.

"Timezone" is actually handier than you might think, as it allows you to select multiple time zones. You can then right-click the time display, choose Show Timezone, and select from the submenu which time zone to use. The Eee PC is easy to take with you as you travel the globe, so this feature is very useful if you travel frequently.

Some other nice features on the right-click menu are Show Calendar, which simply displays the current month calendar, although you can pan forward and backward by month and year, or simply type in the month and year. You can also use a drop-down list to select any week in the year.

Copy to Clipboard in the menu does what it says, but you get to select the date format. That's also handy when you simply don't want to type the date.

One of the omissions in the Eee PC is the inability to sync to an NTP time via ntpdate server. Asus does include the rdate command to sync to an rdate server. (Chapter 9 discusses how to download and use ntpdate, if you want to use it. However, you can just as easily use a time server for rdate.) Because I'm in North America, I use time.nrc.ca to use the time server provided by the National Research Council, Ottawa, Canada. Substitute your own closest server in the command to set the time:

```
> sudo /usr/sbin/rdate -s time.nrc.ca
```

If you want, you can put this command into a file and copy it to the /usr/bin directory. I named my file gettime. Change the permissions on the file to allow it to execute by right-clicking the file in the Administrative File Manager, selecting Properties, and setting all the execute permissions. To set the file to execute from the command line, enter the following:

```
> sudo chmod +x gettime
```

If you want to see this work, simply set the time to something wrong on your Eee PC and then, from the command prompt, issue the gettime command. It'll instantly set the time back to its proper value.

Setting the Volume

In Easy Mode, you can access a simple volume and balance control, reminiscent of the Windows volume control, from either the system tray or by clicking the Volume icon on the Settings tab.

In Full Desktop, the Eee PC has a Sound Mixer application that you can use to set the various input and output volume levels. It also provides both internal and external microphone boost channels. Of course, there's also a mute control. To access the mixer, right-click the speaker icon in the system tray and select the function you want (see Figure 1.10).

FIGURE 1.10

Selecting the Master Channel.

If you choose Select Master Channel, you can select the various input and output channels. The Mixer Window has some of that functionality, and also has the volume and balance controls. The Input tab lets you select between the internal and external microphones.

For command-line fans, you can also pull up alsamixer (it is installed). I personally find the semi-GUI interface for alsamixer to be a little rough (see Figure 1.11). If you want to try it out, launch a terminal window by pressing Ctrl+Alt+t. At the prompt, issue the following command:

```
>  alsamixer
```

You control alsamixer through a combination of the Tab key and the arrow keys. The vertical bars are either output or input levels. Use the Tab key to navigate between the "views" (toward the top of the interface), and use the right and left arrow keys to navigate between the channels. The up and down arrow keys turn the output or input levels up or down.

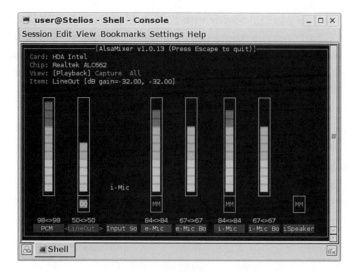

FIGURE 1.11
The alsamixer GUI.

Cleaning Your Eee PC

You can wipe the outside of the case with a slightly damp sponge. You can use a drop of mild dish detergent on the sponge if you like. You can clean the dirt around the keys with a cotton swab (alcohol works well here). Vacuuming around the keyboard also works well.

Cleaning the display is best done with an eyeglass cleaning kit. Do not spray the cleaner directly on the screen, but rather use one short spray on the cloth. In fact, never spray or drip anything into any of the machine's openings.

Getting to the Full Desktop

No introduction to the Eee PC would be complete without learning how to switch between the two desktops. Asus literature variously calls the Linux KDE Desktop both the Full Desktop and Advanced Mode. Either way, the KDE desktop is a handy way of controlling your Eee PC, with a lot more flexibility than Easy Mode.

There's a utility that you can easily download and install that adds an icon in the Shut Down menu you can click to switch to the Full Desktop. From the Full Desktop, there's a command on the Launch menu to switch back to Easy Mode. So you will now have the best of both worlds.

This will be your first foray into the world of downloading and installing Linux packages. Packages are bundles of executable and library files that comprise a complete application. The Eee PC's Xandros operating system can download and install packages for you. For now, we'll use the command-line interface but Chapter 8 will go over all of the ways to do this, both via a GUI and from the command line.

From Easy Mode, press Ctrl+Alt+T to launch a terminal window. In the terminal window, type the following two commands:

```
> sudo apt-get update
> sudo apt-get install ksmserver kicker
```

When the packages are installed, click the close box on the terminal window or type the following command:

```
> exit
```

Before switching desktops, make sure that close all of your applications. If you don't, they will be closed for you. Click the Shut Down icon at the right of panel at the bottom of the screen (see Figure 1.12). It's a red circle with a white horizontal line. Click the new Full Desktop icon to switch desktops. When in Full Desktop, click the Launch button at the left of the panel, and select Easy Mode. Once again, close your applications before doing this or they will be closed for you.

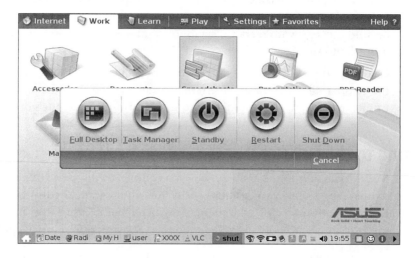

FIGURE 1.12

The Full Desktop icon in the Shut Down Menu.

If you wish to boot directly into the Full Desktop, in Easy Mode click the Settings Tab. Click the Personalization icon and then select Full Desktop mode under Login Mode (see Figure 1.13). Click OK and it's set. When you boot directly into the Full Desktop, it takes a little longer to start the Eee PC. This is because you are first booting under the Easy Mode (momentarily) and then launching the Full Desktop.

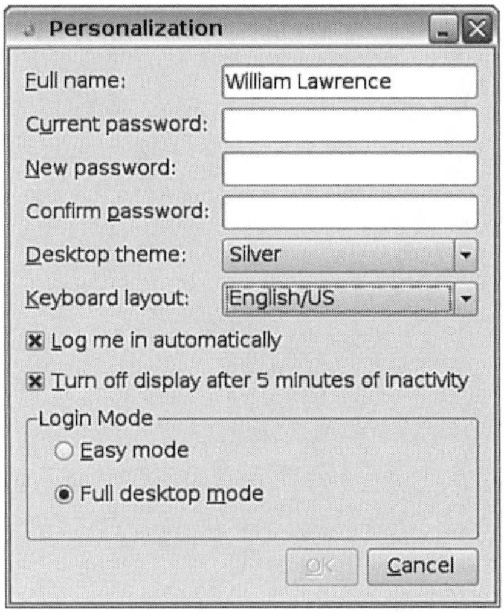

FIGURE 1.13

Selecting Full Desktop as the default desktop.

Summary

In this chapter, you got a good introduction to the Eee PC, its main controls and connections, and some of its basic features. You also learned to launch a terminal window in Easy Mode and used the Linux Bash command shell to run an application and to download and install a package.

You also got to see a side of the Eee PC you may not have known was there: Full Desktop. We'll spend a lot of this book with Full Desktop, as it's really the best way to do advanced tasks in the Xandros Linux operating system.

Adding Peripheral Devices

If you plan to sit at a desk and do some heavy-duty typing and lots of work on your Eee PC, you'll want to connect an external monitor, keyboard, and mouse to it. You might also want to add an external CD/DVD drive and attach the Eee PC to a printer. If you plan to use the Eee PC only as an ultra-portable machine, you probably don't need to consider the expense of these items, though a portable mouse is always a good investment if you don't like to use the touch pad.

Except for the monitor, everything plugs into a USB port; however, the machine only has three USB ports. So, if you plan to connect more than three USB gadgets to your Eee PC, you'll also want to add a USB hub, as described first.

This chapter explains how to connect various external devices to your Eee PC. Adding a keyboard and mouse is pretty much a simple matter of plugging them in to a USB port. I've plugged in several keyboards, mice, and a trackball to my Eee PC and all worked flawlessly. Therefore, this chapter doesn't cover this simple procedure.

Adding a USB Hub

Hubs usually come in four- and eight-port varieties. Unless you're going to add a USB lava lamp and USB rocket launcher, four ports should be fine. With a four-port hub, you can attach a keyboard, CD/DVD drive, full-sized mouse, and printer. The really great thing about using a USB hub is that you only need to unplug the hub USB connector from the Eee PC and you're ready to go. When you want to tie into everything again, there's only one USB connector to attach.

Hubs are very generic items these days and extremely inexpensive. Your local discount or electronics store is almost certain to have several models. I recommend that you get a "powered" USB hub, meaning that it does not rely on the Eee PC for power. Because you'll be using the hub at a desk where there's probably power available, why not have a powered hub? No matter which type of hub you choose, just plug it into an open USB port on the Eee PC and you've instantly expanded the number of ports available.

Adding Flash Storage

The Eee PC will accept MultiMediaCard (MMC), Secure Digital (SD), and the new higher-density Secure Digital High Capacity (SDHC) flash memory cards in the slot on the right side. Just plug in a flash memory card to add an extra drive. When you add the flash memory card, Xandros automatically mounts it and makes it accessible via a Linux cross directory connection (called a symbolic link) from your user directory. The best way to see this is through the File Manager, as shown in Figure 2.1. You can launch the File Manager from the Work tab in Easy mode.

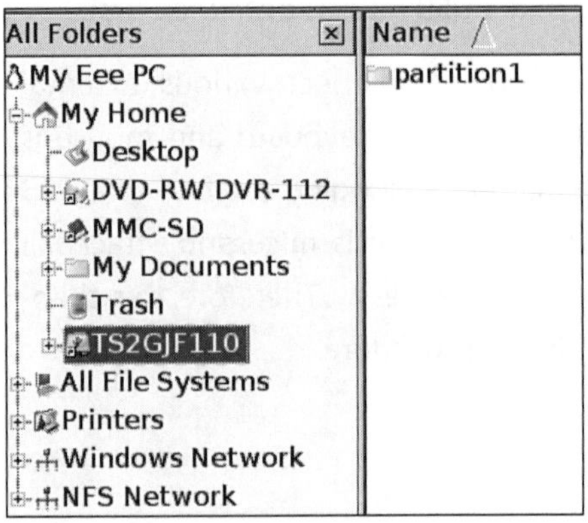

FIGURE 2.1

File Manager showing the symbolic link for the flash drive.

Note that, by default, the MMC-SD mount starts with the first directory or directories as the partition(s) when viewed this way. However, if you open it with the Administrative File Manager in Full Desktop, the partition, still shown as a directory, is on the All Folders side and the mount is parallel to the main file system, as shown in Figure 2.2. Either way, the result is the same and you can navigate there.

```
┌────────────────────────────────────────────────────────────────────────┐
│ 🗅 /media/MMC-SD/partition1 - File Manager              _  🗗  X          │
├────────────────────────────────────────────────────────────────────────┤
│ File  Edit  View  Go  Bookmarks  Window  Tools  Help                     │
├────────────────────────────────────────────────────────────────────────┤
│ ⇤ → ↑  X ↻  ⤵ 🖿 🖺  ⤵ 📑  🖵 📊 🖵                               ◎      │
├──────────────────────────────┬───────────────────────────────────────────┤
│ All Folders              ⊠   │ Name                    Size  Type ▽    A   │
│ ⚠ My Eee PC                  │ 🗀 Documents                  File Folder  dr │
│ ├─🏠 My Home                  │ 🗀 downloads                  File Folder  dr │
│ │  ├─🖥 Desktop               │ 🗀 music                      File Folder  dr │
│ │  ├─📇 MMC-SD                │ 🗀 pix                        File Folder  dr │
│ │  ├─🗀 My Documents          │                                             │
│ │  └─🗑 Trash                 │                                             │
│ ├─🖳 All File Systems         │                                             │
│ │  ├─🗀 /                     │                                             │
│ │  └─🗀 /media/MMC-SD/partition1                                           │
│ ├─🖨 Printers                 │                                             │
│ └─🖧 NFS Network              │                                             │
│                              │                                             │
│                              │ ◂▸                                          │
├──────────────────────────────┴───────────────────────────────────────────┤
│ 4 object(s)        128KB                      🖳 This Computer             │
└────────────────────────────────────────────────────────────────────────┘
```

FIGURE 2.2

Administrative File Manager showing the mount for the flash drive. From the command line, you'll find a symbolic link to the mount at /home/user, which is quite convenient.

It would be good at this point to discuss how you can tell how much space is available on any drive. In Easy Mode, you can use the Disk Utility on the Settings tab to check remaining space internally.

You can also use the File Manager to check the amount of space left internally or on any drive that you plug in (SD/MMC card, USB drive, or external hard drive). You can access the File Manager on the Work tab, or by choosing Launch, File Manager in Full Desktop. You can't check the space used and available by selecting a symbolic link for the drive; instead, you must select the actual mount for the drive in the file system. The symbolic link has a little arrow in the icon; the "real" partition is shown under All File Systems.

To check the remaining space, right-click the drive at its mount and select Properties from the shortcut menu. You'll see values for the total storage on the drive, the amount used, and the amount remaining. If you see numbers only for Size and Size on Disk, you're looking at a symbolic link, not the actual partition.

Connecting an External Hard Drive

External hard drives and most flash drives typically work simply by plugging them in to a USB port.

When you plug in an external disk drive or a flash drive, the Removable Device dialog box pops up (see Figure 2.3), giving you the choice of opening the drive in the File Manager, Music Manager, or Photo Manager. You can also just close the box by clicking Cancel.

note I did encounter a problem with U3 smart drives that have the built-in password protection application set. Because U3 smart drives are designed to launch on Windows, they simply don't work on the Eee PC, and the flash drive won't open. Removing the U3 application fixes that nicely enough. The easiest way to make these drives usable is to plug them into a Windows machine and format them as FAT 32.

FIGURE 2.3

The persistent Removable Device dialog box for removable media.

Flash drives, like SD cards, are mounted in /media and have a symbolic link under My Home (/home/user). You may see some very odd names for flash drives when viewing them in the File Manager.

If you want to remove a flash drive, you should first unmount it. This doesn't remove power, which is unnecessary on the Eee PC as it supports "hot-swapping," but disconnects it from the file system. To unmount a flash drive on either the Full Desktop or in Easy Mode, you'll find a USB symbol icon in the bottom panel. Right-click the USB symbol and click the Safely Remove command. The Eee PC will unmount it from the system.

Connecting a CD/DVD Player

CD/DVD players are somewhat problematic in one aspect: playing DVDs. There is a library missing that we'll discuss in Chapter 9 that will allow you to easily play DVDs.

Other than that, most external CD/DVD drives work just fine and are essentially plug-and-play. When a data/audio CD or data/video DVD is in place, the Eee PC mounts the drive under My Home via a symbolic link in the File Manager (it's really under /media). However, there aren't any applications residing on the Eee PC that will write data CDs or DVDs. Moreover, you can't rip DVDs.

To make matters worse, none of the CD/DVD disk-burning packages in the default repositories for Xandros (and none of the packages I recommend) actually works on the Eee PC. However, Chapter 8 discusses adding additional package repositories and Chapter 9, "Must-Have Utilities," discusses K3B, which enables you to burn DVDs, rip audio CDs, and do pretty much everything else you might need with CDs or DVDs. Chapter 9 provides a link to the website from which you can download a .deb package for Xandros that works perfectly on the Eee PC.

Connecting a Printer

Xandros Linux has excellent support for printers, and setting up a printer is almost trivial. About the only tricky thing is hooking up to a printer that is shared on a network. Even that's pretty easy if you've already set up the Eee PC on the network. See Chapter 1 for information on joining the Eee PC to a Windows network.

You can easily set up a printer from either Easy Mode or the Full Desktop. In Easy Mode, click the Settings tab and then the Printers icon. In the Full Desktop, run Control Center (Launch, Control Center, Control Center). From there, choose Peripheral Devices and then Printers. Just click the Add button to get started with the Add Printer Wizard, shown in Figure 2.4.

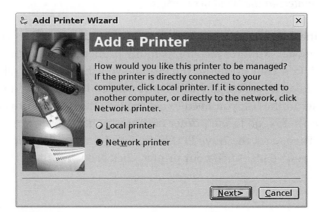

FIGURE 2.4

First step in adding a printer.

The wizard first asks you to specify whether the printer is attached directly to the Eee PC or attached to another computer on the network. (If attached directly to the Eee PC, this is another reason to have a powered USB hub.) Click Next when you've made your selection.

If it's a network printer, it must be attached to another computer and "shared." To access such a printer, click the Browse button to find it (don't bother filling in the name at this point). In the Browse For Network Printer dialog box, shown in Figure 2.5, navigate to the computer and then to the printer it's sharing (just click on the workgroup, then the machine, and finally the printer). Click OK. Now you can give the printer a name. It's a good idea to give it a name that indicates the model. The printer name can't contain spaces. You can substitute an underline character (_) for a space if you like. When you are finished, click Next.

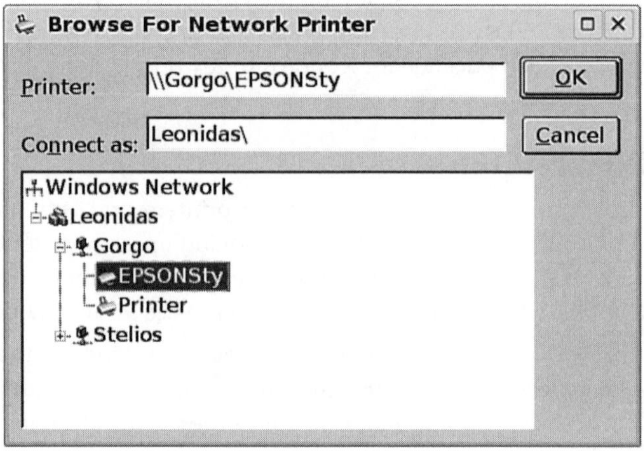

FIGURE 2.5

Browsing for printers in the Windows workgroup.

On the next wizard page, shown in Figure 2.6, select the printer manufacturer and model. Xandros recognizes many printers, so odds are in your favor that you'll find your printer in the drop-down list. When you select your printer, the dialog automatically fills in the correct driver. If you do not find your printer in the list, you need to get the PPD file (printer driver) for it. To do so, open Firefox, go to the printer manufacturer's website, and download the PPD file. Then, click the Have PPD button and navigate to it in the file browser. After you've identified your printer, click Next.

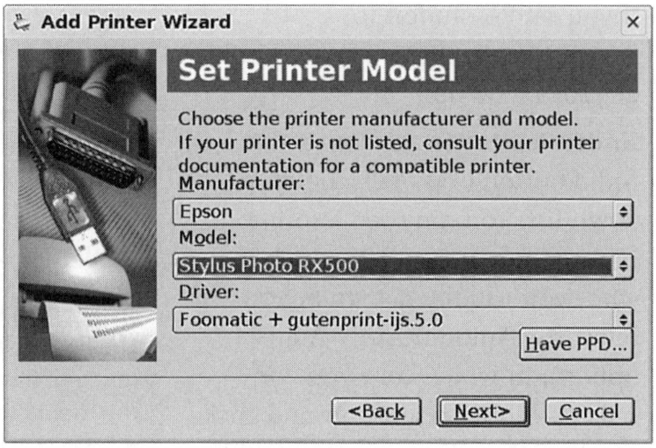

FIGURE 2.6

Selecting a printer from the list.

The final wizard page has you print a test page. I've found just about every printer I have access to on the menus, and I suspect you will, too.

Connecting an External Monitor or Projector

The screens on the 701 and 900 series are sufficient when you're on the go or for just casual web surfing, emails, and so forth, but if you plan to, say, write a book, mix audio tracks, or retouch photographs, you'll want to hook up an external monitor. Fortunately, this is simply a matter of connecting a VGA monitor cable into the port on the side of the Eee PC, connecting the other end to your monitor, and selecting to use the monitor through the External Monitor dialog box.

Adjusting the Screen Resolution

I've tried a number of monitors with my Eee PC, and they all work up to a 1024×768 resolution. However, recall from Chapter 1 that the Eee PC specifications indicate that it is capable of output up to 1600×1280 dpi. So what gives? Well, in some instances the Eee PC apparently doesn't recognize what the monitor can handle.

Suppose you plug in a monitor that can handle up to 1280×1024 and you'd really like to use it at that resolution, but the option isn't offered. You may still be able to use that resolution by doing a little configuration file tweaking. Follow these steps:

1. Open the External Display dialog box. In Easy Mode, click the Desktop Mode icon on the Settings tab. In Full Desktop, choose Launch, Control Center, External Display.

If you set Resolution to Automatically Adjust, you usually get 1024×768 dpi.

note In the External Display dialog box, you can choose to output video to the internal display only (the display on the Eee PC itself), the external display only (your monitor), or to both. When you run both, which I normally do, you don't get a true split-screen display. Instead, the Eee PC display shows only as much of the top-left portion of the monitor that fits its limited display space.

2. Under Resolution, click the Manual radio button and open the drop-down list. You may see resolutions higher than 1024×768 (which is what you usually get when you select the Automatically Adjust option), in which case you can select a higher resolution and click Apply. Otherwise, you need to edit the /etc/X11 xorg.conf file.

3. Open the /etc/X11 xorg.conf file either from the command line with your favorite text editor (remember to preface the command with sudo so that you have permission to save the file) or by navigating to it in Full Desktop mode with the Administrative File Manager. The Administrative File Manager can be accessed through Launch > Applications > System > Administrator Tools > File Manager (Administrator). From the Administrative File Manager, right-click the file and choose Open With, Text Editor.

4. Look for the section called "Screen". Change the Virtual entry for each of the four color depths (Depth; i.e. number of bits per pixel) from 1024×768 to whatever the maximum resolution is that your monitor will handle. The following shows my settings for the file:

```
Section "Screen"
        Identifier "Screen1"
        Device     "Device1"
        Monitor    "Monitor1"
        DefaultDepth    16
        SubSection "Display"
                Depth    8
                Virtual  1280 1024
        EndSubSection
        SubSection "Display"
                Depth    15
                Virtual  1280 1024
        EndSubSection
        SubSection "Display"
                Depth    16
                Virtual  1280 1024
        EndSubSection
```

```
        SubSection "Display"
                Depth      24
                Virtual    1280 1024
        EndSubSection
    EndSection
```

5. Save the file and exit.

6. Open the External Display dialog box, and you'll see new resolutions in the Manual drop-down list going up to whatever resolution you entered in the xorg.conf file, as shown in Figure 2.7.

7. Select the resolution you want and then click Apply. You get to try out the new resolution (to see if it works) and you have 15 seconds to accept it. If you don't accept it in that time, the resolution will return to the previous setting. This is designed to prevent accidentally setting an unusable resolution.

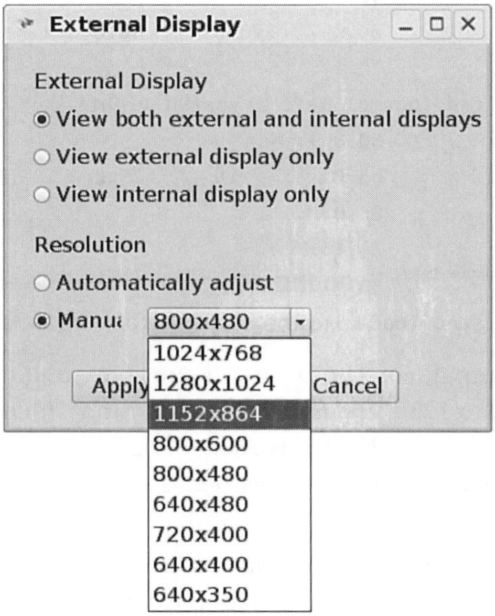

FIGURE 2.7

The expanded resolutions list.

Rotating the Display to Resemble a Kindle

Now that you have set the resolution, it's time to discuss the handy command-line video-control tool called xrandr. You can use xrandr to change the resolution as well, but it also enables you to do other nifty things such as rotate the screen. You need a command prompt to use this tool. In Easy Mode, press Ctrl+Alt+T. In Full Desktop, use your favorite method for launching an xterm window (or just choose Launch, Run Command and issue the Konsole command).

First, find out what your video display can do. To do that, from the command prompt, enter the following command:

```
> xrandr -q
```

You should get output that looks similar to the following:

```
Screen 0: minimum 320 x 200, current 1152 x 864, maximum 1280 x 1024
VGA connected 1152x864+0+0 (normal left inverted right) 310mm x 230mm
    1024x768        75.0 +    84.9        75.1
    1280x1024       59.9
    1152x864        74.8*
    800x600         84.9        75.0
    800x480         60.0
    640x480         84.6        75.0        60.0
    720x400         70.1
LVDS connected (normal left inverted right)
    800x480         60.0 +
    640x480         85.0        72.8        75.0        59.9
    720x400         85.0
    640x400         85.1
    640x350         85.1
TV disconnected (normal left inverted right)
```

From the output, you can see that I can command video resolutions for my monitor up to 1280×768 (which I set) and that the maximum the Eee PC internal display can handle is 800×480. Each resolution is followed by one or more numbers, which are the vertical scan rate(s), measured in Hertz, supported at that resolution.

Also note that normal, left, inverted, and right are available for both displays. Suppose that you have a monitor that will rotate to provide a "page" orientation display (higher than wide). You can use xrandr to rotate the display image to match this orientation by entering:

```
> xrandr -o left
```

Rotating your Eee PC display in this way enables you to have a display similar to that of an e-book display device such an Amazon Kindle. Load e-book reader software (such as Adobe Acrobat) and you have a very similar format for reading to that of a real book.

To return the display to normal, issue the following command:

```
> xrandr -o normal
```

By the way, using `inverted` flips the display upside down, which is just plain weird. It makes for a lovely practical joke, though.

If you want to set the resolution from the command line, use the `-s` argument. For example, the following sets the resolution to 1024×768:

```
> xrandr -s 1024x768
```

Setting the Clock

You can set both the clock and how it displays time. The procedure and available options are different depending on whether you are in Easy Mode or Full Desktop.

Setting the Clock in Easy Mode

To set the clock in Easy Mode, double-click the time display in the system tray. This opens the Date and Time dialog box, in which you can set the time, the date, and the time zone, and view a calendar.

You can also display a World Clock from Easy Mode by clicking this icon on the Internet tab. Just hover your mouse over one of the cities shown on the world map and you'll see the current time there displayed in the tool tip. If you maximize the window first, you'll find it easier to pinpoint the spot on the map that you want.

Establishing an Ethernet Connection

To get your network connection working by Ethernet, you first must find out whether the IP address for the Eee PC will be fixed (a static IP address) or dynamically assigned (via DHCP). Either your Internet Service Provider (ISP) or, if you are joining a LAN at an organization, your network administrator will provide this information.

If the IP address will be static, you need the following additional information:

- IP address for the Eee PC.
- Subnet mask. This is the same for all the addresses in your subnet (the machines hooked to a single router).
- Gateway address, if your network has gateways.

If the IP address will be dynamically assigned via DHCP, you probably don't need to know the preceding details (but if you're joining a large-scale network, ask your network administrator, because there are optional settings that you may need to use). When the Eee PC sends a DHCP request across the network, the DHCP server takes care of assigning the IP address (and how long you can keep it, which may be forever) as well as the gateway address, DNS addresses, and the subnet mask.

If you're using a static IP address, you need to know the IP addresses of the DNS (Domain Name System) servers. DNS servers translate machine names and web addresses into IP addresses, and therefore provide human-friendly domain and machine names instead of IP addresses for the network. Usually, there is more than one DNS server, and you should find out in what order they should be entered (one is usually a secondary DNS server).

For example, in a Windows LAN a machine might be named //marysue; however, the static IP address for the machine might be 199.66.24.11. No one wants to remember //199.66.24.11 when it's much easier to remember Mary Sue's machine's name.

Your network probably doesn't use WINS servers, because DNS is the standard these days, but if it does, find out if you need to put in an override WINS address. (WINS is only sort of like DNS, but has dynamically assigned mappings.)

Sharing is an unlikely event on an Eee PC, but possible. Sharing refers to using the Eee PC to connect to the Internet by either ethernet or wireless and using the unused wireless or ethernet NIC to connect to one or more other computers. All other computers therefore connect to the Eee PC in order to connect to the Internet. Given that the Eee PC is noted for its portability, this isn't a likely scenario. Besides, in the age of cheap routers and wireless, why bother?

Armed with that information, you're ready to establish an Ethernet connection. If you're connecting via a wire, you're likely either joining a home network through a router or, in very rare cases, via a cross-over cable directly to the Ethernet port of another computer. For example, lots of industrial hardware has Ethernet connectivity and built-in web servers, so you simply connect the Eee PC via the cross-over cable to the machine, set the IP address for your Eee PC, and point your web browser to the IP address of the machine's web server.

If your connection is through a router, it's probably a DHCP connection, which is pretty trivial to set up. If you're joining a larger LAN at some organization, you'll probably need all of the above information.

You configure your setting in the Local Area Connection Properties dialog box, shown in Figure 2.8, available by clicking the Network icon on the Internet tab in Easy Mode or by choosing Launch, Control Center, Network Connections in Full Desktop.

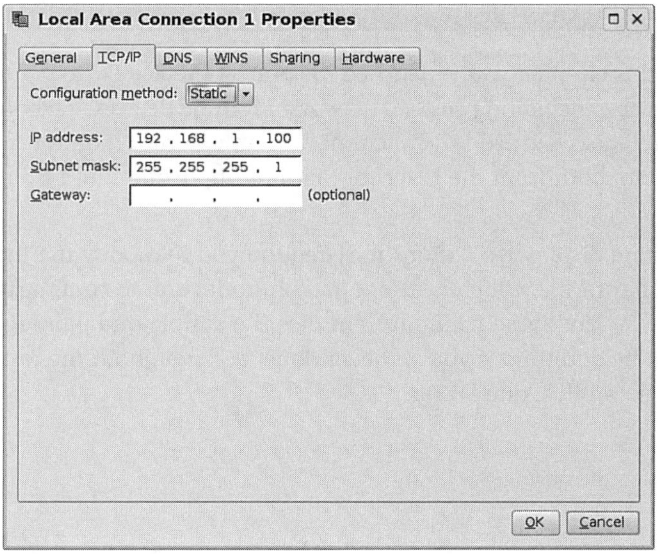

Local Area Connection 1 Properties

General | TCP/IP | DNS | WINS | Sharing | Hardware

Configuration method: Static

IP address: 192 . 168 . 1 . 100
Subnet mask: 255 . 255 . 255 . 1
Gateway: .   .   .   (optional)

OK   Cancel

FIGURE 2.8

Network properties.

All of the settings discussed have their own nice, neat tabs, and setup is straightforward. If you'd prefer a wizard to ask you these sorts of questions, you can use the Connection Wizard, the first page of which is shown in Figure 2.9. You launch it in Easy Mode by clicking the Network icon on the Internet tab and then clicking the Create button and launch it in Full Desktop by choosing Launch, Applications, Internet, Connection Wizard. The wizard can actually set up both Ethernet and wireless connections.

Connection Wizard

Connection Wizard

This wizard allows you to easily configure the method by which your system will connect to a network such as the Internet.

Please select the type of connection:

Connection type:

Cable
Dial-up
Dial-up - AOL
GSM / 3G (UMTS) / HSDPA
DSL - Point-to-Point Over ATM
DSL - Point-to-Point Over Ethernet
Wireless Point-to-Point Over Ethernet
Local Area Network
Local Area Network - Wireless

Next >   Cancel

FIGURE 2.9

Opening page of the Connection Wizard.

Summary

In this chapter, you've learned to connect the Eee PC to a variety of peripheral devices, including printers, networks, storage devices, keyboards, and drives. You'll also learned how to connect to an external monitor and control its resolution, both from the External Monitor application and from the command line.

Setting display resolutions may require you to modify the the /etc/X11 xorg.conf file, which is also a good introduction to configuring devices in Linux. Modifying configuration files is a simple and painless process, but it can be daunting if you've never done it. Throughout the rest of the book, we'll be doing that quite a bit.

Configuring Internet Applications

The Thunderbird email client (from Mozilla, which also offers the Firefox web browser) can manage all of your email accounts (both web email and ISP-based email) and your RSS and Usenet subscriptions. This chapter explains how to use Thunderbird to connect to email providers and to subscribe to RSS feeds and Usenet groups. (Subscribing to RSS feeds via Firefox is also covered.)

This chapter also covers how to use Pidgin, the instant messenger application installed in Xandros. The Eee PC has some other pretty nifty Internet applications installed under Xandros: Skype and VNC. As explained in this chapter, you can use Skype to make free phone calls to other Skype users and use VNC to remotely access another computer.

Accessing Email via Thunderbird

This section covers using Thunderbird to:

- Set up a new email account
- Work with an existing email account
- Manage your mail storage

Setting Up an Email Account

There are two general protocols for exchanging email with an email server: POP3 and IMAP (actually IMAP version 4). IMAP is a newer, somewhat more capable protocol, although both are very much in current use. These protocols are used to retrieve email from email servers. Both methods rely on SMTP (Simple Mail Transfer Protocol) to send email. Setting up either system is relatively simple and the procedure is fairly similar. This section covers setting up POP3 and then explains the few differences in setting up IMAP. Although the focus is on setting up email through an ISP, this section also covers configuring Thunderbird for Google's webmail system: Gmail. Thunderbird does have a wizard for setting up Gmail, but it doesn't quite set things up properly, so I'll show you how to fix it.

Setting Up a POP3 Account

Although the following example is primarily intended to demonstrate setting up POP3 access from an ISP and Gmail, the procedure is pretty much the same for almost any webmail source. From any webmail system, you must activate POP3 access. Also, webmail systems tend to use secure transfers on certain ports, and you have to set Thunderbird to match these requirements. Webmail providers also provide detailed instructions for setting up POP3 access to their systems, so look for a link that provides help on settings.

You can launch Thunderbird in Easy Mode by clicking the Email icon on the Work tab. In Full Desktop, you start it by choosing Launch, Applications, Internet, Thunderbird Email Client.

To set up a POP3 account:

1. Choose File, New, Account, as shown in Figure 3.1. This opens the Account Wizard.

2. Select Email Account and click the Next button to move to the Identity wizard page, shown in Figure 3.2.

3. In the Your Name field, enter your name as you'd like it to appear in the From field of your email messages.

4. In the Email Address field, enter your email address. Your ISP should have provided this when you opened your account, usually on some sort of account information form.

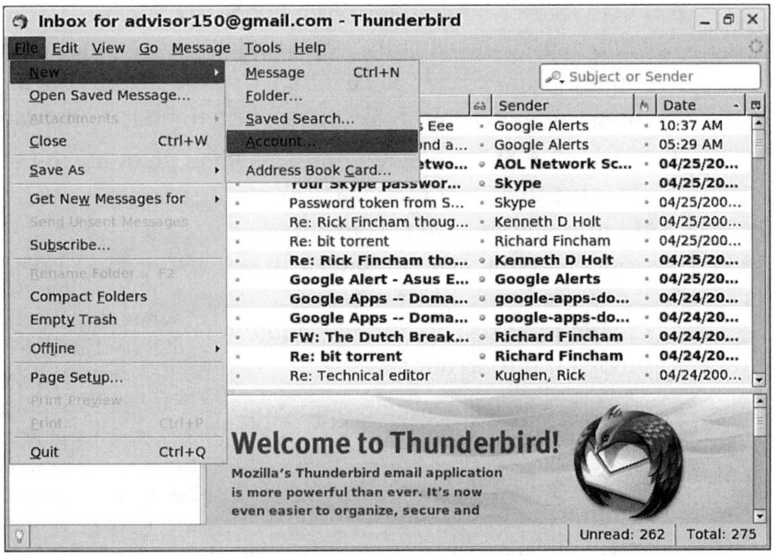

FIGURE 3.1
Adding a new account in Thunderbird.

FIGURE 3.2
Filling in the Identity wizard page.

5. Click the Next button.

6. On the Server Information wizard page (see Figure 3.3), click the POP radio button and enter the name of the server for incoming email. This is usually mail.*whateveryourISPis*.com, pop3.*whateveryourISPis*.net, or something like that. Look on the account information form from your ISP.

7. If you plan to have more than one email account, you might want to clear the Use Global Inbox check box. If this is checked, all new email from all accounts accumulates in the single Local Folder account. Clearing this sets up an individual inbox for this account.

8. If this is the first email account, you can also enter the name of your Outgoing Server on this dialog box. Again, refer to the information from your ISP. This will be something like smtp.*whateveryourISPis*.com.

note If you're setting up multiple accounts, Thunderbird has an annoying habit of using the default SMTP server and not providing a way to change this during account setup for subsequent accounts. If you run into this problem, fear not because it is easy to fix by editing the account information, as described later in this section.

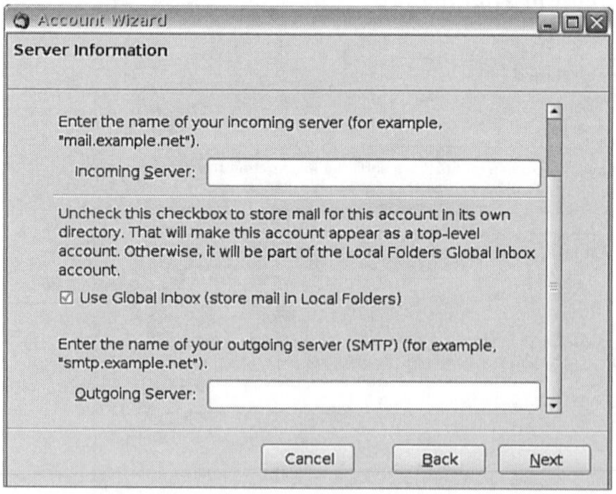

Account Wizard

Server Information

Enter the name of your incoming server (for example, "mail.example.net").

Incoming Server:

Uncheck this checkbox to store mail for this account in its own directory. That will make this account appear as a top-level account. Otherwise, it will be part of the Local Folders Global Inbox account.

☑ Use Global Inbox (store mail in Local Folders)

Enter the name of your outgoing server (SMTP) (for example, "smtp.example.net").

Outgoing Server:

Cancel   Back   Next

FIGURE 3.3

Selecting POP3 protocol.

9. Click the Next button.

10. On the User Name wizard page, enter the username that your ISP (or webmail provider) assigned to you. This too should be on the account information form from the ISP. If this is the first email account you've set up, you can also enter the Outgoing User Name.

11. Click the Next button.

12. On the Account Name wizard page, enter the name you'd like to give to the account within Thunderbird. For example, if it's the account from your ISP and you also have webmail accounts, you might want to call this one "Home."

13. Click the Next button.

14. Congratulations! The wizard page gives you a chance to review the information for your account. If it isn't correct, you can use the Back button to go back and fix it, or you can complete the wizard and then edit the account. Editing the account is sometimes preferable because you can't set the more advanced properties through the Account Wizard. Clear the check box if you don't want to try to download your email now. Clearing this is a good idea if you know you have to change settings.

15. Click Finish and you're done.

At no point in this entire process were you asked for the password. Thunderbird requests this when you actually connect to the account, at which point you also have the option to have Thunderbird remember the password.

Setting Up an IMAP Account

The steps for setting up an IMAP account are almost exactly the same as for the POP account, except that you select IMAP instead of POP. The same subtle shift of the functionality of the wizard applies: you can only enter the name of the outgoing server when setting up the first email account. All subsequent accounts assume that the SMTP server will be the same, and don't give you a chance to enter a new different SMTP server in the wizard. You must edit the account to change the SMTP server.

Editing an Existing Email Account

Let's edit the account and take a look at the sorts of things you might want to fix. To do that, select the account in Thunderbird (you'll see a screen similar to Figure 3.4) and then click View Settings for This Account on the right. If you clicked Local Folders, after opening the settings you may have to select the appropriate account on the tree to the left.

If you need to create a new SMTP server listing, scroll the tree (on the left) to the bottom and click Outgoing Server (SMTP). To add a new entry, click the Add button on the right and enter the information about the outgoing server in the SMTP Server dialog box.

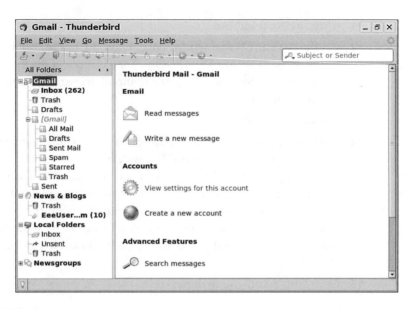

FIGURE 3.4

Editing an account.

Setting Up Gmail

Gmail uses a secure connection, so when setting up Gmail, the settings in the SMTP Server dialog box should match those shown in Figure 3.5.

FIGURE 3.5

SMTP server settings for Gmail.

If you're using Gmail, you also need to set the POP3 server properties. Scroll to the top of the tree and click Gmail. Click View Settings for This Account to open the Account Settings window. Gmail requires that you select SSL and set the port to 995.

Setting up a Gmail IMAP account is very similar to setting up a POP3 account, but with a few deviations:

- On the Account Information page of the Account Wizard, you must select IMAP instead of POP3.
- The Gmail setup uses port 993 for the imap.gmail.com server, as shown in Figure 3.6. Note that TLS must be enabled.

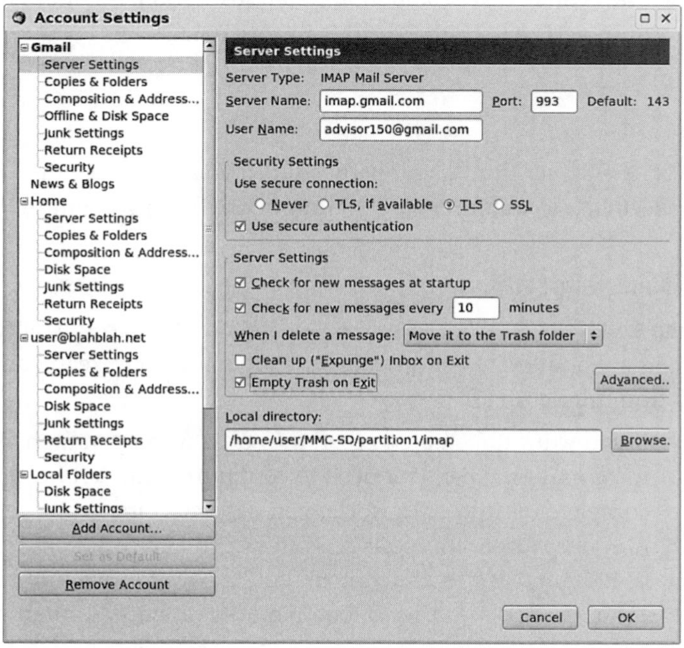

FIGURE 3.6

Server settings for IMAP (Gmail).

Managing Storage with Your Email Accounts

Once you have email set up, you need to consider how to handle downloads, because storage space on the Eee PC is very limited. If you download all the email to your Eee PC, you need to carefully monitor how much email you store on the computer. You'll need to either clean up your email quite often or reset the location in which downloads are stored (such as an SD flash drive). Some methods for minimizing the amount of email stored on your Eee PC follow.

Store Email on an SD Flash Drive

To change the location in which you store email to your SD flash drive, follow these steps:

1. Open the Account Settings window for your account.

2. Click Server Settings under the account name.

3. On the Server Settings properties sheet, click the Browse button next to the Local Directory field and choose your SD drive. If you're using the internal display of the Eee PC, this field is hidden as the dialog has been sized to fit the screen. The workaround for large windows is to Alt+drag them with the mouse. In this case, Alt-drag the window up until you can see the bottom, then just drag the bottom downward until you can see the Local Directory field.

Empty Trash on Exit

Also on the Server Settings properties sheet, you can check the Empty Trash on Exit check box to automatically clean out anything you put in the trash.

Space Saving Thunderbird Settings

On the Offline & Disk Space properties sheet of the Account Settings window, you can configure a few more settings that will help to keep your solid-state drive from filling up:

- If you want to be able to read messages when you aren't connected to the email provider, you need to configure Thunderbird to download complete messages. However, you can set Thunderbird to not download messages larger than 50KB, as shown in Figure 3.7. So, if someone sends you a 10MB attachment, you'll have to save that manually (Thunderbird won't download big attachments automatically).

- You can set Thunderbird to automatically delete messages more than 30 days (or some arbitrary time) old (see Figure 3.7).

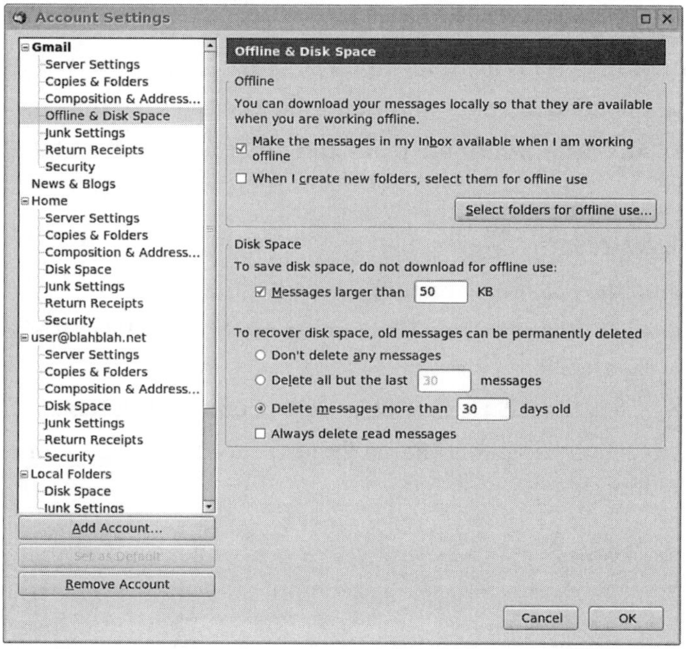

FIGURE 3.7

Space-saving settings for offline email reading.

Setting Up RSS Feeds

Really Simple Syndication (RSS) is a way to subscribe to receive headlines and synopses of updates to blogs, general news sources, and almost everything else that's available on the Web. Basically, an RSS document, or "feed," is an XML file that has a link to the full article or blog entry along with the title and a synopsis.

RSS feeds are provided by many web sites, including news sites, blogs, company and organizational sites, and almost anything else you can think of. Subscribing to a site simply requires linking to an XML file at the site. Your RSS reader periodically reads the file and the file's contents describe the current headlines.

The RSS reader software downloads the headlines, which contain links to the main articles, and organizes them such that they appear like a set of email headers in your inbox. If you find a particular entry interesting, you can either expand it to look at the synopsis or click the link to open the complete article in Firefox.

Subscribing to RSS Feeds via Thunderbird

Subscribing to feeds in Thunderbird is a two-step process:

1. Create an account to contain the RSS feed subscriptions.
2. Add feeds, which are really URLs that point to the XML files.

Setting Up an RSS Account

To set up the RSS feeds account:

1. Click File, New, Account to open the Account Wizard, shown in Figure 3.8.
2. Select the RSS News & Blogs radio button. Click Next.
3. Give the account a name (or just leave the default name of News & Blogs).

FIGURE 3.8

Adding a new RSS account in Thunderbird.

Adding RSS Feeds

The easiest way to explain how to add RSS feeds is through an example:

1. Point Firefox at http://www.space.com.

2. Scroll to the bottom of the page and click the orange XML button on the left. (This is a typical location for the button.) A page of available feeds appears.

3. Click the link for any feed, and you'll get a page that shows the current content available under that feed, each containing the headline and the synopsis (see Figure 3.9).

4. Select the web address in the Address field and copy it (Ctrl+C) to the clipboard.

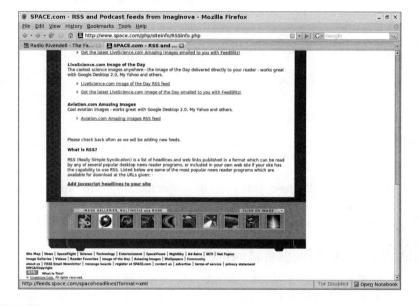

FIGURE 3.9

Finding the XML button that leads to the feeds.

5. In Thunderbird, click the News & Blogs (or whatever you named it) top-level folder in the folder tree, and then click Manage Subscriptions on the right.

6. In the RSS Subscriptions dialog box, click the Add button.

7. In the Feed URL field, paste the web address of the feed (Ctrl+V). To save on disk space, you might want to select the Show the Article Summary Instead of Loading the Web Page option.

   The Import button provides a way to load an OPML or an XML file for an RSS feed. OPML files are sets of RSS feeds, and many RSS readers can save their subscription sets to an OPML file. You can use the Export button to save your set of RSS feeds as an OPML file, which you can then share with others.

8. Click OK. Thunderbird downloads the various feed entries (see Figure 3.10).

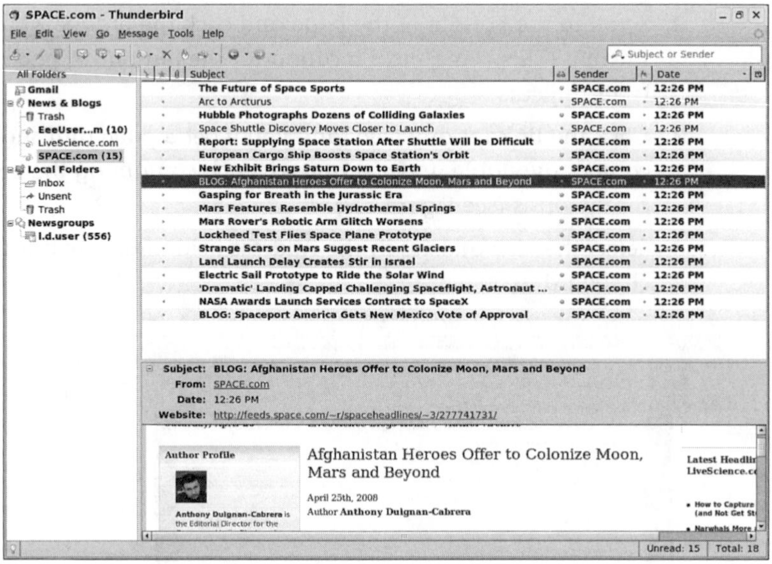

FIGURE 3.10
Viewing RSS feeds in Thunderbird.

To view an RSS feed, just open its folder like any other mail folder. Click a link and Thunderbird will load the related article in the bottom pane. Click the website link and it'll load that article into Firefox. Pretty cool, eh?

Subscribing to RSS Feeds via Firefox

In the previous section, you navigated to a web page and found the orange XML button to list the RSS feeds. Well, that's pretty much all that's required to subscribe via Firefox. When you get to a page listing RSS feeds, click the Subscribe Now button (see Figure 3.11).

To see your RSS feeds, go to the Bookmarks menu and select the Bookmarks Toolbar folder. When you hover the mouse pointer over the name of the feed source, such as Space.com, you'll see the latest feeds. Just select a feed and the article will load in your browser.

Accessing Usenet Newsgroups via Thunderbird

Usenet is old technology (well, for the Internet at least) and is basically a set of thousands of categorized online forums. A word of caution about Usenet: there are adult forums and usenet is mostly not moderated (on moderated forums, the post is sent to a moderator before it goes to the group). In unmoderated groups, anyone can post anything they want. These are some of the reasons that Usenet has fallen out of favor, and many folks prefer moderated forums on Yahoo or other web portals, blogs, and RSS feeds. Still, there are useful technical forums on Usenet.

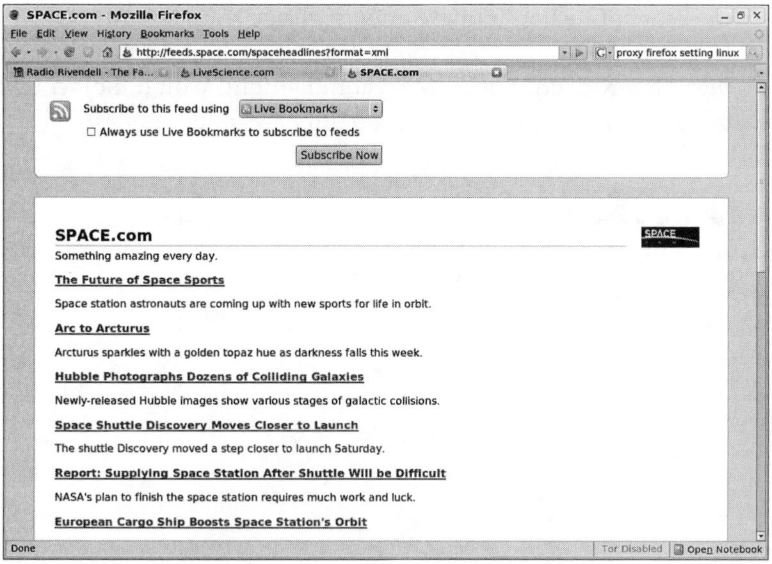

FIGURE 3.11

Click the Subscribe Now button.

Many ISPs offer access to news servers that provide access to newsgroups. If you'd like to build an account to access a news server in Thunderbird, follow these steps:

1. Click File, New, Account to open the Account Wizard.

2. Select the Newsgroup Account radio button. Click Next.

3. Enter your name and email address. Click Next.

4. On the Server Information wizard page, enter the name of the news server from your ISP (see Figure 3.12). The format for this is usually news.*yourISPdomain*.com (or .net, or whatever). Click Next.

5. Give the account a name (such as New or Usenet). Click Next.

6. Verify that the settings are correct. Click OK, and you're ready to go.

If a login and password are required, you'll be prompted for this when Thunderbird first connects with the server.

Now the fun begins. There are literally thousands of Usenet groups, some of which are decidedly unsavory. How do you navigate this morass? Fortunately, people keep lists of what the various groups are. One of the best of these lists is at http://www.dmoz.org/Computers/Usenet/. Peruse the links on this page and you'll be able to find what you're looking for. Alternatively, you can use the Search function for newsgroups within Thunderbird itself. To use this, click Newsgroups (or whatever you called the account) in the All Folders tree and then click Manage Subscriptions on the right. Wait a moment, because it takes a while to download a list of all newsgroup names.

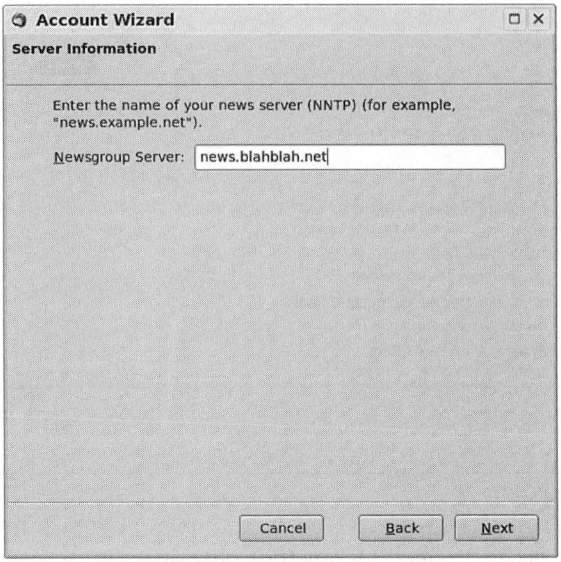

FIGURE 3.12

Setting up a news server in Thunderbird.

Suppose, for instance, that you want to look up forums about Debian Linux. Well, just type Debian into the Show Items that Contain field and a set of forums is listed. Check the boxes for the forums to which you'd like to subscribe and then click the Subscribe button.

Once you've successfully subscribed to some forums, just click one in the Newsgroups folder in Thunderbird and you'll see a set of posts on the right. Clicking the Get New Messages button downloads the latest set of posts. Click the post and, unless it's too old and has "expired," you'll see the post in the bottom pane. Double-click it and it gets its own window.

You can manage subscriptions just by right-clicking them in the Newsgroups folder, as shown in Figure 3.13. So, if you decide that you no longer want a subscription, just right-click and choose Unsubscribe.

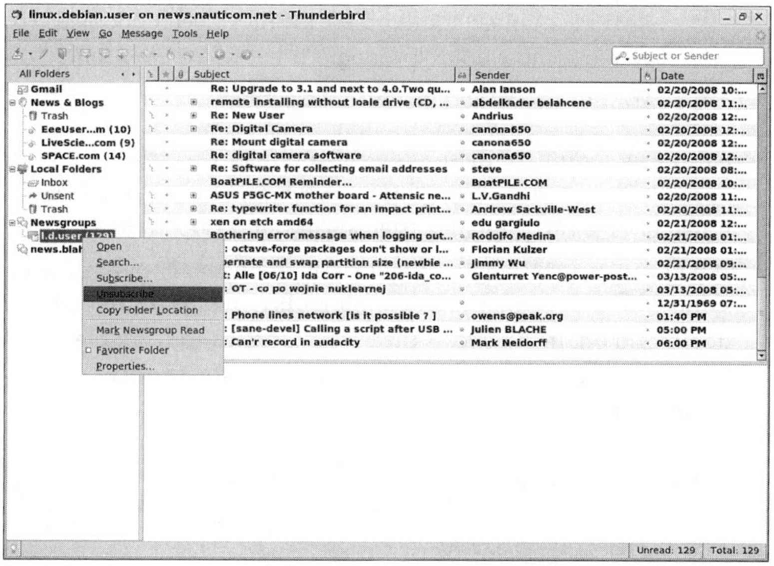

FIGURE 3.13

Unsubscribing from a Usenet forum.

Using the Pidgin Instant Messenger Client

Pidgin is the instant messenger application installed in Xandros. You can load it in Easy Mode by clicking the Messenger icon on the Internet tab. In Full Desktop, start it by choosing Launch, Applications, Internet, Pidgin Internet Messenger. The thing about Pidgin is that it's merely a client, meaning you must add an account from an existing IM system to make it work.

The supported set of IM systems includes:

- **AIM:** The ubiquitous AOL Instant Messenger.

- **Google Talk:** The chat client that you get with Gmail.

- **Groupwise:** The IM component of the Novell collaborative platform.

- **ICQ:** The first IM system.

- **IRC:** Internet Relay Chat, a really old system mostly used for conferencing between groups of people (the so-called "channels").

- **MSN:** The Microsoft entry into the IM world.

- **QQ:** Really Tencent QQ, the most popular IM system in China.

- **Simple:** This is also called SIP/SIMPLE. Pidgin supports the chat component of this open standard, which also includes Voice over IP (VoIP).

- **Sametime:** The IBM/Lotus IM system.

■ **XMPP:** An open standard for IM that's been adopted by a number of systems, most notably Google Talk and Apple iChat.

■ **Yahoo:** The Yahoo instant messenger.

Of course, for any of these systems, you first need to set up an account. You need a valid username/ID plus a password. This section shows you how to set up Pidgin for two popular systems: AIM and Google Talk.

When you launch Pidgin in Full Desktop, it simply places the green-ball chat symbol on the toolbar. If you don't realize this, you can end up launching it again and again. To access the Pidgin application, double-click the toolbar icon. You can also right-click the icon to see the shortcut menu shown in Figure 3.14.

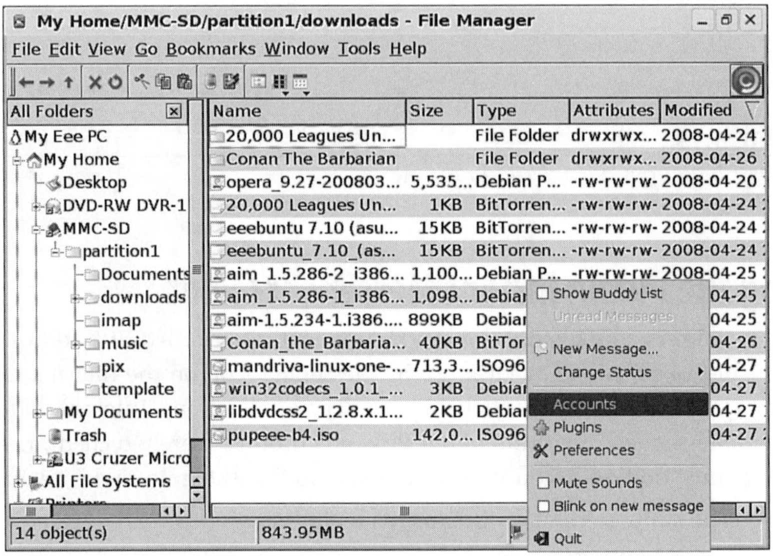

FIGURE 3.14

The Pidgin shortcut menu on the toolbar.

To set up an account from the Pidgin application:

1. Choose Add/Edit from the Accounts menu (from right-clicking the toolbar icon).

2. In the Accounts dialog box, click the Add button.

3. In the Add Account dialog box, in the Protocol list, choose the system that you want to join.

4. For an AIM account, you simply need to enter the ID and password, as shown in Figure 3.15. Everything else is taken care of automatically.

For Google Talk, you also need to know the domain name. This is almost always gmail.com. It matches the domain name of your Gmail account.

> **tip**
>
> When you check this box for Google Talk, you can double-click the email status bar in the Pidgin application to launch the browser and load Google.

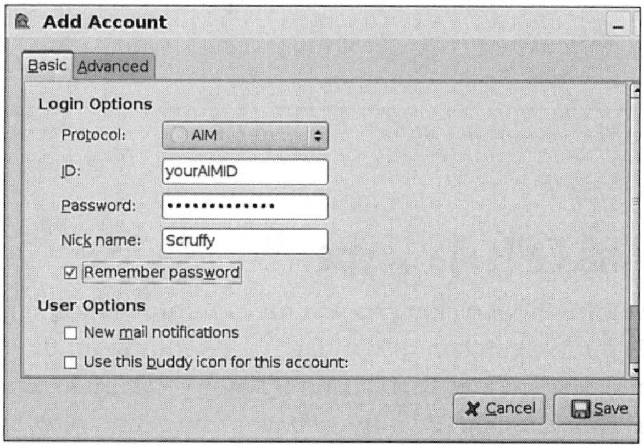

5. If you want to be notified when you have incoming email, check the New Mail Notifications box.

6. Click Save to save the account.

FIGURE 3.15

Setting up AIM in Pidgin.

AIM provides all sorts of goodies, including the AIM Bots (automated services). You can also check your AOL email from here.

The bar at the bottom of the application provides choices for your current status in AIM, such as available, away, offline, and so forth. The Buddies menu contains the controls for starting a chat or joining one. You can also check the current status of others (via User Info).

When using any of the instant messaging networks, if you choose to log the messages, which you'll find under the Pidgin Tools menu by choosing Preferences (it's on the Logging tab), you can also view the logs of previous conversations with specific users. You can also use the Preferences dialog box to customize the look of the application.

Conversations in Pidgin work just like in AIM or any of the chat applications. Figure 3.16 shows a conversation in progress.

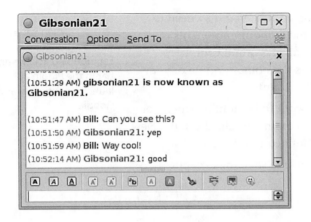

FIGURE 3.16

Pidgin in action chatting via an AIM account.

Making Free Phone Calls via Skype

Skype is a free-to-use tool as long as you are communicating only with other Skype users. For a fee, you can also make phone calls to landline phones and wireless phones. The focus of this section is what you can do via the Eee PC for free on Skype. This is where the nifty webcam comes into play for video conferencing. You simply need to set up a free Skype account and you're ready to video conference.

Setting Up a Skype Account

Setting up a Skype account is quite simple:

1. Launch Skype. In Easy Mode, click the Skype icon on the Internet tab. In Full Desktop, choose Launch, Applications, Internet, Skype.

2. Click the Don't Have a Skype Name Yet? link.

3. Complete the Create a New Skype Account dialog box, shown in Figure 3.17. All the information is required except the optional Full Name field.

4. Click the Sign Up button.

During the rest of the signup process, unless you really want to use Skype as a phone service, simply ignore all the extra services and places where you can put in credit card numbers, Pay Pal accounts, and so forth. What you're after is a free account, so you just need to set your screen name (the choice of which is not always easy, considering Skype has 309 million accounts with screen names) and your password. Once you finally fight your way through all of that, you're ready.

FIGURE 3.17

Signing up for a Skype account.

Using Skype

After you sign in with your screen name and password, do a sound check. Make sure that your speakers are on or your headset is plugged in.

Just to make sure things are working, click the Echo/Sound Test Service link and record a message. This will check your microphone and speakers or headset. If

> **tip** A cheap headset unit with an ear bud and tiny microphone works fine. Mine plugs into both the headphone and microphone ports, and is nice to have for places like Internet cafes where I want to use Skype but don't want my entire conversation to be public.

you need to make some changes to the input or output volume, see Chapter 1, "Getting Started," for a description of the volume controls.

When you're ready, click the little green ball at the bottom of the Skype application window to access the contacts list. Just for "grins," I typed Eee into the search list and found lots of Eee users. Just start adding your contacts, and you're ready to make calls.

The green phone icon in the Skype application is your call button. Select a contact and click the icon to ring the contact. Once connected, make sure that your video is on. You'll be able to see your own camera in a little window within the video conference window, as shown in Figure 3.18.

FIGURE 3.18

Skype video conferencing through the Eee PC.

Remotely Accessing Another Computer Using VNC

Using VNC is a way to remotely access another computer. The Eee PC has a VNC server and client built in. You can access both the server and client in the same menu in Full Desktop by choosing Launch, Applications, System, Remote Desktop Sharing. The server, which allows other computers to see your video and operate the GUI, is the Share My Desktop part. To do this, the remote computer must have a VNC client installed. The other computer's owner can get the VNC client, plus a server, for free at http://www.realvnc.com.

To run these in Easy Mode, you must first launch a terminal window via Ctrl+Alt+T. The command to run the client is krdc and the command to run the server is krfb.

Inviting a Remote Computer to Access Your Eee PC

Assuming that the remote computer is equipped with the VNC client, all you have to do to enable someone using that other computer to remotely access your Eee PC is to:

1. Launch Share My Desktop from the Launch menu.

2. In the Invitation – Share My Desktop dialog box (see Figure 3.19), you'll see a couple of buttons for creating invitations. Click the Create Invitation button.

3. This simply creates a password for logging and displays your URL and port. Jot down the password for logging in and the URL and port and give this information to the person who'll be logging into your Eee PC remotely.

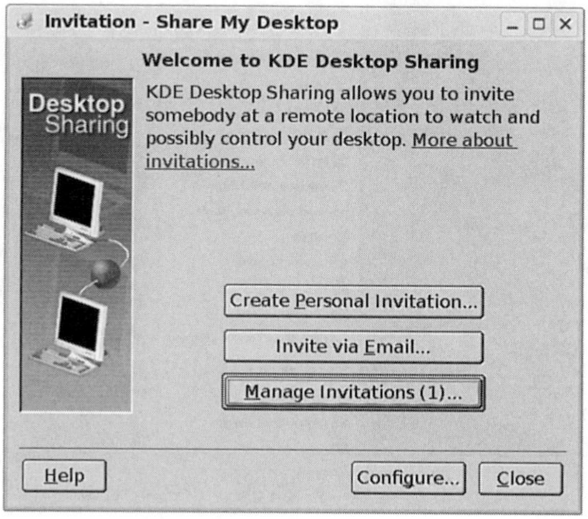

FIGURE 3.19

The invitation choices.

You can also try to use the Invite via Email button, but it's frankly worthless. It does indeed launch Thunderbird, but neglects to put the information necessary into the email, and there's no way to access the information for that invitation. So, you might as well do this manually.

The great thing about the invitation system is that it provides a way to deactivate the password. Just click the Manage Invitations button and you can delete invitations you've created.

Accessing a Remote Computer from Your Eee PC

To go the other way and log into a remote computer, you need precisely the same information from the other computer: IP address and port (or machine name and port) plus a password. Actually, it's possible that the remote computer may not require a password, in which case you'll just suddenly see the remote computer's desktop. Launch the Remote Desktop Connection application and enter the address of the remote computer (don't forget the colon and port) in the Remote Desktop field. Click the Connect button. If there's a password, you'll be challenged to enter this. Enter the password, and you'll see the screen from the remote computer on your screen, as shown in the example in Figure 3.20. You're now running the remote computer from your keyboard and mouse.

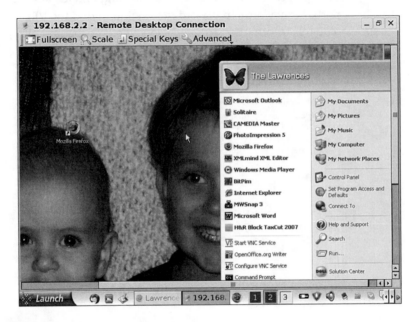

FIGURE 3.20
Running a Windows XP PC remotely from the Eee PC.

Summary

In this chapter, you learned how to set up the various Internet communications packages that come with the Eee PC. Much of this information is general enough that you now can apply it to both other Linux applications or to applications in other operating systems.

With the exception of the VNC tools, all of these applications are available on the menus in both Easy Mode and the Full Desktop. If you need to access VNC in Easy Mode, you can do so via the command line.

Customizing Easy Mode

Easy Mode is one of the attractive features of the Eee PC. I've watched a three-year-old child master it in little time. For casual users and non-geeks, Easy Mode is a wonderful thing. It's amazingly simple and intuitive, and runs nicely in the limited space of the Eee PC's onboard screen.

Easy Mode is a well-thought-out adaptation of a window manager that was optimized for the Eee screen and the default applications. Frankly, if you're not interested in the capabilities of the Eee PC beyond the set of applications exposed through Easy Mode, you can do all of your day-to-day tasks with it.

This chapter covers how to customize Easy Mode and how to liberate the underlying window manager and use it to its full potential. You can completely change the look and feel of Easy Mode, making it a much more advanced interface to the Eee PC.

What Is a Window Manager?

Microsoft Windows provides a single windows manager, which is the interface the defines the look and operation of windows, the location and contents of menus, and even the "physics" of how you interact with windows via the mouse. Linux provides many, many windows managers to choose from. By the time you finish this book, you will have encountered most of the major Linux Windows managers and some of the more interesting minor ones.

In the Linux world, window managers interact with the underlying windowing system called "X-Windows." X-Windows provides the basic framework for drawing windows, interacting with input devices (such as the mouse and keyboard), and everything else required to construct the user interface.

Easy Mode is actually based on the Ice Window Manager (IceWM), and is customized for the Eee PC. IceWM is actually not one of the two most popular Windows managers in the Linux world, and holds a position as a "minor player." The irony is that customizing Easy Mode is much harder than customizing the Full Desktop (as covered in Chapter 5), which is based on the KDE window manager. The Easy Mode desktop provides the tools for only very minor customizations Therefore, to customize Easy Mode requires customizing the Easy Mode configuration files.

Because Easy Mode is a specific implementation of a user interface for the Eee PC, applications do not provide ready-made icons for Easy Mode. Perhaps this will change over time as the Eee PC gains in popularity. Unfortunately, this currently means that adding icons for new applications onto specific tabs is not trivial. In fact, it requires more than a little skill with a high-end graphic package as well as modifying configuration files.

Given the difficulty of making modifications to Easy Mode, why do it at all? There are several reasons:

- You intend to use your Eee PC without an attached monitor most of the time. Easy Mode works especially well with the limited real estate on the default display.
- The primary user of the Eee PC is a young person, and you want to set it up with additional software.

- Your school, library, or other group has purchased a number of Eee PC machines for your students, and you want to customize them for your group. One of the primary goals for the Eee PC is to provide a simple and inexpensive computer for students. Therefore, you may need to make customizations to Easy Mode for a large number of machines. To do so, customize one as outlined in this chapter and copy the icons and configuration files to the other computers.

Beyond merely customizing the tabbed interface, you can augment or even abandon the tabbed interface of Easy Mode and rely instead on the IceWM window manager without the Eee PC customizations. In fact, you can customize IceWM until its capabilities rival that of the KDE desktop in Full Desktop mode. The latter portion of this chapter covers how to do this.

Even if you don't decide to do anything with Easy Mode, consider this an introduction to the fun of Linux as well. Microsoft Windows is pretty much about doing your day-to-day tasks and that's all. Linux is about exploring, pushing the limits, and seeing what happens when you "do this." It is not always necessarily about the end result, but what you learn in the journey to reach that result. That's why Linux provides so many possibilities and choices for doing practically anything.

Adding Application Icons to the Favorites Tab

Working with applications in Easy Mode is simplicity itself. You click a tab and then click an icon to launch an application. Chapter 8, "Getting More Linux Applications," discusses adding and removing applications in general to the Eee PC. The following provides the steps for adding the additional applications to Easy Mode.

The Favorites tab is the Easy Mode method of adding additional applications icons to the desktop, but its functionality is limited. You can add icons for most preinstalled programs to the Favorites tab by clicking the Customize application icon (see Figure 4.1). Simply select in the Available Favorites list the application you want to add, and click the Add button to add it to the Current Favorites list on the right. The Up and Down buttons let you move the currently selected application icon up and down the list, which sets the order in which it appears on the Favorites tab.

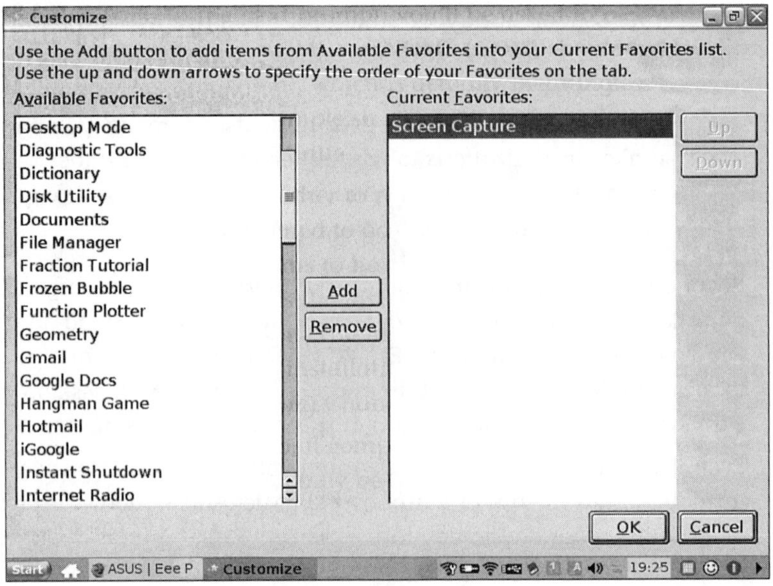

FIGURE 4.1

Adding icons to the Favorites tab.

Unfortunately, if you want to add applications that aren't listed here, you need to start editing configuration files and creating icons, covered next. You can add such icons to any tabs, you are no longer limited to Favorites.

Adding Application Icons to the Easy Mode Tabs

If you've added applications to your Eee PC (which is covered in Chapter 8), you may wish to add them to the appropriate Easy Mode tabs. For example, if you add the GIMP image editor, which in fact is a very good idea for creating new icons, its icons should be on either the Work or Play tabs. You need to do a few things to add icons to these tabs:

1. Create a local customizations directory for Easy Mode.

2. Set up a work folder for icons and load the Easy Mode icons into it.

3. Create custom icons for your applications. Each application needs five icons: one for normal display and four for the four Easy Mode themes.

4. Add the custom icons to the the appropriate tabs.

The first two tasks are pretty simple, but building icons that look good is quite a challenge. Moreover, the challenge is three-fold: you must drop out the background (make it transparent) for the icon art, scale the icon to match the other icons, and copy the icon onto a separate layer on all four background icons (one is required for each of the Easy Mode themes).

What make creating custom icons a little tougher is that the paint program installed with Xandros, MTPaint, really isn't up to the task. You need a more capable paint program, such as GIMP. Chapter 8 explains how to download applications such as GIMP. You could also use any other advanced paint package as well, although the instruction here are specific to GIMP.

This section covers this process in detail, from setting up the working directories to actually building the icons. At present, unfortunately, the best way to customize the tabbed Easy Mode interface is still to build the icons in a competent graphics program.

Setting Up the Work Area for Icons

First off, let's go over what you're going to do and why you're doing it that way:

1. Set up a local customizations directory for AsusLauncher, which is the proper name of the Easy Mode interface. This directory will contain the customizations to the Easy Mode user interface. Having a local customizations directory means you're free to modify files in that directory without changing the master files for the system.

2. Set up a working directory for icons. This can be anywhere under your home directory tree; however, if you have an SD card installed, you might as well put it there and save wear and tear on the solid-state drive.

This may sound a little odd, but you won't be doing these tasks in Easy Mode. You can, but you'll need to restart X Window System to test things anyway, so why not start out in Full Desktop where it's a little more convenient to work? Actually, I have my Eee PC set to boot into Full Desktop for this.

Also, although you can do all of this from the command line (and you'll mostly be using the command line throughout this chapter), you'll use the File Manager to preview the icons. This is simply for convenience, as you simply double-click a graphics file to preview it. It's a good idea to preview the icons to make sure they look right before you copy them into place and restart X Window System.

First, build the local customizations directory for AsusLauncher. Launch an xterm or console window (choose Launch, Run Command, and then enter Konsole) and check the current directory by looking at the shell prompt. The current directory location should be /user/home.

Issue the following command to build the working directory:

```
> mkdir .AsusLauncher
```

You don't need sudo because it's your home directory. Now copy the simpleui.rc file to .AsusLauncher:

```
> cp /opt/xandros/share/AsusLauncher/simpleui.rc .AsusLauncher
```

Next, make a pristine backup of the configuration file, just in case things go awry. Sure, you can always get another one from the /opt tree, but it's really good to get into the habit of backing up configuration files before you twiddle with them.

```
> cp /opt/xandros/share/AsusLauncher/simpleui.rc AsusLauncherOriginal.rc
```

Next, create a working directory for the various icon files. I'm assuming that you have an MMC-SD card installed, so the command will look something like this:

```
> mkdir /media/MMC-SD/partition1/icons
```

If you don't have an MMC-SD card, simply create the directory within /user/home. Now copy the icon files you need to build your new icons:

```
> cp /opt/xandros/share/AsusLauncher/*icon_background.png /media/MMC-
➥SD/partition1/icons/
```

Adding Icons to the Easy Mode Configuration File

A bit of background first. The simpleui.rc file is the configuration for the Easy Mode interface. Like many newer configuration files, simpleui.rc is an XML file. XML is actually much easier to work with than the older formats and enables you to easily see where something begins and ends. Each element, or tag, has a clear beginning, in the format <element>, and ending, in the format </element>. As long as you maintain this balance of beginning and ending tags and carefully type in what's shown, you can't go wrong.

The tag structure in the simpleui.rc file mimics the structure of the Easy Mode desktop, with its tabs that contain either application icons or folders. Folders in the desktop can also contain application icons, so that structure exists in the simpleui.rc file as well. In general, the structure is something like this:

defines a tab.

defines a folder.

defines an application icon and the logic to launch the application itself.

A `<parcel>` element contains a `simplecat` attribute, which defines the icon's location in the tab structure. In XML, an *attribute* is a way of specifying something within a tag. In this case, if the icon is on the Internet tab, the attribute value will be `simplecat="Internet"`. Pay close attention to the equals sign and make sure the value that's specified, `Internet`, is in quotes. If the icon happens to be in a folder, then you use a convention similar to a directory structure, with the tab and folder names separated by a slash. For example, to place an application icon in the Webmail folder on the Internet tab, the attribute value would be `simplecat="Internet/Webmail"`.

By the way, as I've learned from hard experience, if you make a mistake with the `simplecat="xxxx"` attribute, you'll drive yourself nuts wondering what happened to the icon or folder you've created. It simply won't appear. Therefore, double-check that your syntax and capitalization are correct.

First, change the directory to .AsusLauncher:

```
> cd .AsusLauncher
```

You don't need to "be" in this directory to work, but I find it more convenient.

Next, you need to edit the simpleui.rc file. The file was copied from the /opt tree, which means its permissions are such that you need root access to edit the file. You can change the file permissions if you like with `chmod` (change mode); however, it's just as easy to open the file with `sudo` prepended to the command. (For more information about the `chmod` command, see Chapter 11, "Introduction to the Linux Command Line.") If you're doing this from the File Manager, you need the Administrative File Manager (available in Full Desktop Mode) to open the file in your editor of choice and be able to save your changes. That's another good reason to do all of this from within Full Desktop: accessing the Administrative File Manager is a lot easier.

I'm an old xemacs kind of guy (I installed XEmacs via Synaptic), so I open the file with the following command. Substitute your text editor of choice for `xemacs`.

```
> sudo xemacs simpleui.rc &
```

For this example, I'm going to add an Opera browser icon to the Internet tab. (I've already installed Opera via the .deb package I downloaded, and I've made sure that works; for instructions on installing Opera and other applications, see Chapter 8.) All I have to do is insert an entry for the Opera icon in the simpleui.rc file. First, I need to search for some other icons on the Internet tab. Icons are placed on the tab in the order in which they appear in the file. I want to put the Opera icon right beside the Web icon for Firefox, because they are related applications. So, I'll look for Firefox. This is a bit tricky, because Firefox is actually used for many icons, so I need to find the correct one. To do that, I search for Firefox and look for an entry within a `<parcel>` element that has the `simplecat="Internet"` attribute. After I find that, I'll add a few extra blank lines for some working space after the `<parcel>` element. The entry for Opera looks like this:

```
<parcel extraargs="/usr/bin/opera" simplecat="Internet" selected_
icon="opera_hi.png" icon="opera_norm.png" >
<name lang="en">Opera</name>
</parcel>
```

A bit of translation is required:

- The `extraargs` attribute defines the command necessary to run the application. In this case, I just need to run the opera executable file. I need to provide the full path to this from the root of the file system.

- The `simplecat` attribute defines this icon as residing in the Internet tab.

- The `selected_icon` attribute points to the PNG (Portable Network Graphics) format graphics file that will be used when the icon is selected (this is the `hi`, or highlighted icon). The `selected` attribute means that either the mouse is hovering over the icon or the icon has been clicked. The `icon` attribute points to the normal (`norm`) icon PNG file. The normal icon file is the one used to simply display the icon on the tab.

- The `<name>` element defines the word used under the icon for the language (`en` for English) that I use. Check the other entries to get the right language code if your native language is something other than English.

- The end tag `</parcel>` closes the XML element. As I previously mentioned, this is very important. XML parsers do not like tags that don't end.

Note that the graphics files do not require a complete path as did the `extraargs` attribute. The Easy Mode launcher knows to look in the /opt/xandros/share/AsusLauncher directory for icons.

Check over your entry and then save the file.

Building the Icons

To follow the instructions in this section, you need to use the graphics program GIMP. If you haven't installed it, refer to Chapter 8 for instructions. Using GIMP to create icons is a bit tricky, because you must work with transparencies and layers. This section gives detailed instructions, so you should be fine even if you are new to GIMP.

Your first big problem is getting a suitable graphics file to use as the basis of the icon. For Opera, I simply used Google's Image Search and looked for

"Opera" and "icon." While GIMP is perfectly capable of sizing a graphic down to the resolution you need, you may get some nasty-looking edges if you take a really big, high-resolution graphic and reduce it down to the 120×120-pixel size that's required. I found one that was 128×128 pixels, which I was able to scale down to 120×120 pixels.

A suitable icon consists of a file that's 120×120 pixels in PNG format and that has a transparent background. Because GIMP is a highly capable graphics editor, it's possible to take graphics files of pretty much any format and create a suitable icon.

Assuming that you have found an image (via a search engine perhaps) for the icon that you wish to build, save the graphic to the icons directory you just created. Now you can either load the graphics file into GIMP by right-clicking it in the File Manager and choosing Open With, GIMP Image Editor or you can edit it from the command line by using the GIMP command followed by the image file on the command line.

After you load the image, you need to resize it to 120×120 pixels. To do this within the GIMP menus, choose Image, Scale Image to open the Scale Image dialog box, shown in Figure 4.2. Enter 120 in both the Width and Height fields. If the resolution for X and Y isn't 72 dpi, set it to 72. Check that all the settings are as described and then click the Scale button to set the image at the right size and resolution. Make sure that the clarity of the scaled image is acceptable. If the image is blocky or fuzzy, find another on the web.

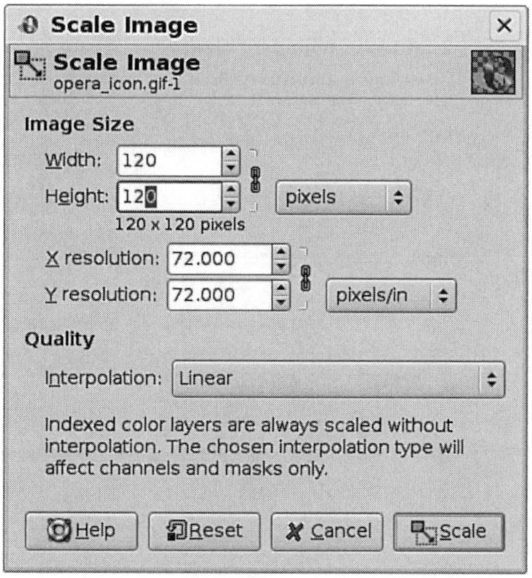

FIGURE 4.2

Sizing a graphic in GIMP.

Now you have the image at the right size. However, you need to reduce just the picture portion of the image to 80×80 pixels. The entire graphic, or graphic frame, however, must remain at 120×120 pixels. This requires cutting the icon portion of the frame, creating a new frame, and pasting it there. Next, you'll scale the frame to 80×80 pixels. This trick gets the image to the necessary 80×80 size that leaves room for the title of the icon. Then you'll extend the layer boundaries back to 120×120 pixels, centering the scaled picture in the frame. Finally, you'll select the picture portion and move it up a bit, leaving a little extra room at the bottom for text.

To put the picture on a new layer:

1. Using the square selection tool from the main GIMP tool window, drag a selection box around the icon portion of the frame.
2. Press Ctrl+X to cut the picture from the frame.
3. In the window that contains your graphic file, choose Layer, New Layer.
4. Press Ctrl+V to paste the picture into the new layer.

To resize the layer and picture:

1. Choose Layer, Scale Layer to open the Scale Layer dialog box.
2. Set the Width and Height to 80 pixels.
3. Click Scale.
4. Choose Layer, Layer Boundary Size to open the Set Layer Boundary Size dialog box, shown in Figure 4.3.
5. Set the Width and Height to 120 pixels.

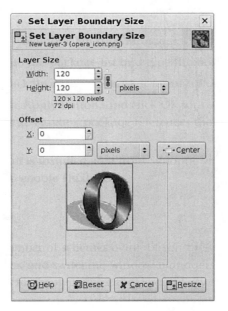

FIGURE 4.3

Setting the Width and Height to 120.

6. Click Center.

7. Click Resize.

Now you have an 80×80-pixel picture in a 120×120-pixel frame.

To move the picture up in the frame:

1. Using the square selection tool from the main GIMP tool window, drag a selection box around the picture portion of the graphic.

2. Drag the picture up, leaving the bottom fifth or quarter of the frame free for text.

The background image is ready, but you need to do a few more things before you're done. Just to make sure that image is an RGB color model (especially if you're converting from GIF, which has a fixed palette), choose Image, Mode, RGB. If RGB is grayed out, it is already using the RGB color model.

You'll want to save a copy of the file in the GIMP native XCF format first, because the format for Easy Mode icon files, PNG, doesn't support layers. This means that the image will be "flattened," and you may want to keep your layers. This might not be absolutely necessary for the plain icon, but for the "hi" (highlighted icon) versions it's essential, because the base layer of the image has the highlight fill, and you need to keep the picture portion as a separate layer so as to not disrupt the bottom layer fountain fill while sizing and moving the picture portion.

The file-naming convention is extremely important, by the way. If you don't get the file naming right, your icons won't work. For the standard icon, the filename must be *name*_norm.png. Each file of the five files must start with the *name* that you choose, and the base file must end in _norm. I list the highlighted icon names in a bit, so you can get them absolutely right.

Save the file first as an XCF file (to preserve the layers) by choosing File, Save As. In the Name field, enter *name*_norm.xcf and click Save.

Next, save the file as a PNG file by choosing File, Save As. This time, use .png as the extension, clear the Save Background Color option, and then click Save. You'll be told by GIMP that you need to export the file first (this flattens the layers) and then save. Just go ahead and do this.

One file down, four to go. Remember when you copied *icon_background.png from the AsusLauncher directory to the new icons directory? This copied four files: accessibility_icon_background.png, business_icon_background.png, home_icon_background.png, and student_icon_background.png? Each of these is a building block for the highlighted icons for four desktop themes. Regardless of whether or not you ever intend to switch the Asus Eee PC built-in themes, you have to build all of these. Now that you have your base icon file, this is going to be fairly simple. You load each background icon file into GIMP

(GIMP can have multiple open files) and save it with the appropriate filename within this list of names:

accessibility_*name*_hi.xcf

business_*name*_hi.xcf

home_*name*_hi.xcf

student_*name*_hi.xcf

Again, you initially save the files as XCF files to preserve the layers. After you've created each of these files, create a new layer by choosing Layer, New Layer, just as you did with the base icon. Now each has a blank layer (above the background fill pattern) into which you can copy the picture portion of your icon.

If the *name*_norm.png file isn't open, load that into GIMP as well. You'll use the PNG file because you're only interested in copying the icon portion of the frame. Use the square selection tool again, and select the entire picture area.

Press Ctrl+C to copy the picture. Click one of the background graphics and press Ctrl+V to paste the picture onto the upper layer. It should paste in exactly the correct position (if not, choose Select, None and then reselect it and drag it). Repeat this for each of the background files, saving each as you go.

Now for the last part. Save each file with precisely the same name but with a .png extension. You'll be prompted to "export" for each, which you must do, and then you're done.

Click each of the files in the File Manager and make sure that the pictures are all in the correct position in the graphics frame. For the highlighted icon (hi) files, the background should have a tint, but should also show the "checker-board" pattern that denotes that the background is transparent.

From the command line, use the `cd` command to change the directory to your icon working directory. Issue the following commands to copy the files into place:

```
>sudo cp *name_hi.png /opt/xandros/share/AsusLauncher/
```

```
>sudo cp *name.png /opt/xandros/share/AsusLauncher/
```

You're now ready to give the icon a try. Select Easy Mode from the Launch menu to switch modes. Once in Easy Mode, check that your new icon is in position on the tab you designated (see Figure 4.4). Hover the mouse pointer over it to ensure that it "highlights" like the other icons. If so, click the icon and check that it opens the application. If all works well, congratulations!

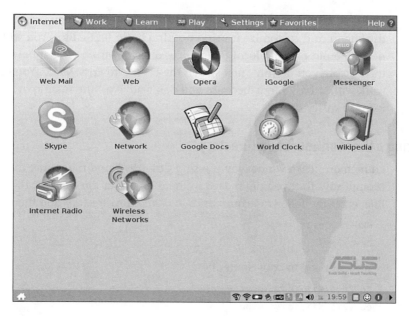

FIGURE 4.4

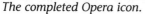

The completed Opera icon.

Common things that can go wrong include the following:

- A syntax error in the XML in the simpleui.rc file. If you don't see your icon at all, check this. The `simplecat` attribute must contain the tab name precisely as it appears in similar entries in the file. The end tag, `</parcel>`, must be present to properly close the `<parcel>` tag. Quotes must be on both sides of the attribute values.

- No transparency in the base icon file. This means that the base icon, and all of the "hi" versions, will look a little odd. Make sure that you save the file to .png format with the Save Background Colors option deselected.

Enabling the IceWM Start Menu

As mentioned at the beginning of the chapter, Easy Mode is a custom version of IceWM. According to the official IceWM website (http://icewm.org), "The goal of IceWM is speed, simplicity, and not getting in the user's way." Sounds perfect for the Eee PC, doesn't it?

In the Easy Mode Eee PC implementation, many IceWM features are turned off. One really nice feature is a Start menu (similar to the Windows Start menu or KDE Launch menu). From within Easy Mode, you can easily turn on this menu and customize it using nothing but a text editor. You will, however, need to build another local preferences directory from your /home/user directory. Before you do that, first switch the Eee PC to Easy Mode. You can now work within Easy Mode because you don't have all the fussing around with icons to worry about.

Making a User Configuration Directory

Launch an xterm window by pressing Ctrl+Alt+T and make sure that the prompt says that you are indeed in the /home/user directory. At the command line, enter the following commands to create the directory and then switch to it:

```
> mkdir .icewm
> cd .icewm
```

Now, you need to copy some files:

```
> cp /etc/X11/icewm/preferences .
> cp /etc/X11/icewm/menu .
```

The trailing dot is shorthand for the current directory, and is required because the cp command needs a destination argument.

You'll be editing both files, so you need to either use sudo to issue the command to load the file into the editor of choice, or change the file permissions to read/write. I mentioned before that this is done through the chmod command, which is explained in Chapter 11. To change the permissions on the files, issue the following command:

```
> chmod 666 *
```

The 666 sets the permissions bits to read and write for the user/group/world permissions.

Now you can easily edit either of the files without sudo. This time, use the built-in kwrite editor:

```
> kwrite preferences &
```

The & spawns a separate process for the editor, and it's no longer tied to the terminal window. Use the Find command in the Edit menu and look for the following string: TaskBarShowStartMenu.

You should find a section that looks like this:

```
#   Show 'Start' menu on task bar
# TaskBarShowStartMenu=1 # 0/1
TaskBarShowStartMenu=0
```

Change the last:

```
TaskBarShowStartMenu=0
```

to

```
TaskBarShowStartMenu=1
```

This will enable the Start menu. It's fairly anticlimactic, but that's all there is to it. Save the file, close all of your files and save any information. Restart X Window System by pressing Ctrl+Alt+Backspace.

Using the Menu

When Easy Mode is back in business, you should now have a nifty Start menu. The Start menu in its raw state has a lot of cool things on it and also a lot of nonfunctional things. The Eee PC doesn't have some of the programs that normally reside in IceWM environments, so there are a few nonfunctional items. For the most part, the menu system does actually hide things that aren't there and picks up things that are. On my Eee PC, I've added both the XEmacs graphics editor and GIMP, and they both show up. You may also find a few default entries that don't do anything on the Eee PC.

Because things are missing that you might want to use, the next task is to modify the Start menu to pick up things that you want to add and remove things that you don't want. To do that, edit the menu file:

```
> kwrite menu &
```

The structure of this file is pretty easy to follow. The pound sign # at the beginning of a line is a comment. The separator statement alone on a line creates a separator line in the menu. menu starts a menu item, which contains a folder. prog is a program. So, for example, to add the Xandros File Manager before the Applications folder, you would add something like the following:

```
separator
menu "File Manager" folder {
    prog "Xandros File Manager" /usr/bin/XandrosFileManager
XandrosFileManager
}
separator
menu Applications folder {
 .
 .
 .
```

The menu "File Manager" folder statement adds a menu item, which is a folder (that is, it contains other items) to the menu. The item itself will show

up as File Manager. The open curly brace ({) is followed by the prog statement, which has "Xandros File Manager" as the submenu item name, and two
ways to invoke the program (one if its directory is in the PATH environment
variable and one with the full path). The closing curly brace ends the statement. Save the file and check your menu; you don't need to restart the X
Window System environment. Try it out and select the Xandros File Manager
to launch it. Pretty cool, eh?

If you want to remove something, you can put a comment character (#) at the
beginning of each line in its entry. That's really all there is to this. Just make
sure you put a comment before each line in a group.

IceWM has a few more goodies that you might like. On the Start menu, you
can change themes by choosing Start, Settings, Themes and then selecting a
theme from the menu (see Figure 4.5). The infadel2 theme is especially nice,
with its black metallic look.

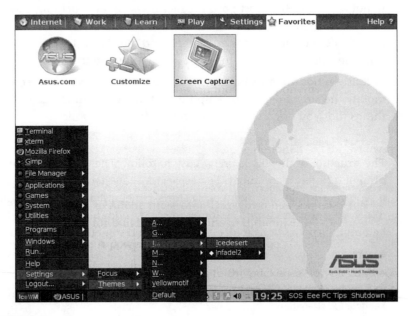

FIGURE 4.5

Selecting a theme.

Also, take a look at Start, Windows. This provides a window from which you
can select one of four virtual desktops. This is basically the same functionality
as in the virtual desktops offered by the KDE and other Linux window managers.

Choosing IceWM as Your Window Manager

If you really like the more typical IceWM interface, other than the Easy Mode implementation, you can make that interface your default.

The whole idea, which is detailed at http://www.ProductiveLinux.com, is to provide the functionality of the various desktop tools using a lightweight, multipurpose file and system management tool called ROX-Filer. ROX-Filer has menu-like windows to launch applications, functions for setting the computer wallpaper, and even its own taskbar-like structure. Supposedly the combination of IceWM and ROX-Filer is as functional as the KDE but faster.

caution After you've made IceWM your default window manager, you won't be able to switch to Full Desktop (KDE) without first undoing some configuration settings.

To actually set up the ROX/IceMW environment, you need to:

1. Install the ROX-Filer package.

2. Modify the configuration file that invokes AsusLauncher for Easy Mode.

Fortunately, you can load ROX-Filer directly from Synaptic using the repositories that Chapter 8 sets up. If you want to pursue using ROX, jump ahead to Chapter 8 and set up the repositories and learn a little about Synaptic. After you do so, you can proceed here.

Installing the ROX-Filer Package

Launch the Synaptic Package Manager from a terminal window with the sudo synaptic command. If you haven't reloaded the repositories in a while, click the Reload button in Synaptic.

Click one of the packages in the list, and start typing "rox." (If you use the Search function, look in Chapter 8 for instructions about clearing the error that Search causes in Synaptic.) You're looking for a package called rox-filer, as shown in Figure 4.6. Once you've found it, mark it for installation by checking its check box and then install it.

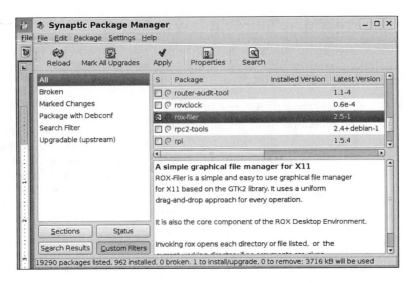

FIGURE 4.6
Loading ROX-Filer via Synaptic.

Modifying the AsusLauncher Configuration for ROX-Filer

After Easy Mode is loaded, press Ctrl+Alt+T to launch an xterm window. What
you're going to do is make a copy of the /usr/bin/startsimple.sh shell script.
This is the script that starts the desktop. If you want to return to a configuration with Easy Mode and Full Desktop, you'll want a pristine copy of this
script. To copy the script, issue the following command at the prompt:

```
> sudo cp /usr/bin/startsimple.sh /usr/bin/startsimple.sh_OLD
```

Next, load the startsimple.sh shell (see Figure 4.7) into your favorite editor,
invoking the editor with sudo so that you have permission to write a modified
version of the file. I'll use xemacs and launch it this way:

```
> sudo xemacs /usr/bin/startsimple.sh &
```

Use the Search function in your editor to find the line with
/opt/xandros/bin/AsusLauncher &. Put a comment character (#) as the first
character in the line. This line now won't be executed. You've now disabled
AsusLauncher, so Easy Mode and Full Desktop are no longer available. You'll
need to replace that line with ROX. Look for a line that contains wapmonitor &.
Insert a blank line below that and enter the following into the blank line:

```
Rox -S &
```

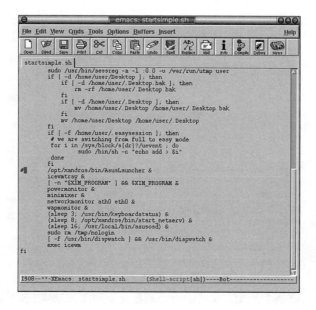

FIGURE 4.7

Editing startsimple.sh.

A little explanation is required. The -s switch invokes ROX in the ROX-Session mode, which launches the ROX Desktop. The & character spawns ROX as a new process and makes it independent of the script. You can now save the file, exit your editor, and reset the X Window System environment by pressing Ctrl+Alt+Backspace. The Eee PC will now load the IceWM and ROX-Session, and you'll be in a brave new world.

ROX takes a little getting used to, but its convention of treating everything in a drag-and-drop way is quite convenient. Actually, ROX has lots of conveniences. For example, you can load any of the Eee PC wallpapers quite easily from ROX via the Background function. This is pretty cool, as all you really need to do is drag the background graphic file icon from a ROX file manager window onto the Set Background dialog box (see Figure 4.8).

You can get Eee PC wallpapers from lots of sources. Just run a Google search for "Eee PC" and "wallpaper." Download the wallpaper file anywhere you like, and then use the Set Background dialog box to load the wallpaper. Once loaded, you can stretch it, center it, and so forth right from the Set Background dialog box.

Figure 4.9 shows the ROX Desktop with the IceWM taskbar running the Infadel2 theme. This shows the Applications window, which is really just the file manager showing the /usr/share directory.

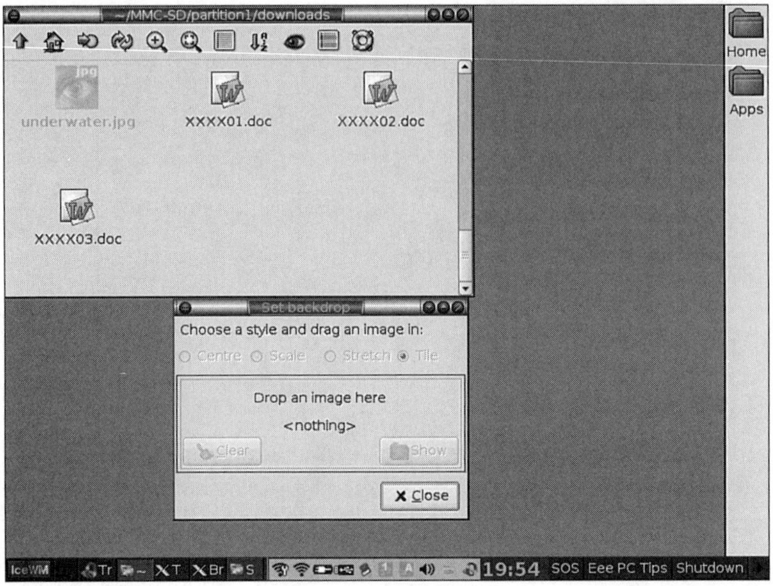

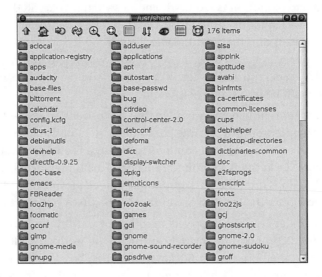

FIGURE 4.8

Preparing to drag-and-drop the wallpaper file.

FIGURE 4.9

IceWM and ROX.

Although the combination of IceWM and ROX is nice, I frankly prefer the KDE desktop. If you tire of the IceWM/ROX environment, simply reinvoke the original AsusLauncher by deleting the usr/bin/startsimple.sh file and copying /usr/bin/startsimple.sh_OLD to /usr/bin/startsimple.sh. Remember to use `sudo` with the `cp` command if you do this.

If you want to find out more information about IceWM, check out http://www.icewm.org. There's documentation and themes that you can use. As for ROX, you'll find everything you need at http://roscidus.com/desktop/.

Summary

This chapter took a rather deep dive into Linux configuration focused on Easy Mode and its underlying window manager. If you are going to support extensions to Easy Mode, it provided the necessary instructions. If you're a fan of the IceWM window manager in general, it also provided instructions for removing the Eee PC customizations and using it in a more "default" look-and-feel.

If you wish to build custom icons for Easy Mode and find this difficult, check the various Eee PC forums and web sites and use Google to search for "easy mode editor." When this was written, the manual method of building icons described in this chapter provided the best quality icons. However, someone may have come up with an Easy Mode editor that does a good job with icons, and that will save you considerable effort.

Working with the Full (KDE) Desktop

The Full Desktop, or more properly the KDE Desktop, provides more capability than the Easy Mode. One wonders why it was actually hidden in the Eee PC. Clearly, given that it was configured to work well with the Eee PC, it should have been easier to launch. In Chapter 1, you learned how to access the KDE Desktop. In this chapter, you'll learn more about how to use it and tailor it to your liking.

Back in the 1990s, when UNIX boxes roamed the earth, I worked on a project that had a component from X/Open (actually, it was called the Open Software Group then) known as the Common Desktop Environment (CDE). It was kind of "clunky," but at the time, it was one of the easiest-to-use desktop environments in the UNIX world. One of the big drawbacks was that there were very few applications that ran under the CDE, and most were just old UNIX applications that really had very different (and very odd) user interfaces.

Around 1996, a German student named Mathias Ettrich started the ball rolling toward development of an easy-to-use desktop, the K Desktop Environment (KDE), and a toolkit for developing applications. Today, the KDE is still largely built by volunteers, although Mandriva and a few other companies actually contribute resources to the project.

I work with a lot of desktops and operating systems, and while the standard Macintosh desktop (Aqua) is really quite nice, I still prefer the KDE. It's easy to use, efficient, massively customizable, and a lot less cluttered than the interface in various Microsoft Windows versions.

The Xandros Eee PC KDE incarnation has all the preloaded software nicely installed in the Launch menus. Moreover, most applications that you load via the Synaptic Package Manager or apt-get automatically install in the Launch menus. Really, care and mainte-

note There's a terminology issue that you'll encounter in this chapter and in your everyday computing as well: folder and directory. They both mean the same thing, but "directory" is often used when discussing the file tree from the perspective of the command line, whereas "folder" is commonly used when discussing a graphical user interface (GUI). I use the terms interchangeably.

nance of the KDE is pretty easy. With easy customization of various applications by "dot" directories from your home directory, no Windows registry to worry about, and a really powerful command line, it's a great environment for every day computing.

Introducing the KDE Panel

From Easy Mode, you can launch the KDE (Full Desktop) from the Shutdown icon on the taskbar. (The taskbar is called the "panel" in the KDE as well as most Linux desktops. This section introduces the various parts of the basic KDE panel, shown in Figure 5.1, and then explains how to customize the panel.

FIGURE 5.1

The basic KDE desktop.

The panel or "kicker," on the bottom of the KDE screen has the following components from left-to-right:

- Launch button, which (when clicked) gives you access to the application and system menus as well as some direct actions such as running a command, switching to Easy Mode, and logging out.

- Firefox.

- Thunderbird.

- File Manager (this version has your user privileges and isn't the Administrator version).

- The Show Desktop button (click this to minimize-all-applications).

- Beyond the application buttons lie the buttons for currently running tasks (this part of the panel is also called the Taskbar).

- Next are the two virtual desktop buttons. Virtual desktops is a concept recognizable all the way back to the CDE. The idea is that you can clutter up your desktop all you want, and when it's full, you can just click another button to start over with another desktop. Actually, the concept is quite useful. While writing this book, I used three virtual desktops: one for writing, one for experimenting, and one to manage graphics. It's a tremendous convenience to be able to switch between desktops at the click of a button. You can also right-click a button and select Configure Desktops to add more (up to 20 if you really want to get carried away).

- Next along the panel is the power icon, which tells you whether you're plugged in (the plug appears) or on battery power. Hovering over this icon provides a tool tip with the current battery charge level.

- The bug-on-the-shield button launches the antivirus control panel. The Xandros antivirus application isn't an interactive, all-intrusive, processor-cycle-devouring application like that on Windows. It doesn't scan emails or constantly run in the background. From the Anti-virus panel, you can update the virus database or scan all or any part of the file system (including a single file). You can also schedule auto-scans and auto-updates. Given that Linux isn't the target of large-scale, concerted efforts to take over machines or steal information (yet), this antivirus protection is adequate. Actually, it's much more useful for protecting Windows machines that might share a network with your Eee because the Eee might download files that contain viruses which would affect Windows.

- Next is the MMC-SD storage control. If you hover over this icon, the tool tip will tell you how much space is left. Right-click this icon to see a menu with a single choice: Safely Remove the Flash Memory Card. This control will be followed to the left by USB Flash Drive controls, for any flash drives plugged into the Eee PC. The work in the same fashion as the MMC-SD storage control.

- The Volume Control provides a slider for the output volume to the speakers or the headphones.
- The keyboard control provides options for keyboard configurations, including layouts that are specific to certain languages.
- Next is the Network button. Click this to connect to and disconnect from both wired and wireless networks. You can also set up new connections, configure existing connections, and so forth.
- Finally, at the end of the panel is the Lock button. Unless you've set a user password during your initial Eee PC start up, *do not* click this button. You'll lock yourself out and you'll need to reboot. It won't take "no password" for a password. You can use this menu to display the Logout button, which is kind of handy.

Our tour of the panel completes with roll-up buttons. Click one of these and the panel rolls to the right or left (if you are on the default screen and have two buttons), exposing more of the screen. Click again and the panel rolls back out along the bottom of the screen.

On the 701 Eee PCs, you can't see the clock unless you connect to external monitor. Click the right roll-up button to see the clock. You can right-click the clock to set the time, change the clock mode, and bring up the calendar. This is covered in detail in Chapter 1, "Getting to Know Your Eee PC." There are a few more tricks lurking in the panel. If you hover your mouse to the upper left of any button or icon on the panel, a tiny triangle appears. Click that to produce a menu to move, remove, or launch the related application or function.

Configuring the Panel

Right-clicking a one of the narrow blank spaces between the taskbar and virtual desktop buttons opens the panel menu. The panel menu provides commands to add buttons to panels, remove existing buttons, and configure the panel itself (actually, the panel menu is also available from the button menus).

The variety of ways in which you can customize the panel is actually pretty amazing. You do most customization through the Panel screen of the Configure KDE Panel window (Configure Panel is available from the Panel Menu), shown in Figure 5.2.

Arrangement Tab

On the Arrangement tab (see Figure 5.2), you can position the panel on the top, right, left, or bottom (default) of the screen. In the Length section, you can use the slider or field to set the panel's length, or can choose to have it expand as required to fit the contents.

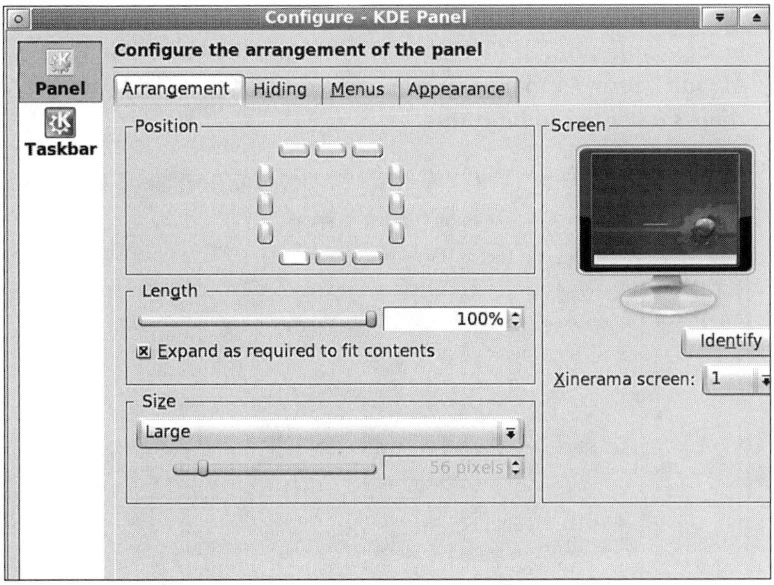

FIGURE 5.2

Configuring the panel.

The Size setting is actually very useful on the Eee PC, because you can set the height (or width, depending on the orientation) of the panel. The Tiny option works great on the built-in Eee PC screen, and Large is useful if you have a very high-resolution monitor attached.

Hiding Tab

The Hiding tab (see Figure 5.3) has some controls that are really appropriate to the Eee PC's default screen size. You can choose either to hide the panel or to allow applications to cover it. If you choose to allow applications to cover it, you can set a designated edge or corner of the screen to recover the panel. Thus, you can get the panel back by placing the mouse pointer at that designated location. If you want to use the panel but don't want to give up the screen real estate, select Hide Automatically. Just put the mouse pointer toward the bottom the screen to get the panel back.

Menus Tab

The Menus tab lets you configure the Launch menu. You can add additional menus as well as edit the contents of the Launch menu. One particularly useful menu is the Quick Browser, which combines the functionality of a file manager with the speed and simplicity of a menu. From its top level, you can jump to the home folder, root folder, or (and I really like this) to the various system configuration directories. So, if you want to play with your X11 or emacs configuration files, just follow along the cascading menus. The number of Quick Browser menus shown can get quickly out of hand, which is why there's a control to limit this.

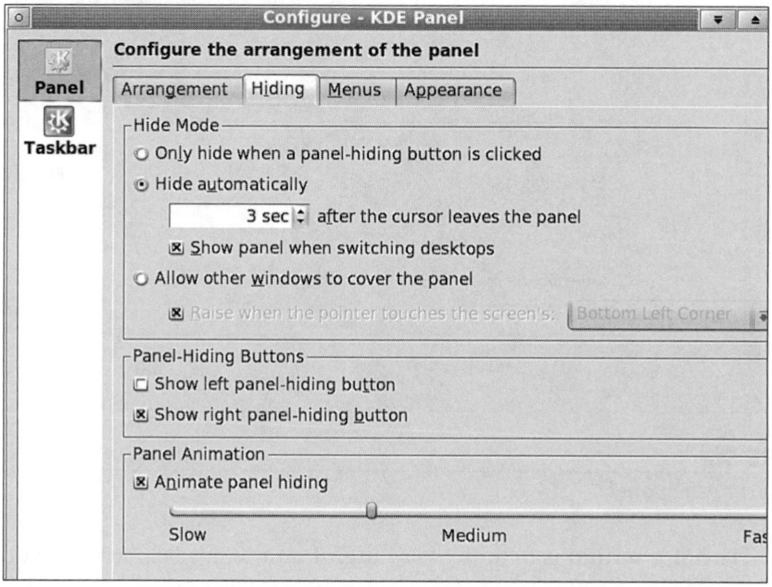

FIGURE 5.3

The panel-hiding controls.

Clicking the Edit Launch Menu button brings up the Menu Editor, which is covered in more detail in Chapter 8, "Getting More Linux Applications." Suffice it to say that you can add, delete, and otherwise control all the entries in the menu.

Appearance Tab

The Appearance tab gives you tools to customize the look of the panel. Aside from the color schemes for various buttons, you can customize the look of the panel itself. The panel even has its own wallpaper. You can turn this off by enabling transparency, which allows the desktop wallpaper to show through.

The Advanced Options button offers additional tweaks, and you can set the size of the panel in pixels and the amount of tint if you have transparency active.

Taskbar Button

Clicking the Taskbar button in the upper-left corner of the Configure KDE Panel window provides a few more space-saving functions you might appreciate on the Eee PC's small screen. You can show only application buttons from minimized windows, instead of buttons from all windows. That can limit the number of buttons on the panel. You can also set the taskbar to group similar applications to save space.

Add to Panel Command

If you remove all items from the taskbar, you can right-click the open space and produce a menu that includes the Add to Panel command. The Add to Panel command offers some really useful (and

> **tip** If you decide to remove the Performance Monitor, use Remove Applets, not Remove Display. Remove Display simply takes away the graph and leaves the empty box to clutter up the panel.

nonuseful) tools. You can keep track of the available system memory and your current CPU load with the Performance Monitor (it's under Applets).

Under Panels, you'll find some alternative panels. Be careful here, because I've managed to actually lock out the regular panel simply by trying to use the Universal Sidebar. I'd stay away from that. If you do manage to lock out the panel, you'll need to reset the X Window System with the magic Ctrl+Alt+Backspace key combination. The KasBar is a simple, and I think ugly, panel alternative.

Configuring the KDE Interface

The KDE is extremely configurable, with many more options than are available in Microsoft Windows. In fact, the array of ways to configure the KDE is absolutely dizzying.

There are two routes to configuring the desktop, which lead to two separate interfaces that pretty much do the same thing:

- **Display pane of the Control Center:** Choose Launch, Control Center, Control Center, Display.

- **Display Properties window:** Right-click an open space on the desktop and choose Properties.

This section discusses the second option, the Display Properties window, because that's the easier one to use. The Display Properties application, shown in Figure 5.4, has a number of buttons on the left, each of which opens a different set of options on the right when you click it, as described next. The Panel options are not described because they are the same options described in the previous section, "Configuring the Panel."

Background

Clicking the Background button provides controls for setting the wallpaper, as well as a very nifty way to get additional wallpapers.

By the way, wallpapers are stored in the /user/share/wallpapers folder, should you ever want to manually install a wallpaper or delete a few to save space. Unlike Windows, the KDE can use SVG wallpapers, which are significantly smaller than the JPG, GIF or PNG bitmap formats that it also supports.

On the Background settings, you can choose to have wallpaper for each virtual desktop, or not. If you choose not to have wallpaper, you can select other nice visual effects, such as fountain fills, patterns, and colors. If you do select a wallpaper from the list, you can see a preview of it on the right.

Now for the fun part: clicking the Get New Wallpapers button gives you access to the wallpapers available at http://www.KDE-Look.org, which has a nice collection of KDE-themed (and other) wallpaper. You can browse by Latest, Most Downloads, and Highest Rated, as shown in Figure 5.4. You can also preview each wallpaper in the right pane.

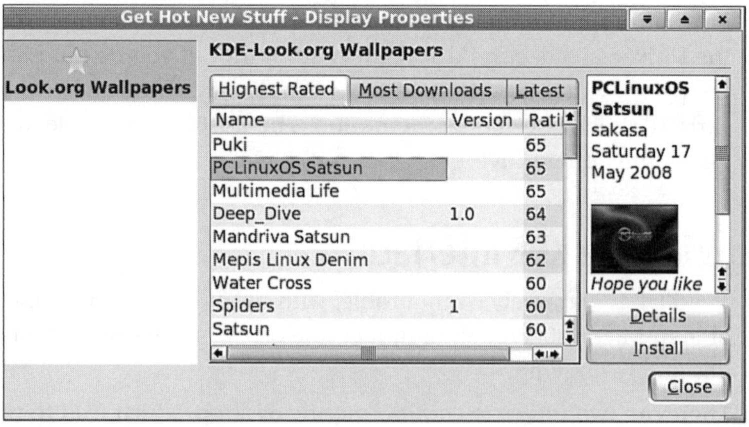

FIGURE 5.4

Previewing wallpapers to download and install.

Colors

Clicking the Colors button provides controls for setting the window color schemes. The top pane provides examples of items in the interface, which you click to select and can then change their colors. You can also load preset color schemes for the desktop, as well as create your own. Additional color schemes are available from http://www.KDE-Look.org, and if you download any of these, you can load them through the Import Scheme button.

Fonts

The Fonts icon provides controls for changing the fonts for the various parts of the desktop, or changing all fonts. You can also change all fonts throughout the interface at once through the Adjust All Fonts button. If you wish to tinker with the anti-aliasing, you can do that from here as well.

Icons

Click Icons and you'll find tools for switching the icon sets, as shown in Figure 5.5. Note that only one icon set is shown in the list. Once again, http://www.KDE-Look.org comes to the rescue as a convenient repository for new icons. Download an icons file (they run about 15 to 20MB as a rule) and load it via the file browser from the Install New Theme button.

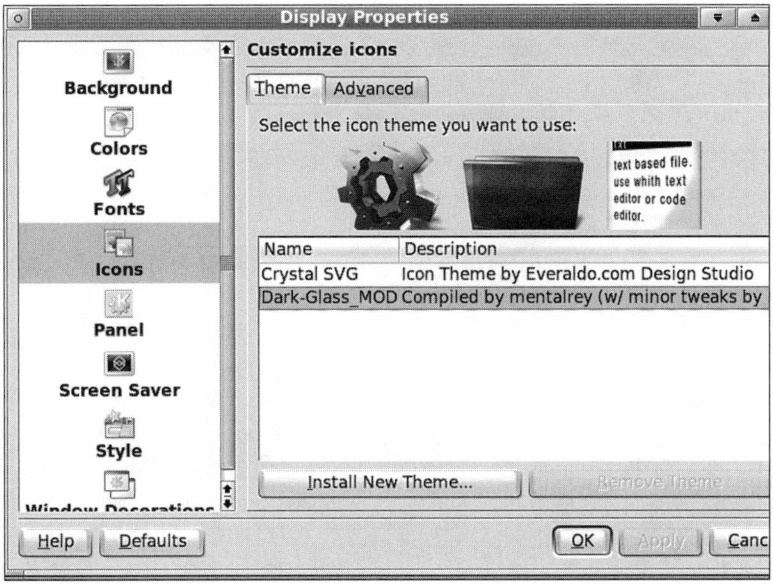

FIGURE 5.5
Selecting icon sets.

Screen Saver

Clicking Screen Saver is a bit of a disappointment, because there are no screen-savers installed. If you want to install a screensaver, the easiest way is to do a search through the Synaptic Package Manager (just search for "screensaver"). Due to a bug in the Synaptic Package Manager on the Eee PC, you'll need to run the `fix` command twice after each search before you can download a package. Once a screensaver is installed, you can configure it from this screen.

Style

The Style controls configure the look and feel of the radio buttons, check boxes, and so on that appear in the various dialog boxes. Note that you can adopt some of the old UNIX looks, such as SGI (Silicon Graphics) and CDE, as well as newer styles developed for Linux. As you select different styles, the example controls change to provide a preview.

Window Decorations

The Window Decorations controls (see Figure 5.6) actually rather radically change the behavior and appearance of windows in the desktop. Try each one and note the changes to the look of the windows and the controls. For some window schemes, the Buttons tab allows you to add extra control buttons to the windows.

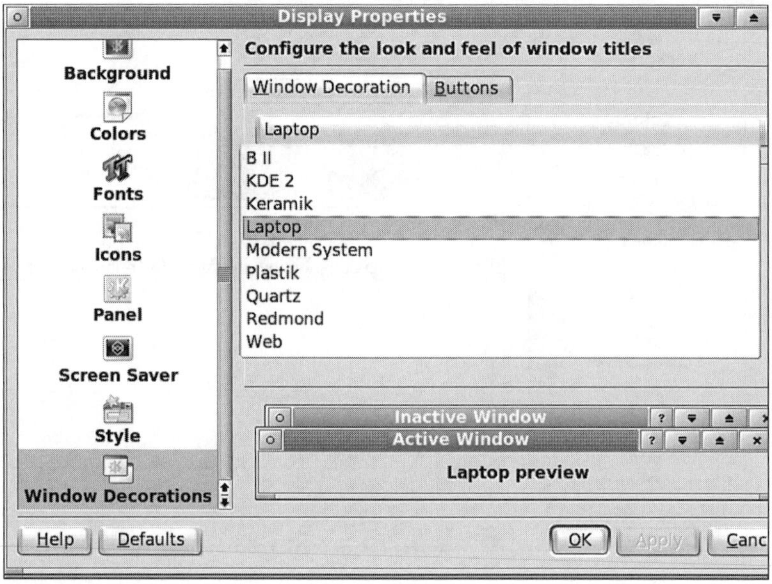

FIGURE 5.6
Selecting the window decorations.

Touring the File System

If you're new to the Linux file system, you'll notice that the major difference from Microsoft Windows (aside from the forward slash instead of a backslash to separate folders in a file path) is that the entire file system is one tree. The top level is called "root" and is shown as /. Linux does not use the MS-DOS notion of a C: drive, D: drive, etc. When you plug in a flash drive or add an MMC/SD card, they are automatically mounted into the file system as folders under /media. The same is true if you add a CD or DVD drive.

The second convention that you need to understand is the concept of a "home" directory. While the early versions of Windows, and its predecessor DOS, were essentially single-user operating systems, UNIX and Linux are essentially multiuser operating systems. Thus, the idea of a separate home directory for each user was created. While the Eee PC is a single-user implementation of Xandros (a Linux variant), it still has the concept of a user and a home directory. This is /user/home.

There are plenty of file managers in Linux, and the Eee PC's default KDE desktop exposes two of them from the launch menu: File Manager (blue) and Administrative File Manager (red). These are actually based on the XandrosFileManager application. The main difference between the two is that the Administrative File Manager runs with root privileges. This makes the Administrator version capable of changing things in the nonuser part of the file system. This is both good, in that you have a graphical way to do this, and risky, in that you can mess things up quite a bit.

Given that the File Manager (blue) is designed for managing user-related files, it opens to the /home/user directory with the subfolders under it opened in the tree. The Administrative File Manager also opens to the /user/home directory, but it has an additional default entry in the tree called All File Systems (see Figure 5.7), which opens to reveal the root of the file system plus any folders under /media. In the File Manager (blue), you can also see the rest of the file system via the View > Show All File Systems command. However, you can't modify files outside of your user directories with this File Manager.

These folders correspond to the top of the file systems for the USB storage devices and MMC-SD drive.

To make it easy for you to reach the file trees under /media, symbolic links are automatically created when you plug in an storage device. These symbolic links connect the home directory to each of device file trees. The symbolic link is deleted when you use the panel control for that device to remove it. A *symbolic link* is a direct connection from one branch of the file tree to another. It's another advantage the Linux file system has over Windows XP, because it allows you to make convenient connections throughout the file system.

You'll find a folder called My Documents in your home directory, which leads to subfolders such as My Music and My Office. Keep in mind that this is on the internal file system and space is a premium there, so it's a really good idea to store documents, music, photos, and so forth on an MMC/SD flash card instead.

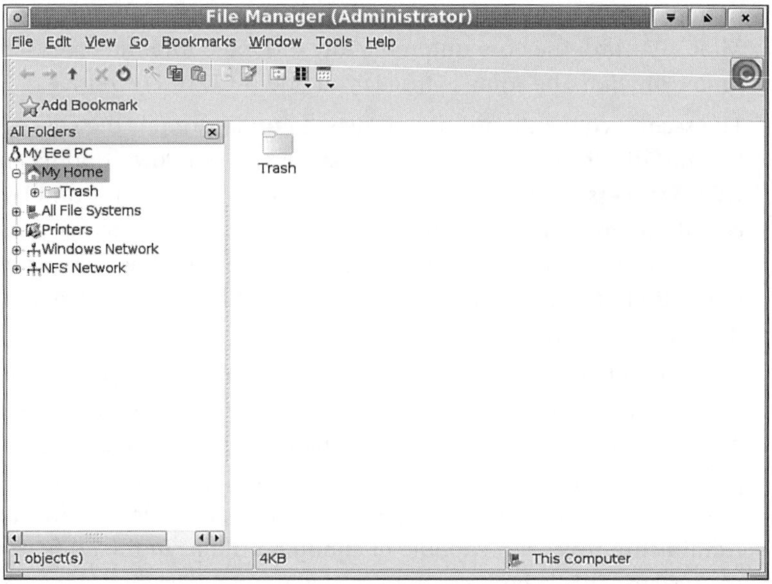

FIGURE 5.7

Administrative File Manager with expanded file tree options.

Linux has the concept of local configuration files, which are stored as subfolders to your home directory. These invariably begin with a "." (which normally makes them hidden) and contain various configuration files and log files. Log files contain a history of events for the application and are often useful in trying to figure out what went wrong when things go awry. If you want to see your configuration directories in the File Manager, simply right-click a blank spot in the folder (right side of the File Manager) and select Show Hidden Files. You can also select View > Show Hidden Files from the menu. When you can see the folders in the File Manager (see Figure 5.8), you can navigate to them.

The File Manager tree also opens network file systems, such as a Windows Workgroup or a UNIX/Linux network file system (NFS). You can browse through machines and any shared parts of their file systems as well.

Although you can't browse the entire file system with the File Manager, you can with the Administrative File Manager. Also, if you choose to edit a file with the Administrative File Manager (by selecting the Open With command from the File Manager's right-click menu), the editor also has root privileges so that you can actually write to the file even if it's outside of your user tree. Chapter 11, "Introduction to the Linux Command Line," goes into detail about file permissions and navigating the file system with commands.

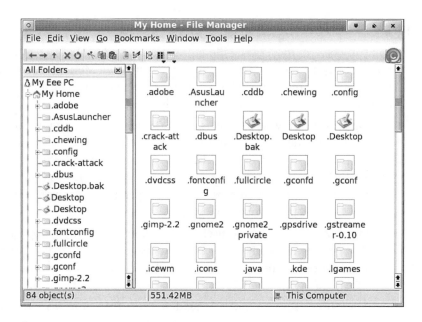

FIGURE 5.8

Hidden folders, revealed in the File Manager.

The following lists some of the points of interest in the file system:

/bin: The executable files that provide the basic commands and tools for Linux. This is used to start the Eee PC, but also by you as the basis for the various Linux commands.

/boot: Startup, shutdown, and system configuration files.

/dev: Device files that represent the various devices installed on the Eee PC.

/etc: Where Linux keeps its configuration files.

/home: The branch of the directory tree that leads to the various account directories (or, in the case of the Eee PC, the user directory).

/media: The directory branches (mount points) that lead to the files systems of various devices plugged into the Eee PC.

/opt: The branch that includes many (but not all) of the software packages you install. Others are installed under /usr/bin.

/sbin: More programs, usually related to administering the system.

/usr: Includes most of the programs you install, in the /bin directory.

/tmp: Where the temporary files used by the system live.

/var: The home of many log files, print spooler files, and the like.

Using the File Manager Right-Click Menu

You can perform most of the file-manipulation tasks that are required in running your system directly from either of the two File Managers (user and administrative) by right-clicking a filename. The following list describes the function of each of the menu commands:

Open: For many types of files, the KDE has a default application that is considered the editor of choice. For some types of files, such as OpenOffice.org Writer files, there's probably only one editor on the Eee PC that can open those files. For other file types, such as graphics files, there may be many choices. Selecting Open instructs the KDE to open the file with the default application.

Open With: This is most useful when there are multiple applications that can open the file. The KDE presents you with a menu of applications that could be used. Selecting Other allows you to browse the list of known applications.

Find: If you select a folder instead of a file, Find provides some basic search tools to look for files of various types, a specific file, or a set of files. The Find tool matches on the filename, and you can use the * wildcard to match any set of characters. For example, my*.txt will find any files with the .txt extension that begin with the two-letter string "my." You can also search the contents of files.

Cut: Places the file(s) or folder(s) on the clipboard (think of it as a temporary staging area) in preparation for a file move. When you paste an item, it's moved from its original location to the destination.

Copy: Places the file(s) or folder(s) on the clipboard in preparation for a file copy. When you paste an item, it is copied rather than moved; that is, the original item is left in its original location.

Paste: Pastes the file(s) or folder(s) from the clipboard into the designated folder. The operation can be either a move or a copy operation, depending on what command placed the item(s) onto the clipboard.

Move to Trash: When you use either File Manager to remove a file or folder, you have a choice of whether to really get rid of it or simply move it to the Trash directory. If you right-click a file and select Move to Trash, the item is simply moved to the Trash directory. Trash is a staging area for things that you probably want to delete, but aren't entirely sure about. On a system with as little storage as the Eee PC has, it's a good idea not to keep a lot in the Trash. To delete the Trash, simply right-click the Trash folder and select Empty Trash; then the deleted items are gone for good.

Delete: Removes the selected file or folder completely. Be bold; space is at a premium!

Rename: Opens the file or folder name in a text field so that you can rename it.

Add Bookmark: Places the file or folder in the File Manager's bookmark list (under the Bookmark menu). This gives you a way to quickly get back to certain files or folders.

Create Symbolic Link: Enables you to create a symbolic link between the currently selected file or folder and any other folder in the file system.

Scan with Anti-Virus: Enables you to scan the selected file or folder for viruses. This is a really convenient way to scan anything that you download.

Add to ZIP Archive: Add the currently selected file(s) or folder(s) to a ZIP file. This not only combines the files into a single file, for later unpacking, but compresses the size as well.

Create TGZ Archive: A combination of the Linux tar file repository and gzip (GnuZip) commands, to create a tg.zip or tgz file. The resulting file is often called a "tarball." It's similar to a ZIP file, but tarballs are native to the Linux/UNIX world.

Edit File Type: Displays a dialog box that you can use to change the file associations for applications that can open the file.

Properties: Enables you to change the filename and its permissions for owner, group, and other (the chmod function). For more about chmod, see Chapter 11.

Konqueror

Because Xandros has its own file manager, it decided to not place the most popular KDE file manager, Konqueror, on the menus. That doesn't mean Konqueror isn't installed, however. Actually, Konqueror is far more than a file manager; it's also a web browser and system administration tool. Konquerer has much more capability than the Xandros replacements.

You can launch Konqueror from the Launch menu Run command with this simple command: Konqueror. The Konqueror initial screen, shown in Figure 5.9, provides choices to manage your files, manage network file shares, or reach system administration screens. Like ROX (introduced in Chapter 4, "Customizing Easy Mode"), Konqueror is a do-it-all application. It is even a complete and standards-compliant web browser. If you type a URL into the Location field, it will browse to that website.

FIGURE 5.9

Konqueror.

Backing Up Your System

Now that you know how to work with the file system, you'll want ways to back it up. There are two types of backups:

- **Simple file backups:** To protect your data
- **Complete system backups:** To restore your system to a particular working state if necessary

File Backups

For file backups, the easiest thing to do is to back up the system onto a DVD. A DVD enough capacity to store the whole file system, minus the MMC/SD flash drive, so that makes it somewhat simpler. The best way, and really the only reliable way that I've found, to do DVD backups on the Eee PC is through the K3b program. Chapter 8, "Getting More Linux Applications," Chapter 9, "Must-Have Utilities," provide instructions for adding applications in general and K3b in particular, respectively.

K3b has a simple drag-and-drop interface (see Figure 5.10). To create a backup DVD with K3b:

1. Launch K3b via Launch > Multimedia >K3b.

2. Click the New Data DVD Project button.

3. Drag the directories you'd like to write from the top file list to the bottom list.

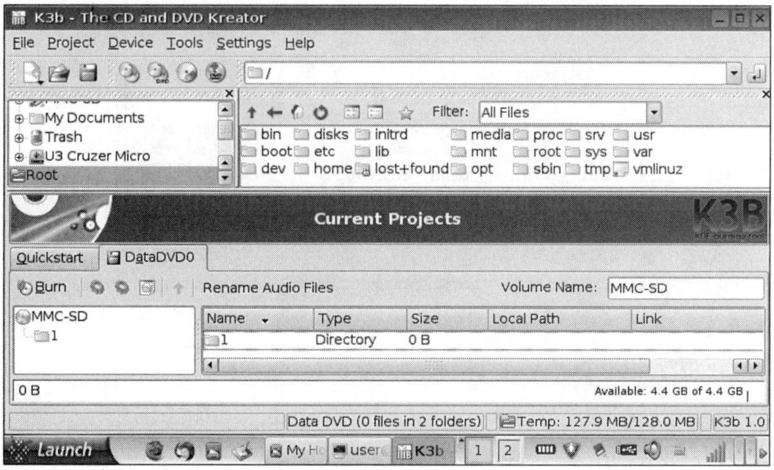

FIGURE 5.10

K3B, with directories selected and ready to burn.

4. Click the Burn button (at the left of the screen).

5. In the DVD Project dialog box, select Create Image and Remove Image. Keep in mind the the ISO image (which is as large as the data itself) must also fit somewhere temporarily on the Eee's available storage. You can select the location for this in the Image tab. If the location doesn't have sufficient space, you'll be told when you click the Burn button in the DVD Project dialog box.

6. Click the Burn button in the dialog box.

7. A dialog box will appear with options to store the directories referenced by the links, not to follow links but merely put the link file on the DVD, or ignore links entirely. Select the symbolic link option you wish to use.

8. The progress window, shown in Figure 5.11, shows the writing process.

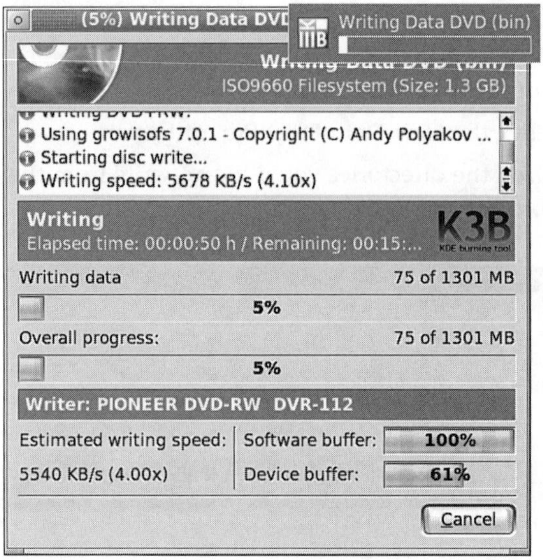

FIGURE 5.11
Backing up with K3b.

Complete System Backups

Backing up the complete system sometimes is called making a drive image or "ghosting" (after a rather famous program for this purpose, called Ghost). This provides a snapshot of your current system that you can restore to bring the system back to its precise state at that time (thus overwriting any changed data). Although this isn't horribly difficult to do, it does require some technical know-how and self-confidence. There are three ways to go about building system images, and they require that you have an attached CD drive:

- Write the image to a large enough USB flash drive. The flash drive must be 4GB or greater for a 4G, and 8GB or more for an 8G, and 12 or 20 GB or more for the 900 series.

- Write the image to a USB portable hard drive. This lets you save multiple images, which could be helpful if you want to switch among several systems (Xandros, Windows XP, and Ubuntu, for instance).

- Write the image to a network drive. In this case, you must have another machine on your network to which you can write the image file. In this case, the network must be working under DHCP. Make sure the network drive has enough space!

The following are two programs that you can use to make system images. Both are downloaded as ISO files. An ISO file is itself a disk image that you must burn to a CD or DVD:

- **PING (Partimage Is Not Ghost):** You can obtain this from http://ping.windowsdream.com/ping.html. It's fairly easy to use and can be used to back up to a flash drive (memory stick), USB portable drive, or a network location. The website provides detailed instructions. Follow them to the letter.

- **Clonezilla:** You can obtain this from http://www.clonezilla.org/. I recommend this one only for backing up to a flash drive (memory stick) or a USB portable drive. It has a somewhat "clunkier" interface, but works just fine.

Both programs provide "live" (that is, bootable) Linux CDs with the imaging software installed on the CD. To use either program, you must change the boot order of the Eee PC so that it boots from the CD first. To do this, reboot the system and, while it's first starting up, press the F2 key. Find the boot order and make the first entry of the three the CD drive. Save and exit and the Eee PC will reboot normally.

Next, download the ISO image file for the utility you intend to use. Once downloaded, because it's a CD image, you can double-click it in the File Manager to "burn" the image to CD. It's only DVDs that are problematic; they require K3b.

After you have a completed CD, label it and then put it into the CD drive. Install your flash drive as well, and then reboot the system. The Eee PC will boot the version of Linux on the CD and will give you an option to load the utility. Do so. In either utility, you need to move around the menus in the interface with the arrow keys.

To back up the native Xandros Linux using PING, you'll want to select hdc1 and hdc2 to back up. These are the two Linux partitions on which Xandros is written. For some reason, PING sees an installed MMC-SD card as SDA1. You do not need hdc3 and hdc4. For Clonezilla, you want to back up SDA1 and SDA2. You can tell the correct partitions because of the sizes and the file system type. On a 4G, the two partition sizes for Xandros are 2468MB and 1513MB. The file systems are EXT2 and EXT3 respectively.

If you're using PING, make sure that you have created or connected (if it's on a portable storage device) the destination directory for the image before you run the program. If you're using Clonezilla and you're putting the image on a USB device, wait until it prompts you and then connect the device. With either application, backups to take some time.

You'll also need the CD or USB flash drive to restore the image. Keep in mind that restoring an image is a destructive affair. Back up your data (via K3b or simply by copying files to a flash drive) before restoring an image.

Summary

In this chapter, you got an introduction to configuring one of the major Linux desktops: the KDE. You also got a tour of the file system and the GUI file management tools. Given the number and variety of customizations available for the KDE, you should have no trouble tailoring it to suit your needs and tastes.

You also got a look at some of the ways that you can back up your information on the Eee PC, including a couple of ways that you can make a restorable image. Once you have configured the KDE the way you want, you can back up Xandros and your configuration.

Using Other Window Managers

The previous chapters covered configuring the Easy Mode (IceWM) window manager and the Full Desktop (KDE) window manager, but what if you're a huge fan of GNOME instead of the KDE? What if you want to run something extremely lightweight, such as Fluxbox? What if you'd like to try the really cutting-edge Beryl, with its "rubbery" windows and 3D cube? This chapter explains how to load and use these three window managers. First, it offers a few factors to consider before you load one of these window managers on your Eee PC.

Quick Comparison of Beryl, Fluxbox, and GNOME

Whereas Beryl and Fluxbox are pretty lightweight and should fit with ease on a 4GB system, GNOME, with all of its applications, is very hefty indeed. On a 4GB Eee PC, loading GNOME is marginal but certainly within reason. Moreover, you don't need all the applications that come with the KDE if you have GNOME (or vice versa), so you can make room by removing redundant applications. If you have an 8GB Eee PC, or a 900 Eee PC with its whopping 20GB, running GNOME isn't a problem. If you have a 2GB unit, forget it.

Here's a quick overview of the three window managers, including their advantages and disadvantages.

Window Manager	Will run on a 2GB Eee PC?	Main Advantages	Main Disadvantages	Considerations in Using	Difficulty to Remove
Beryl	No	Advanced functionality and special effects.	Requires more processing power than KDE.	Can be run with the KDE so that you can switch between the two.	Easy to remove using the package manager.
Fluxbox	Yes	Minimalist approach, with a basic desktop. Because it is "light weight," it runs efficiently.	Lacks some of the convenience and customization features of the KDE.	Can be run with the KDE.	Easy to remove using the package manager.
Gnome	No	The alternative to the KDE. Includes its own set of applications.	Because it is bundled with so many applications, it takes up a lot of space.	To free up space on a 4GB Eee PC, you must remove many KDE applications.	It may be difficult to remove.

The other thing to keep in mind is that these window managers are alternatives to Full Desktop, the Xandros implementation of the KDE. If you're a devoted fan of Easy Mode (the IceWM window manager) and you wish to customize that interface, check out Chapter 4, "Customizing Easy Mode."

Beryl is a little more challenging to install than GNOME or Fluxbox. In fact, the same technique that is used to switch interfaces with IceWM is what is used to run GNOME and Fluxbox. That is, you edit the /usr/bin/startsimple.sh file to point to another window manager other than KDE (see Chapter 4).

Although these are three separate window managers, Beryl and Fluxbox are both lightweight enough that you can run with both of them installed plus KDE! Beryl's red diamond panel control has a menu entry for switching between installed window managers.

Beryl

Beryl is an advanced 3D Windows Manager with lots of eye-candy and special effects. Some of the special effects include:

- The virtual desktop cube, which presents four virtual monitors as the sides of a cube. To switch desktops, the cube rotates.
- Rubbery windows that wobble as you drag them around.
- The task switcher, with live previews of what's currently going on in the interface of each application.

If you'd like to learn more about Beryl and its capabilities, check our its main web site at http://www.beryl-project.org.

Beryl, and other 3D window managers, are built on a framework called compiz. They all provide lots of eye-candy, which means that they require significant processing power. So, when I saw a page on the eeuser.com wiki (http://wiki.eeeuser.com/) talking about Beryl, I thought, "You've got to be kidding me. No way will something like Beryl run on the Eee PC." I mean, the Eee PC has a pretty modest processor. Still, the lure of my Eee PC being resplendent with a 3D desktop was just too tempting to resist. Hat's off to "Maddocs" who came up with this craziness.

The startling thing is that the Eee PC actually runs Beryl tolerably well, which is a genuine testament to the Beryl folks. If you're sitting at your neighborhood coffee shop running the Eee PC and folks are already staring at your ultra-portable, Beryl's visual effects will make their jaws drop. The downside is that running Beryl is quite a load, and the Eee PC runs palpably slower.

Installing Beryl

To load Beryl, you need the Synaptic Package Manager, or at least the `apt-get` command. It's really much easier to work with Synaptic on a 701 when the Eee PC is hooked to an external terminal, because the dialog boxes fit the screen. The work around is that you can use the Alt-drag technique to drag the oversized window up and down in the smaller screen. With the 900 or later models, you have plenty of room to see the whole application.

Loading the Repositories

First off, you need to add to the Eee PC's repository list the Beryl organization's repository and an additional Debian repository. These are in addition to the repositories identified in Chapter 8, "Getting More Linux Applications." This section uses the Synaptic Package Manager, but you could simply edit the /etc/apt/sources.list in your favorite editor (don't forget to use `sudo`) and then use `apt-get` to pull in the repositories.

From Full Desktop, launch the Synaptic Package Manager via Launch, Applications, System, Synaptic Package Manager. Open the Repositories dialog box via Settings, Repository and then add the following two repositories (see Figure 6.1):

Binary (deb)

URI: http://http.us.debian.org/debian

Distribution: stable

Section(s): main

Binary (deb)

URI: `http://debian.beryl-project.org/`

Distribution:etch

Section(s): main

> **tip** See the "Loading Repositories" section in Chapter 8 for specific instructions on using the Repositories dialog box.

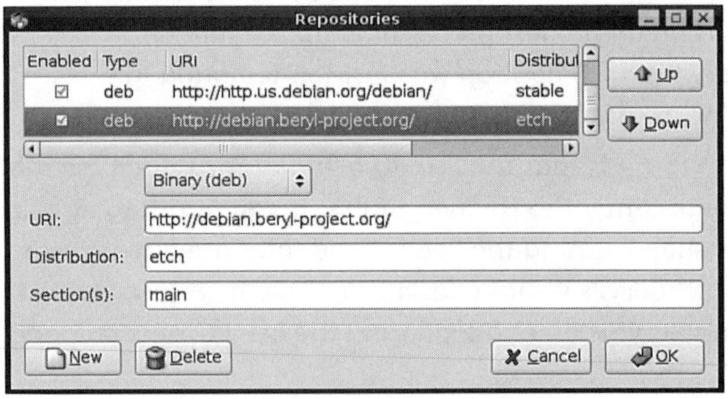

FIGURE 6.1
Adding the repositories required for Beryl.

You may see an error box because you can't access a repository (you lack the necessary key). That's OK, you'll fix that next. Click the OK button, and then exit from Synaptic (momentarily). Bring up a terminal by entering either `xterm` or `konsole` into Launch, Run Command. From the terminal, you'll want to enter the following rather long command. This will add the security key you need to access the Beryl repository.

```
> wget -O - http://debian.beryl-project.org/root@lupine.me.uk.gpg ¦ \

sudo apt-key add -
```

When typing this command, the "\" is a continuation character that was added to show that this should all fit on one line. This is a long command line so look it over carefully to make sure it is correct. It must be precisely right or you won't get the key installed.

After the key is successfully installed, keep the terminal window open (we'll need it again soon). Launch Synaptic again and then click the Reload button to refresh the repository database. Once this is complete, and it may take a while, click on a package in the list and type beryl. Right-click and mark beryl for installation. This will automatically mark the other packages that Beryl needs as well. It looks like a lot of packages (11 when this was written), but really it doesn't take up that much space.

Click the Apply button, and then click the OK button at the prompt windows that follow. When all is installed, exit from Synaptic via File, Exit.

Configuring X-Windows for Beryl

In the terminal window, open the xorg.conf file in your favorite editor, such as kwrite or nano. For example, to edit the file with nano, you'd type:

```
> sudo nano /etc/X11/xorg.conf
```

Find the following line:

```
Option "AIGLX" "false"
```

Change the line to:

```
option "AIGLX" "true"
```

Under the "Device" section, find:

```
Driver      "intel"
```

Change it to:

```
Driver      "i810"
```

Finally, in the "Extensions" section, find the line:

```
Option "Composite" "Disable"
```

Change it to:

```
Option "Composite" "Enable"
```

Save and exit.

Launching Beryl

Now you're ready to crank up Beryl. Choose Launch, Applications, System, Beryl Manager. In a few seconds, you'll see a red diamond in the panel, which indicates that Beryl is running. (If this doesn't work, you may need to run it a second time for the first startup.) "Maddocs" (from the eee.com wiki) recommends some setup options, and they seem to work. Right-click the red diamond and select Advanced Beryl Options to open the submenu shown in Figure 6.2. Set the following options for each of the advanced selections:

Rendering Path: Copy

Composite Overlay Window: Use COW

Rendering Platform: Force AIGLX

Binding: Automatic

Rendering: Indirect Rendering

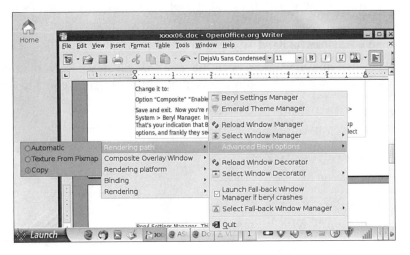

FIGURE 6.2
Advanced Beryl options.

To launch Beryl, right-click the red diamond and choose Select Window Manager, Beryl. That should do it. If not, you can restart X-Windows with Ctrl+Alt+Backspace or restart the Eee PC.

Previewing Some Beryl Tricks

First, drag some windows around and you'll discover that they seem to be made of rubber. (They drag best from the red bar at the top of the window.) Maximize a window and then click-and-drag the left-top corner down and toward the center. You can actually bend the window to see what's behind it (see Figure 6.3).

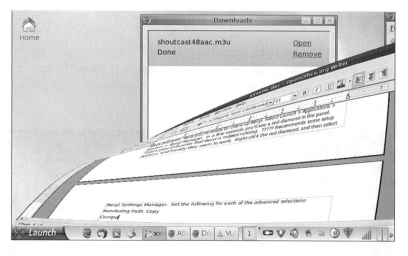

FIGURE 6.3

The amazing bending-window trick.

Next, repeatedly press Alt+Tab. For each press you move through a scrolling, previewing, application selector from which you can select any of the running applications (see Figure 6.4). If you're running in any video resolution higher than the Eee PC 701's native 800×480 pixels, you'll get a similar preview by just hovering the mouse over any of the running application buttons in the panel.

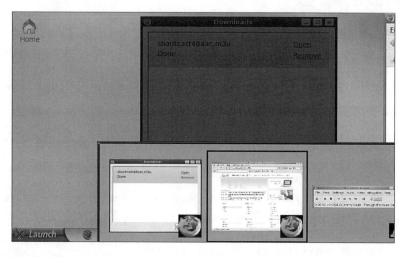

FIGURE 6.4

Alt+Tab application scroller.

Now this is "too cool for school": Press and hold Ctrl+Alt and then click the mouse button. While holding down the keys and the mouse button, drag the mouse from side to side. The desktop is actually a cube, and you're rotating it (see Figure 6.5). You can launch applications on any side of the cube, or even drag them from side to side. This gives you four interconnected virtual desktops that you can simply rotate as you please. If you click any of the panel buttons for running application, the screen cube automatically rotates to the face that contains the application.

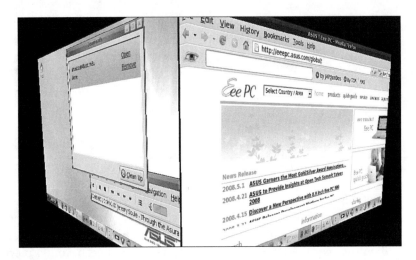

FIGURE 6.5
Rotating the desktop cube.

Just for fun, you can rotate the cube up and down. You'll see the red diamond logo on the top and bottom of the cube. Now, quickly move your mouse pointer to the top-right corner of the screen. This "scales" all the windows onto the current desktop, a la Mac OS X. Select one and they "unscale."

Given the less-than-huge screen size on both the 701 and 900, this is an almost ideal capability for increasing your screen space. This literally quadruples the width of your desktop.

There are many more Beryl tricks, and you can find these at http://www.beryl-project.org/userguide.php. While you're there, explore some of the other resources for Beryl.

> **note** "Maddocs" recommends some changes to the "Emerald" theme, although I don't really mind the defaults. If you want to fiddle with the theme settings (under the Beryl Settings Manager on the red diamond right-click menu), have at it. There are lots more themes at http://themes.beryl-project.org/.

Uninstalling Beryl

If you find the performance degradation of running Beryl to be too annoying, you can use Synaptic to uninstall it. Should you do this, run the `sudo apt-get clean` command to clean up the configuration files.

GNOME

GNOME and the KDE are the two most popular desktop options in the Linux world. In many ways, they are similar, especially in the basic controls for windows, how one interacts with windows using the mouse, and in their application launchers. Both are very full-featured, highly customizable desktops. So which is better? It's really a matter of taste. GNOME does have one advantage in that it is known to take up a little less memory than the KDE.

Like the KDE, GNOME has its own set of associated applications. Most major applications, such as OpenOffice, GIMP, Inkscape, etc., are equally at home under any window manager. However, while KDE has the Konqueror file manager/browser, GNOME has Nautilus. Also, GNOME will install AbiWord on the Eee PC as its default word processor, instead of OpenOffice (which is already there).

While both GNOME and KDE have different sets of "their own" applications, this is to a certain extent nonsense. Applications for GNOME will run quite nicely under KDE and most other Linux window managers. The same is true for KDE applications under GNOME.

Loading GNOME requires that the sources.list file have the repository entries and pinning outlined in Chapter 8. The nearly 180 downloaded packages comprise around 200MB, and the installation itself takes up around 550MB, so you should have at least around 800MB free to attempt this installation.

Installing GNOME

You can install GNOME and its many related packages via the Synaptic Package Manager. To install Gnome:

1. Launch the Synaptic Package Manager via Launch > Applications > System > Synaptic Package Manager.
2. Click into the package list and type gnome.
3. Right-click gnome and mark it for installation.
4. Click the Apply button, and click OK for the various installation dialog boxes. The GNOME package references all of the additional packages that it needs.

This is a very long installation (over an hour with a download speed of 42 kB/s), and it has a catch: After Synaptic completes the download part of the process, but prior to actually installing the various packages, it pops up some windows to prompt you for answers. However, you'll never see these unless you click the Details button in Synaptic's Applying Changes dialog box, so be sure to do that.

Clicking the Details button expands the dialog box to contain a console pane. This makes the dialog box too large for the default 701 display, so use Alt+drag to reposition the window in the screen. Press Return in response to the first prompt. In the next prompt, you'll be asked to pick whether KDE (the prompt refers to it as KDM) or GNOME (GDM) should be the default window manager (see Figure 6.6), which is actually meaningless because this is determined within the startsimple.sh script. However, you need to provide a response or it won't continue.

You'll also be asked whether to replace one of the KDE configuration files. I did not, and things seemed to go okay...well, sort of. One package simply won't install, and it seems to have something to do with the hardware abstraction layer. This is the last package, HAL, and it shows during the gnome-office installation. The installation can't overwrite a file. When you reach this part and the installation stops dead and won't continue, click the close box for the Applying Changes dialog box and then close Synaptic.

When GNOME starts up, it complains about not being able to launch the Power Monitor, and this may be related. However, it seems to run quite well.

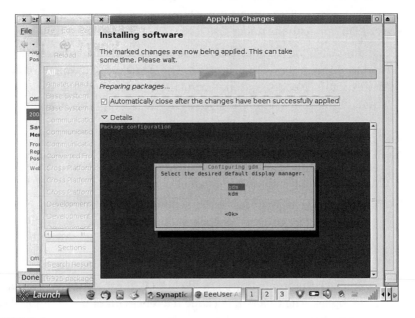

FIGURE 6.6

Configuration prompts that hide under Details.

The next thing to do is to modify the /usr/bin/startsimple.sh script. You need to use sudo when you run your editor to be able to save changes to this file. You're looking for the exec statement that says:

```
exec startkde
```

and you want to change that to:

```
exec gnome-session
```

This exec statement launches the window manager and enables you to fire up whatever window manager you want. Save the file and exit, and then you're ready to try it out.

> **tip**
> I watched my free drive space dwindle away to about 150MB when things were finally all installed. The section, "Freeing Up Space on GNOME" explains how you open up some disk space.

Launching GNOME

Restart the X Window System to get GNOME to start. You can use Ctrl+Alt+Backspace to restart X-Windows. GNOME came right up and found all the devices, installed applications (which were neatly tucked into the appropriate menus), and even the monitor I had plugged in. It does produce a Warning dialog box, on every startup, about not being able to start the dbus system service. Click the Close button when this appears.

In many ways, GNOME seems to fit the small screen on the Eee PC better than the KDE. It also has, by default, better font choices for the cramped 640×480-pixel screen of the 701 models. Everything in GNOME is just a little different from KDE. The Applications menu is, by default, on the top (see Figure 6.7). Four virtual screens are preloaded (the rectangles to the right of the bar at the bottom of the screen). Having four screens is also a good thing when you're starting out with a cramped screen.

FIGURE 6.7

The GNOME desktop, showing the applications menu.

Setting Up Wireless

A very major difference between GNOME and the KDE is the procedure for setting up the wireless network. To set up wireless in GNOME, choose Applications, Internet, Connection Wizard. The wizard walks you though the process of selecting the following:

1. The type of network connection (wireless or wired).

2. The hardware (you've only got one wireless, the Atheros Communications device, so this choice is easy).

3. DHCP or static IP; with most home router configurations, you'll want DHCP.

4. The network that you want to tie into (the wizard provides a list of available wireless networks).

5. The wireless channel number and frequency (you'll typically want to pick Any).

6. The security settings, either WEP or WPA (see Figure 6.8). See Chapter 1, "Getting Started."

7. The name for the network, and whether or not it should be the default and automatically connect. If you set it to automatically connect, you'll simply connect on bootup.

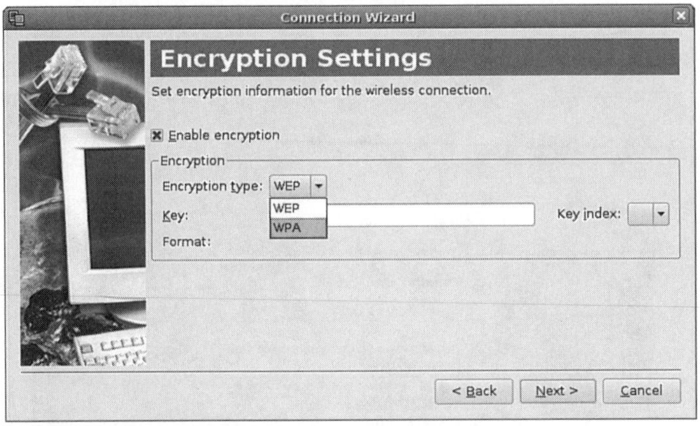

FIGURE 6.8

Encryption type in the Connection Wizard.

GNOME Applications

GNOME has its own complement to almost everything on the KDE, ranging from file browsers to word processors. However, the locations are a little different and the security is a little stricter. Many administrative functions will challenge you for the system password (this is the password you entered when you first switched on the Eee PC).

The GNOME desktop comes with the following additional office applications, all of which may be found under Applications, Office:

AbiWord: A Microsoft Word–compatible word processor. Like OpenOffice.org Writer, it has rather extensive stylesheet capabilities. Oddly, it does not support the OpenOffice.org file format.

Evolution: An email program, which is installed instead of Thunderbird. To my mind, Thunderbird is the superior program. It knows about both POP3 and IMAP (including the newer IMAP standard). It can also function as a news reader. For more information about Thunderbird, see Chapter 3, "Configuring Internet Applications."

Gnumeric Spreadsheet: A Microsoft Excel–compatible spreadsheet program. This supports a lot of odd and legacy spreadsheet formats, such the UNIX Applixware and Microsoft Multiplan (the Excel predecessor) formats. It also can read OpenOffice.org Calc.

Project Management: This is Planner, and is a very useful tool if you're in the world of project management. It can read Microsoft Project XML format, so you've got a way of getting those ubiquitous Project files into the system (see Figure 6.9). The interface is quite similar to Project, so it's really not hard to make the transition.

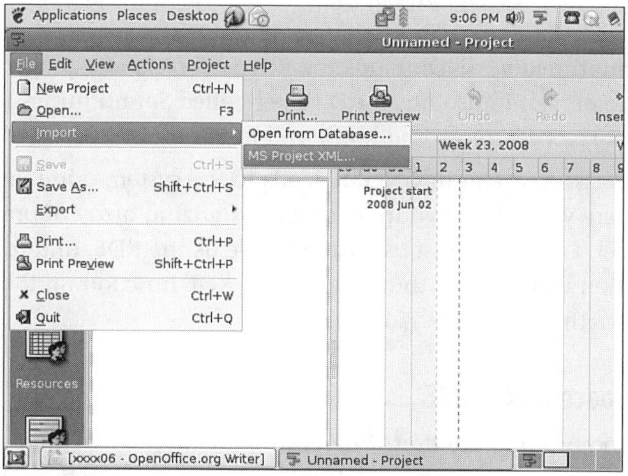

FIGURE 6.9

Planner, showing the Microsoft Project Import command.

For graphics, GNOME comes with two of the must-have Linux applications: GIMP and Inkscape. Like the KDE, GNOME also has a screen-capture program. Unlike the KDE, GNOME comes bundled with Dia (see Figure 6.10), the closest thing to a Microsoft Visio application (other than OpenOffice.org Draw) in the Linux world. It's a little "geekier" than Visio as it emphasizes flow diagrams and the like.

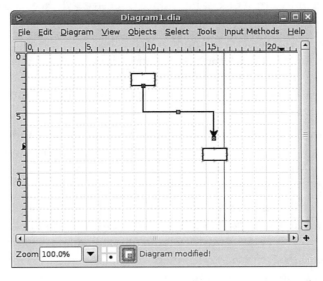

FIGURE 6.10

Running a connector between boxes in Dia.

For multimedia, GNOME has the Rhythmbox audio player and the Totem movie player. It also has a CD ripper called Sound Juicer. Like the KDE, it has sound-recorder, recording-level, and mixer tools.

The Desktop menu in GNOME leads to the system administration menus (this is where you'll find Synaptic) and an amazing array of preferences that you can set. GNOME is just as customizable as the KDE, and the Screen Resolution function works better than the default KDE function on the Eee PC, especially in detecting available video modes.

Freeing Up Space on GNOME

So it occurred to me that, whereas removing the KDE might be somewhat problematic and dangerous, it might be easiest to remove OpenOffice.org to free up some disk space. So I gave it a try to see what happened. To remove any application, such as OpenOffice:

1. Make sure the application is currently not running.

2. Launch the Synaptic Package Manager via Launch > Applications > System > Synaptic Package Manager.

3. Click in the packages pane and then start typing the name of the application. In this instance, openoffice.

4. Right-click the application and mark it for uninstallation.

5. Click the Apply button.

Removing OpenOffice.org gave me back a bit more than 100MB, which provides a little breathing room but not as much as I'd like. So I took out SMPlayer and Thunderbird as well, figuring I could rely on the tools installed with GNOME. Then, to make sure I cleaned out all of the configuration files, I ran:

```
> sudo apt-get clean
```

Suddenly, life was much better. Now I was up to about 500MB of free space. I'm sure with a little diligence I could hunt down even more applications to remove, and probably get back to 600 or 700MB of free space on my 4GB 701.

So, what does this mean? Well, if you're truly a fan of the GNOME desktop, you can pretty easily make this work on a 4GB Eee PC. Just peel away the KDE applications for which you have GNOME replacements. Also, by default, GNOME comes with a lot of games. If you don't want those, you can tear them out, too. Given that GNOME actually seems a little more at home on the Eee PC than the KDE, running GNOME on the Eee PC isn't a bad option.

Uninstalling Gnome

Since the KDE is actually still installed, you can uninstall GNOME by reversing the installation:

1. Launch a terminal window through the Applications > Accessories menu in GNOME.

2. Issue the following on the command line:

```
> sudo gedit /usr/bin/startsimple.sh
```

3. Change the exec statement from:

```
exec gnome-session
```

to

```
exec startdke
```

4. Save the file and exit.

5. Press Ctrl+Alt+Backspace to restart X-Windows and launch the KDE.

6. Launch the Synaptic Package Manager via Launch > Applications > System > Synaptic Package Manager.

7. In the packages pane, right-click each installed package beginning with "gnome" (these have the green box), and mark them for removal. There are several of these so make sure you mark them all.

8. Click the Apply button.

9. After removal is complete, close Synaptic.

10. Press Ctrl+Alt+Backspace to restart X-Windows.

You may find that the Trash icon and Home icons on your desktop are now occupying the same space. Drag Home away from Trash to correct this.

Fluxbox

Whereas Beryl strives for advanced functionality and startling eye-candy, Fluxbox excels at minimalism and speed. It is another excellent choice as a standard window manager, especially for the Eee PC. Fluxbox has a very small memory footprint, running in less than half of the memory space that KDE uses. Fluxbox also provides all of the basics that one needs to run a Linux PC, so it's not a big sacrifice to use it.

Installing Fluxbox

Fluxbox can also be loaded through the Synaptic Package Manager:

1. Launch the Synaptic Package Manager via Launch > Applications > System > Synaptic Package Manager.

2. Click into the package list and type fluxbox.

3. Right-click fluxbox and mark it for installation.

4. Click the Apply button, and click OK for the various installation dialog boxes. The Fluxbox package references the additional package that it needs.

5. When all is installed, exit from Synaptic via File, Exit. Now you're ready to enable Fluxbox.

Launching Fluxbox

There are a number of schemes available on the various Eee PC forums for loading Fluxbox and switching window managers. However, the simplest way of loading it is to simply replace the default Easy Mode (IceWM) with Fluxbox.

Fluxbox can do pretty much anything you can do in the KDE. Simply replace it in the /usr/bin/startsimple.sh. This is exactly the same procedure that was used to launch GNOME.

To start, open an xterm or Konsole window. For example, choose Launch, Run, enter `konsole`, and press Enter. In the Konsole window:

```
> sudo kwrite /usr/bin/startsimple.sh &
```

Find the `exec` line, and change it to:

```
exec fluxbox
```

Save the file and exit. Restart the Eee PC and it will quickly load Fluxbox. You'll be faced with a nearly barren screen and toolbar. The basic controls for Fluxbox are the toolbar and the right-click menu (which you can access by right-clicking any open area of the screen). By the way, the default network connection is launched automatically, so you will have wireless if you're configured for that.

Configuring Fluxbox

Fluxbox seems to do a fairly decent job of populating the menus. Although the various Eee PC forums and wiki pages give advice about how to set up your menus for the Eee PC, the default layout is decent. If you really want to dig into Fluxbox, head off to http://fluxbox.org/ and learn how to configure it and what additional applications are available.

Remember that all of the KDE applications are still there and that they will run just fine under any window manager (including Fluxbox). So, setting up wireless or any other device is easy as you can get to the configuration tools. The administrative console can be launched from the Fluxbox right-click menu. Right-click on a blank area in the desktop and choose Apps > System > kcontrol.

The first thing I did was improve its looks. If you right-click over an empty space and select Styles, you'll get a fairly nice selection of themes (see Figure 6.11). Launch a few windows to play with, and you'll discover that you can switch to adjacent virtual desktops by just dragging them left or right. You can also switch using the buttons at the left of the toolbar. The button near the right end of the toolbar switches which application has focus (or you can just click the Applications button on the toolbar).

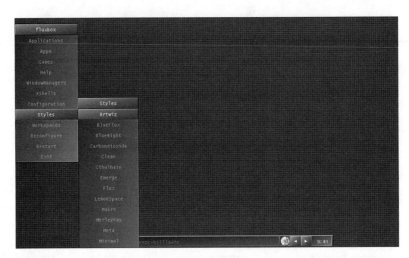

FIGURE 6.11

The Artwiz theme, shown as active, and how to find it in the menu.

The windows have some nice controls that you can access by simply right-clicking the top bar of the window. For example, you can "roll up" the window with the Shade command or move it in front or behind other windows with the Raise or Lower commands.

On its own, Fluxbox picked up almost all the installed applications, and these are under Apps on the right-click menu (see Figure 6.12). Finding them is fairly easy. For example, OpenOffice.org Writer is under Editors and Synaptic is under System. There are a few notable exceptions, such as Firefox, that don't show up by default.

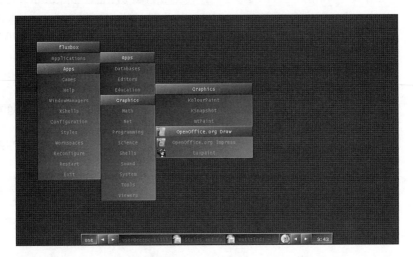

FIGURE 6.12

Finding applications on the right-click menu.

While Fluxbox configuration is largely done through its configuration files, which are in your user directory in .fluxbox, there is a Fluxbox Configuration Tool available through the right-click menu at Configuration (see Figure 6.13). Any changes you make to themes and so forth must be saved by clicking Reconfigure on the main Fluxbox right-click menu.

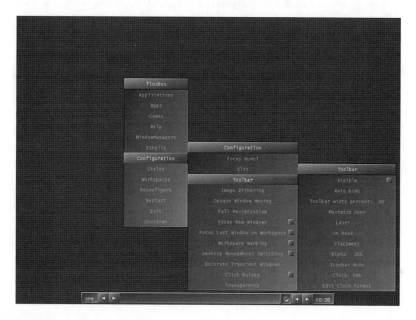

FIGURE 6.13
Fluxbox Configuration Tool.

If you take a liking to Fluxbox, it has a number of advanced functions such as tabbing and something called the "Slit," which is a docking area for applications. It also supports window tabbing, which is a nice feature.

Uninstalling Fluxbox

Should you tire of Fluxbox, simply edit the /usr/bin/startsimple.sh file, and change the `exec` line back to:

```
exec startkde
```

This will restore everything to its previous state, and when you restart, KDE will load instead of Fluxbox.

Summary

In this chapter, you explored several alternate window managers, ranging from the exotic Beryl to the simple Fluxbox. This not only widens your options for interacting with the Eee PC, it demonstrates how to load almost any window manager and run it from the /usr/bin/startsimple.sh file. Having lots of choices and learning to experiment is part of the fun of Linux.

Another lesson from this chapter is that the Eee PC, for all its capabilities, is a limited platform. The 900 and 701 series have limited processing power and many of the 701 models have limited storage. You must take these things into consideration when choosing window managers.

Looking At the Installed Software

T his chapter provides a quick look at some of the installed applications on the Eee PC. There's enough information here to get you started with these applications; however, the best way to learn about what these applications can do is to try them. Experimenting is part of the fun of Linux. So go ahead, dive in and enjoy!

IN THIS CHAPTER

■ Introducing three of the installed set of productivity applications: OpenOffice Writer, OpenOffice Impress, and OpenOffice Draw

■ Learn about the photo viewer, music player, and multimedia player applications.

■ Get an overview of three of the set of learning applications: the typing tutor, the fraction tutor, and the virtual planetarium

Working

The Eee PC ships with the OpenOffice.org suite, which was designed as an open source alternative to Microsoft Office. OpenOffice.org now has, according to its website, 20 years of code development behind it. It is a fully integrated office suite with an amazingly consistent interface throughout. In some ways, it is a better office suite than the Microsoft alternative.

OpenOffice.org started life as StarOffice, from a German company called Star Division. I remember this as being one of the few options back in the early days of PCs and DOS, when WordStar and WordPerfect ruled the Earth. Star Division was eventually bought by Sun, and Sun still sells a commercial variation of the package.

In every case, the OpenOffice.org products are at least comparable to their Microsoft Office counterparts. In the case of Writer, it is clearly a superior application to Microsoft Word. Word is rife with problems, ranging from automatic counters that are almost impossible to manage to long document features that are legendary for their bugginess. Writer is stable, powerful, and has the advantage of a much more thoughtful design. Word suffers from being a collection of add-ons whose sum is, from a usability perspective, considerably less than its parts.

OpenOffice.org has the following major components:

- **Writer:** A word processor with very impressive publishing and long document features thrown in.
- **Impress:** A presentation package designed to compete with PowerPoint. This is a very full-featured package.
- **Draw:** A vector-based illustration package, more similar to CorelDRAW than to Adobe Illustrator. Draw also has some Microsoft Visio functionality for building flow charts and the like.
- **Calc:** A powerful spreadsheet package.

There are fairly frequent updates to the packages, so you can count on at least an upgrade per year. In fact, if you want to use the database package called OpenOffice.org Base, you'll really have to upgrade OpenOffice.org. The version installed has a number of problems, such as nonfunctional wizards. OpenOffice.org has plenty of tutorials, frequently asked questions (FAQs), and the like for basic procedures and tasks. Also, there's an excellent user community to which you can pose questions.

The following sections present a short introduction to the programs and some of their real (and perhaps not so obvious) strengths. These are hardly comprehensive manuals for the applications, but they will serve to get you started. The draft chapters for this book, by the way, were written using OpenOffice.org Writer on the Eee PC.

OpenOffice.org Writer

This is a superb word processor with enough power to rival such advanced publishing programs as Adobe FrameMaker. It's the equal of Microsoft Word in everyday tasks such as reports, memos, homework, and the like. However, its features for building long documents truly excel, and have none of the fabled problems that plague Microsoft Word.

To launch OpenOffice.org Writer in Easy Mode, select the Work tab and then the Documents icon. From Full Desktop, choose Launch, Applications, Office, Writer. The interface is shown in Figure 7.1.

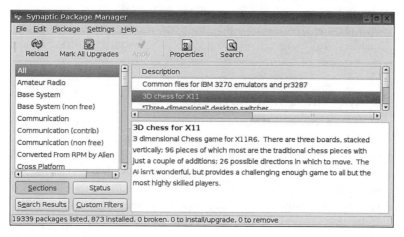

FIGURE 7.1

OpenOffice.org Writer.

There are two ways to format text:

- **Formatting toolbar:** This is a quick way to format short, quick documents that do not need to conform to typographic guidelines and will not be updated over time.

- **Styles and Formatting palette:** This is the best way to format documents that must adhere to style guidelines, such as a corporate or organizational style guide. Also, if the document will be maintained and edited over time, styles are the only way to maintain any consistency from author to author and from version to version.

Using the Formatting Toolbar

The formatting toolbar, just below the menus, has buttons for almost all the functions you'll use. Starting from the left side of the toolbar, you have three file operation buttons (New, Open, Save), a Print button, the Cut/Copy/Paste trio, and, my personal favorite, Undo. In the Font drop-down list, the list of fonts with Xandros is quite adequate, with a few representative serif, sans serif, fixed space, and script examples of text, display, and symbol fonts. To the right of the Font drop-down list are controls for font size, bold, italic, underline, font color, justification, and lists (both enumerated and bulleted).

Below the formatting toolbar, you'll find the ruler, which is also your interactive tab-setting control. Simply click along the ruler to place a default tab (usually a left tab). Right-click an existing tab to change it to your choice: left, centered, right, or decimal aligning. The tab icon in the left corner, just to the right of the ruler, sets the default tab type. Just click this until the default is what you want.

The stops on the right and left of the ruler are interactive indenting markers. Drag them to indent or outdent from either side. Actual page setup controls are under Format, Page. In the Page Style dialog box, you'll find controls to set the page size and margins, number of columns, background, and running headers and footers (as well as some more esoteric settings). You can also set the number of columns with Format, Columns.

Using the Styles and Formatting Palette

The other way of formatting is through the Styles and Formatting palette. You launch this by pressing F11 or choosing Format, Styles and Formatting. The palette appears to the right of the text area. It has a drop-down list at the bottom for the basic categories, such as chapter styles, text styles, and the like. Along the top of the palette, you'll find icons for the various style types: paragraph, character, frame, page, and list. There's also a button for applying styles to a selection and creating new styles. You can also right-click in the palette to create a new style or modify a selected style.

Having paragraph, character, and frame styles provides a lot of publishing power. Paragraph styles are fairly obvious—they format paragraphs. Character styles, sometimes called inline styles, format a selection of text (normally less than a paragraph).

Frames are box-shaped containers for text and graphics that you can create and move around on a page. Frame styles dictate the look of a selected frame. If you set up your paragraph styles and character styles to cover the various required formats in your document, and then religiously apply them instead of using the formatting toolbar, you'll go a long way toward providing a uniform look to your documents.

The Table Editor

The Table Editor is a joy to use. Simply select Table, Insert Table, and you can select the number of rows, columns, and repeating header rows (see Figure 7.2). Clicking the AutoFormat button lets you pick from a number of preset table styles. Once your table is built, you'll get a table toolbar with controls for cells, rows, and columns, as well as for borders and tints. There are also buttons to sort the table or sum the values in a column.

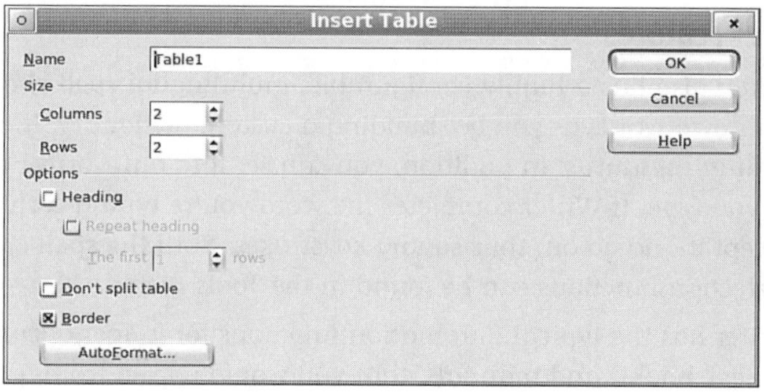

FIGURE 7.2

Table creation in Writer.

To insert a graphics file, choose Insert, Picture, From File. Once the file is inserted, you can double-click the figure to produce the graphics controls, which control how text wraps around the figure, sizing, rules, captions, and many other things.

Writer supports an extremely rich set of graphics formats. In addition to the usual "universal" formats, such as .png, .jpg, .eps, .wmf. and .tif, it also supports a variety of cross-platform and more escoteric formats. For example, Apple Pict and Sun Raster formats are available. It can also import Adobe Photoshop, DXF (a common format from computer-aided drafting applications), and even Kodak photo CD formats.

The Find & Replace tool, available through Edit, Find & Replace, is extremely powerful, and includes full regular expressions plus the ability to search on all sorts of formatting characteristics (see Figure 7.3). Regular expressions are a notation for extremely powerful search queries, and have grown almost into a scripting language over the years. For example, you can use regular expressions to search for not only wildcards, but a range of characters or numbers.

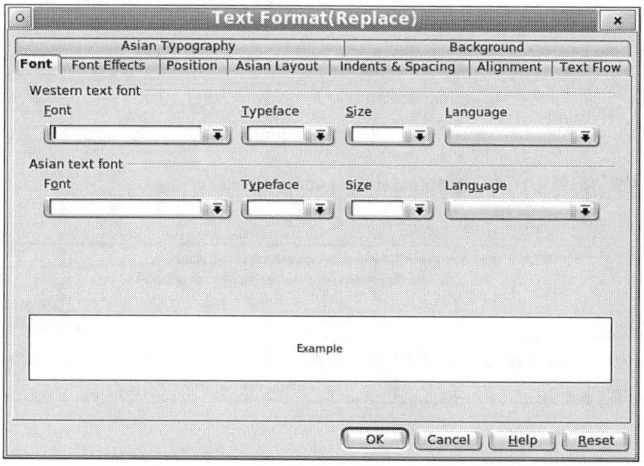

FIGURE 7.3

Some of the extensive Find & Replace options in Writer.

Other Writer Features

Writer also has a highly configurable, multilingual spell checker. You can add your own words as you go, building a custom dictionary. It also comes with a built-in thesaurus. In addition, you can set it to autocorrect and suggest words as you type. If Writer completes the word you're typing correctly, you can accept it and go on, thus saving keystrokes. Both the spell checker and auto-correction functions can be found in the Tools menu.

Writer has the typical automation functions for longer documents, such as papers, books, and manuals, that you would expect from a full featured word processor. Most of these functions may be found in the Insert menu, and you can choose to insert tables of contents, index entries, and cross-references. Under the Tools menu, you'll even find a Bibliography Database command you can use to assist in building a bibliography.

OpenOffice files are all actually stored in eXtensible Markup Language (XML) format. In addition to support the native OpenOffice XML formats, Writer can support other standard XML document formats as well. In the world of technical publishing, DocBook is a standard XML format used by software, aerospace, and publishing companies. Writer also has DocBook import and export filters. I wouldn't recommend this as a general-purpose DocBook editor, but you can get DocBook files into Writer and you can export usable (though somewhat mindless) DocBook files (see Figure 7.4).

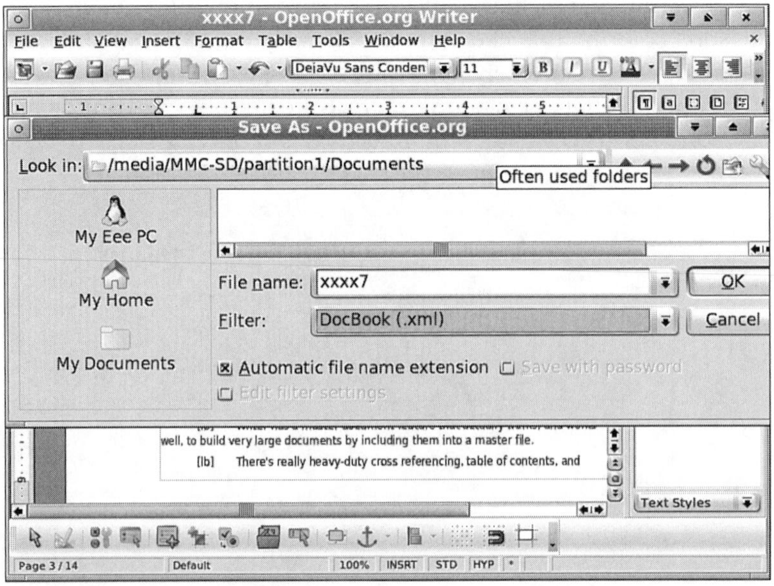

FIGURE 7.4

You can save files as DocBook XML.

Here are a few features that will turn Word fans green with envy:

- You can export your files directly to PDF.
- Writer has a master document feature that actually works, and works well, to build very large documents by including them into a master file.
- Writer includes heavy-duty cross-referencing, table of contents, and indexing functions that won't fall apart in large documents.

Speaking of Word, Writer on the Eee PC is set by default to use Word format. However, it has its own native format, ODT, that's an open standard based on XML. You may want to use that instead of Word format, especially given that such things as the open source Scribus desktop publishing package and Alfresco content management system work so well with ODT format.

Impress

Impress strives to be much more than a PowerPoint wannabe. It has some truly remarkable features, such as excellent illustration tools and lots of special effects. Also, it will output the presentation directly to Adobe Flash, so that you can display it on your website.

You can launch Impress either by clicking the Presentations icon on the Office tab in Easy Mode or by choosing Launch, Applications, Office, Impress in Full Desktop. You're greeted with a three-step Presentation Wizard that will guide you along in creating your presentation.

Using the Presentation Wizard

In Step 1 of the wizard, shown in Figure 7.5, you have a choice of creating a presentation from scratch, selecting one of the templates from the two installed, or importing the styles from an existing template. (See the sidebar for instructions on obtaining additional templates.) After you make your selection, click Next.

OBTAINING ADDITIONAL TEMPLATES

There are lots of sources for additional templates. Doing a Google search on "Impress" and "templates" will produce lots of websites for you to choose from. A UK site, http://www.presentationhelper.co.uk/free-open-office-impress-templates-91.htm, has some particularly nice ones.

To import templates after you have downloaded them, first choose File, Templates, Organize. Next, select Presentations in the left pane. Click the Import Template command in the Commands list on the right and navigate to the folder in which you downloaded the additional templates.

FIGURE 7.5

Step 1 of the Presentation Wizard in Impress.

In Step 2 of the wizard, you select from the palette of presentation backgroups and select the output medium. For example, if you are building a presentation that will be viewed from either a video projector or at least a monitor, you would select Screen. Click Next.

Step 3 of the wizard asks what sort of transition effects you'd like. If you're going to have the presentation run as a Flash file or a standalone, automated presentation, you can pick the duration for each slide and the transition. If you have OpenOffice 2.0.4, click Create at this point to begin working with your presentation. If you have a later version of OpenOffice, click Next.

> **tip** Pick a subtle transition effect. Keeping your audience focused on the message is hard enough without setting off fireworks between each slide.

Step 4 requests metadata about your organization, the purpose of your presentation, and what other messages you'd like to convey. Fill in the fields and continue by clicking Next.

Step 5 asks what page types you'd like to include. Exactly why one would say, "No, please limit my choices!" is beyond me. I always leave everything available. When you're done, click Create.

Once you've finished the wizard, you'll find yourself with a powerful set of tools.

Touring the Impress Work Area

The Impress work area is shown in Figure 7.6. The left panel has the slides that you've created. You can navigate with this panel, as well as edit individual slides and anything attached to them. The center is your main work area, and is where you craft your slides, notes, and handouts. The right panel (Tasks) has selections for master pages (the basic look of the slide) as well as the various formats.

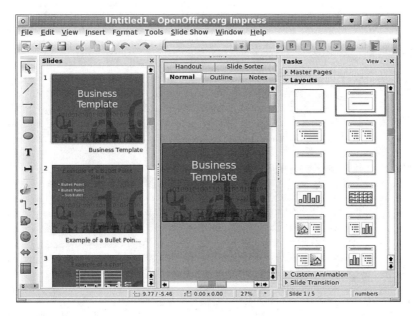

FIGURE 7.6

Impress work area.

Given that screen real-estate is at such a premium on the default Eee PC screen, you'll be pleased to know that the View menu gives you options for hiding and displaying the various work areas.

Note the drawing toolbar along the left side of the screen. Here, you will find basic drawing tools similar to those in Draw. There are also a number of palettes of stock "shapes" you can select and then click-and-drag to draw on the work area (see Figure 7.7). You can reveal the shape palettes by clicking the little triangle on the side of the buttons.

When working with the limited depth of the built-in Eee PC screen, you won't be able to see all the buttons that run the length of the drawing toolbar. The workaround for this is to click the button with the double arrow heads at the bottom of the toolbar. This launches a fly-out palette that contains most of the functions on the toolbar, but not all of them. To see all of the available buttons, hover over Visible Buttons in the flyout palette. If a button is checked, it's on the toolbar or flyout palette. If you want to add a button, just click it.

The top of the window contains a formatting toolbar similar to the one in Writer (an example of the thoughtful consistency throughout the OpenOffice.org toolset).

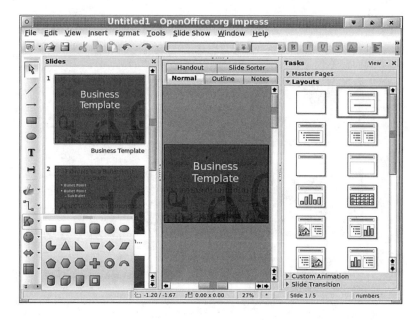

FIGURE 7.7

Some of the shapes in the palette.

You'll also see two text box controls in the drawing palette, one for vertical text and one for horizontal text. Just as with Writer, you can format the text either with the toolbar buttons or with styles. Although the Slides templates have a built-in stylesheet, if you're doing presentations as part of an organization, you'll want to take the time to develop your own stylesheet to provide a standard look and feel that complies with your organization's identity standards.

Any of the shapes or text boxes can be converted into 3D shapes. Simply select the object on the slide, right-click, and select Convert, To 3D. The object is given "thickness" and can then be rotated, skewed, and otherwise manipulated. This is a great effect for text. You can also convert an object to 3D via rotation (Convert, To 3D Rotation Object). This works by "sweeping" the shape 360 degrees around a central axis to make a shape. This works well for objects such as triangles, which sweep to cone shapes (see Figure 7.8). However, it works quite poorly for text, which usually sweeps to something like a set of concentric hoops.

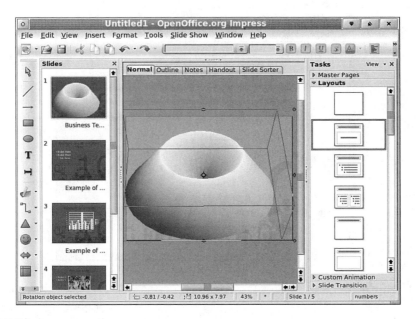

FIGURE 7.8

3D sweep of triangle to a cone, tilted slightly forward.

You can also draw lines and lines with arrow heads. The Connector tool provides Microsoft Visio–like connector objects. By the way, if you seem stuck in some strange editing mode and the slide turns to a pale color, simply right-click and select Exit Group.

Adding Special Effects with Fontwork

If the 3D fonts aren't enough special effects for you, Impress has a tool called Fontwork. This is only visible on the default screen through the Visible Buttons trick.

Fontwork has various colored 3D fonts that follow curved paths instead of a straight baseline. When you launch Fontwork and select an example from the palette, you get a floating Fontwork toolbar. Click the A button to launch the Fontwork Gallery, shown in Figure 7.9. You simply select a Fontwork object from the Gallery, click the OK button, and it appears on your slide. Double-click it and you'll see the text in normal, straight letters. This is the text you edit.

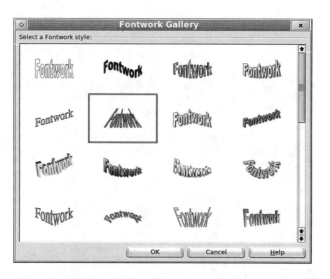

FIGURE 7.9

Fontwork Gallery.

Once you have a Fontwork object, the Fontwork toolbar provides tools for changing the text path, switching case, changing the alignment of a paragraph, and changing the character spacing ("kerning"). These tools provide a remarkable amount of font effects flexibility.

Fontwork provides cool effects, but don't overdo it. Remember that the message you want the viewers to remember isn't that you could do cool tricks with fonts. For the most part, you're better off finding a nice template and sticking with its styles or perhaps styles that conform to your organization's graphics standards.

Adding Animation

Another cool effect, but one that can also be overdone, is animation. Any object can be animated. Just right-click the object and select Custom Animation to open the Custom Animation window, shown in Figure 7.10. The Animation tools appear on the Inpress Tasks palette. You can select to have an object enter the screen, do something to gain attention (Emphasis tab), or exit the screen. You can also set the motion path, and can select such things as an 8-pointed star.

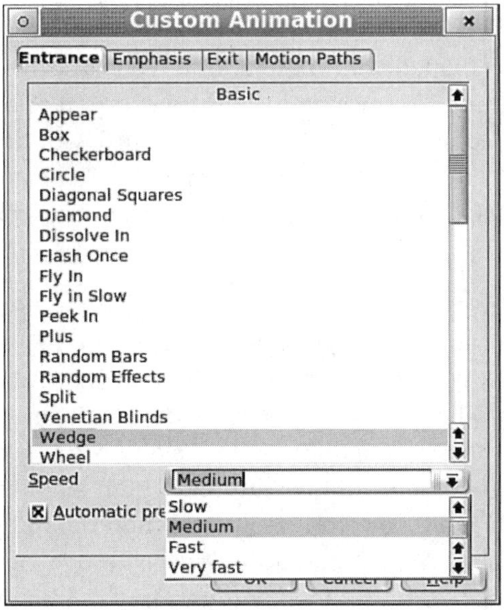

FIGURE 7.10

Setting up animation effects within Impress.

Adding Multimedia Objects

The real power of Impress comes from its ability to insert multimedia objects. There are two sure ways to build a bad presentation:

- Create a long series of bulleted lists that you, as the presenter, simply read to the audience. Your audience will lose focus by the third slide.

- Create a series of slides, each of which uses fancy effects and different transitions, the sum of which obscures your message.

Impress can insert movie files, charts, graphs, and so forth. It can play sound files as well. Even the most modest digital cameras these days provide the ability to capture small movie files, with sound, that you can use to enliven your presentation. Mix interviews, photos, graphs, and other media to make a compelling story, instead of using a list of bullets. In a pinch, you can use the Eee PC itself as your multimedia tool. You can use its built-in webcam and recording capabilities to good effect to capture interviews and narratives.

Exporting Your Presentation

Once you've crafted your presentation, you can save it in either PowerPoint or Impress format. However, you can also export it to an Adobe Flash file. This can be played on any web browser equipped with the Flash plug-in. To do this, choose File, Export, Macromedia Flash. You can also export the presentation as HTML pages, a variety of graphics formats, or as Adobe PDF.

OpenOffice.org Draw

Draw is a vector-based illustration program in the vein of Adobe Illustrator and CorelDRAW. Unlike graphics editors such as Adobe Photoshop or GIMP, Draw works with lines and geometric objects. It can import bitmapped images, but these serve only as objects and can't be edited in any meaningful way. Draw lacks some of the features of high-end illustration packages, but is significantly more powerful and useful than the rather limited drawing editor within Microsoft Word. Moreover, Draw can save files in all of the common vector graphic formats and export graphics in bitmapped formats or as PDF. Draw can also open files in most common vector formats, including files from CAD or technical illustration applications saved in either DXF or CGM formats.

Launching Draw

You can't access Draw directly from the Easy Mode tabbed interface. The easiest way to run it in Easy Mode is to launch a terminal window with Ctrl-Alt-T and the type the following command:

```
> oodraw &
```

You can add it to the tabbed interface if you wish. Refer to Chapter 4, "Customizing Easy Mode," for instructions concerning adding applications to Easy Mode. From the Full Desktop (KDE), you can launch Draw with Launch, Applications, Office, OpenOffice Draw.

Looking at the Draw Interface

After looking at Impress, the Draw interface will be extremely familiar (see Figure 7.11). It has the same drawing tools, this time with the toolbar running along the bottom of the screen. The formatting toolbar has a few additions, such as buttons for arrow heads and line weights. As an everyday Illustrator user, I have to admit that the placement of tools and the icons themselves in Draw is actually more intuitive.

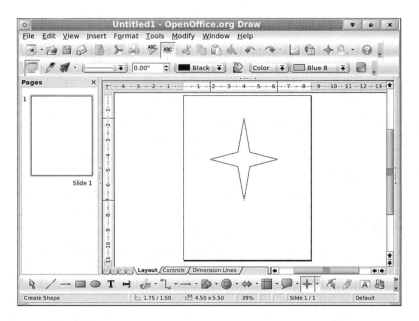

FIGURE 7.11

Dragging a shape from the shape palette.

The theory behind Draw is that you'll create your illustration using line elements, which may be multisided geometric forms of any shape or lines with complex curves, as well as predefined geometric shapes, which can be stretched and skewed as required. Objects have two components: lines (which form the outline of the object) and fills (which form the color or pattern of the interior of the object). You can also add type, including text boxes containing multiple paragraphs.

The combination of text and precision lines makes Draw suitable not only for illustrations but also as a layout package for single-page designs. Although Draw is certainly not the equal of a program such as Adobe InDesign or the open source alternative Scribus, it has enough capability to build ads and flyers.

Working with Freeform Drawing Tools

To truly master any vector-based illustration package, you must learn to draw with the three freeform tools:

- Polygon, which can be used to draw objects with straight sides.

- Curve, sometimes called Bezier Curve, which provides a way, though nonintuitive and a little tricky to master, to draw precise curves with a mouse, touchpad, or trackball.

■ Freehand Curve, which is a reflection of your hand movement and is therefore only as precise as you are. Without an advanced drawing device, such as a digitizer pad, this is difficult. When I've used this tool, I've always ended up "fixing" the curve by editing the "node" within the lines.

Each of these tools can be used as "filled" objects or as outlines (simply select the mode you want to use from the flyout menu). Filled versions automatically fill with the currently selected color and the outline takes the currently selected line color. Outlines simply take the line color. You select colors and line weights on the formatting bar above the drawing area.

The Polygon tool is the easiest to master, and comes in two flavors: Polygon (which may have lines with any arbitrary angle) and Polygon 45 Degree (which is constrained to having all lines at 45-degree angles). Drawing is a click-and-hold-while-dragging operation. The point where you first click-and-hold is the origin point of the first line. You release the mouse button to end a line segment, and then click-and-hold to start the next line segment. Double-click to complete the polygon. To close the polygon, make the last line segment end on the origin point of the first line segment. Figure 7.12 shows a polygon.

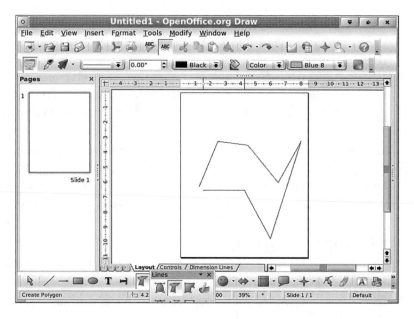

FIGURE 7.12

Drawing a polygon.

You draw curves not by tracing the curve with your mouse but by defining the lines that constrain the curves. For example, to draw an arc, you click-and-hold while dragging to define the path from the origin of the arc to the mid-point (which is also the highest point of the arc). You then release the mouse button and drag the line down toward the endpoint of the arc. When you reach the endpoint, double-click. If you don't double-click, but merely click, you mark a node along the curve and you can start drawing a second curve as part of the line. In this way, you can create compound curves to define very complex shapes. Figure 7.13 shows the sorts of curves that can be drawn.

You'll need to take time to master this technique. If you attempt to learn this under deadline pressure with the idea of building a polished illustration your first time out, you're headed for a very frustrating time. Set aside an hour or so just to get the hang of this tool. It's the basis of much that you will do in Draw, and learning to use it will pay off in the end.

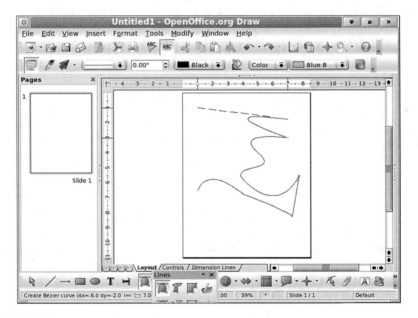

FIGURE 7.13

Drawing a compound curve with the Bezier tool.

The Freeform line tools simply draw a line that exactly tracks your mouse movements. Just click-and-hold while dragging to draw the line. Because your mouse movement won't be a precise curve, the line you create will have bumps and squiggles along its path. You can fix these using the Node Editing tool.

When you click an object with the Node Editing tool, little boxes appear along the path to mark the location of nodes. Click a node and editing "handles" will appear (see Figure 7.14). You can reposition the node, or drag the end-points of the handles to change the angle of the curve from either side. Again, this is a skill that takes a little time to master. Practice this for a while to understand how this works and what the limitations are before you attempt to create "real" drawings.

The Edit Points toolbar provides tools for manipulating the curve via the various nodes. You can add nodes, delete node, split the curve, convert lines to curves, and so forth. The combination of these tools allows you to convert shapes that almost meet your needs into exactly what you want.

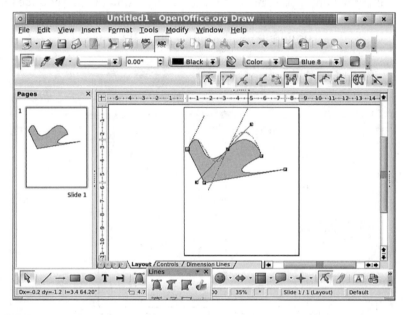

FIGURE 7.14

Changing a curve with node handles.

When using text boxes, keep in mind that you can apply only a single style to a text box. This works very well for such simple things as callout text or captions, but presents problems for large amounts of text with headings and body paragraphs. You'll need to use multiple text boxes for these items and use the Alignment tools.

This brings us to the subject of alignment and arrangement. Objects can be aligned to the top, bottom, either side, or center. To do this, select a group of objects and right-click. Under the Alignment menu, you'll find icons that designate the various alignment choices. Arrangement is the "z-order" for the

various objects; that is, if vertical and horizontal movement represent the x-
and y-axes, then the z-axis defines "above" and "below" or stacking order.
This provides a way in a 2D drawing to place objects over each other. Under
Arrange on the right-click menu, you'll find commands to move an object up
or down in the stacking order, or even to the top or bottom of the stack (see
Figure 7.15).

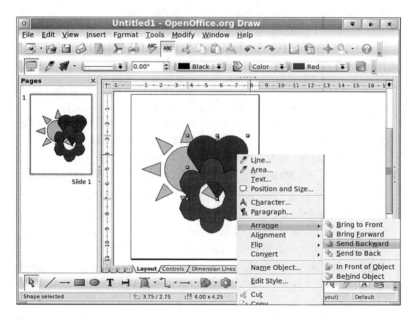

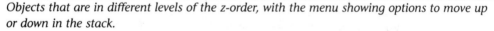

FIGURE 7.15

*Objects that are in different levels of the z-order, with the menu showing options to move up
or down in the stack.*

Another concept you'll find invaluable is grouping. When you "group" a set
of objects, you can manipulate them together. Thus, you can move, size, or
stretch them as if they were a single object. Combined with cut and paste,
grouping provides a great way of building an illustration out of smaller components. Suppose that you have an illustration with a number of electrical
contacts, each of which is a collection of circles (screw heads) and rectangles
(connector tabs). By combining simple shapes, you can build a single contact.
By grouping these shapes and then copying and pasting them multiple times,
you make a set of contacts. By aligning the contacts, you make it visually correct. By arranging the set of contacts, pulled together into a group, over
another object, you've added the contacts to a housing for some device. While
you may not care about technical illustration, the same techniques can be
combined regardless of the type of drawing.

There are lots of other controls and functions you can use, including the 3D functions that were covered under the discussion of Impress (such as the Fontwork tool). There's also a set of flowcharting symbols and connector lines that provides a lot of the functionality you'd find in Microsoft Visio.

As with the other OpenOffice.org applications, you can save your files in the native OpenOffice.org format or export them in a number of common formats for use in other applications. You can also create HTML pages, Flash files, and PDF files from your illustration.

OpenOffice.org Calc

Calc is a spreadsheet program with literally hundreds of functions. It maintains the common OpenOffice.org interface as much as possible, and is accessible and easy enough to produce simple spreadsheets yet has the power to do complex financial and statistical analyses. From Easy Mode, you can launch Calc from the Work tab by clicking the Spreadsheets icon. From Full Desktop, you can run it via Launch, Applications, Office, OpenOffice Calc.

Calc opens into a familiar spreadsheet interface with rows and columns of cells. To type into a cell, simply click it and start typing values or text. You can navigate from cell to cell via the arrow keys or Tab (goes to the right) and Alt+Tab (goes to the left). If you're typing text that isn't a formula, some characters must be "escaped" or they'll be considered part of the formula. For example, the following is the formula to sum two cells:

=SUM(B1:B2)

Normally, that would produce the number that's the sum of the values in those cells. But suppose you want to type the formula as text, without the equals sign being interpreted as the beginning of a formula? Just precede the equals sign with the escape character, a single apostrophe:

'=SUM(B1:B2)

The easiest way to enter formulas in Calc is through the Function Wizard, which you access by clicking the Wizard button (the left-most of the three buttons) on the toolbar above the spreadsheet work area. The wizard opens to reveal a list of all the functions. You can use the Category list to limit the list to only related sets of functions, such as financial or statistical functions. If the function name, such as AMORDEGRC, isn't exactly meaningful to you, just click it and you'll get a description on the right explaining exactly what it does, as shown in Figure 7.16.

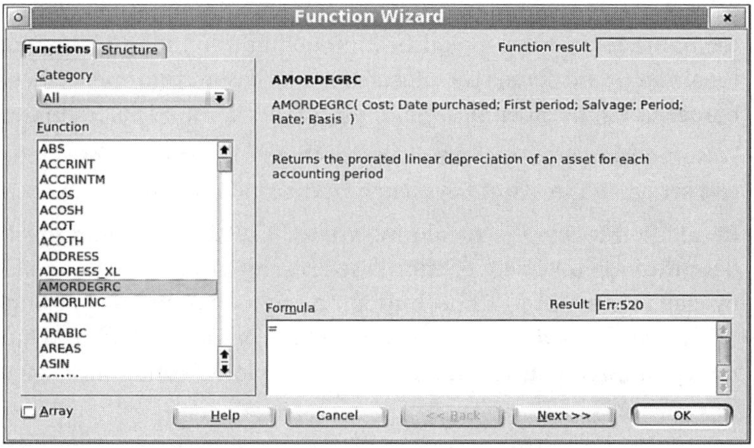

FIGURE 7.16

Picking a function in the Function Wizard.

After you choose the formula you want, click the Next button to choose the cells you want to use in calculating the formula. Each field represents a cell or range of cells. Click the button on the right of the field to select the cells (you can drag to select them, as shown in Figure 7.17) or click the number on the left of the field to apply a nested function to this selection only. You can have up to 30 selections.

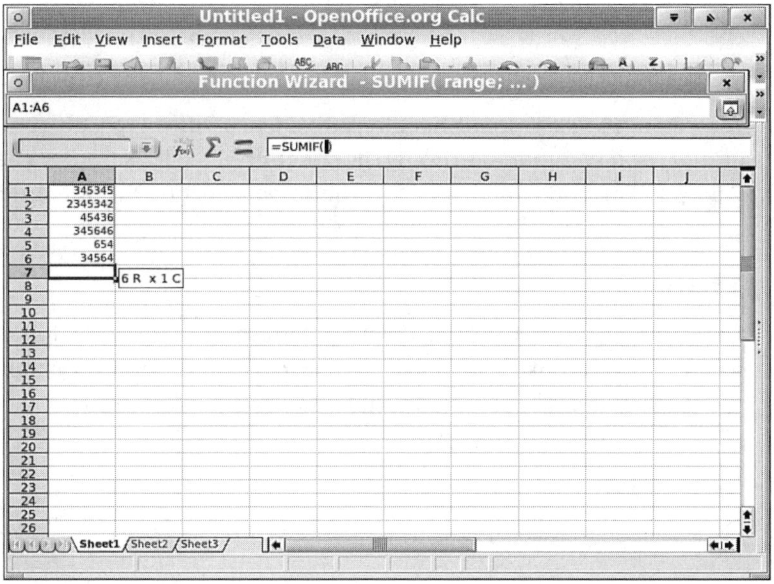

FIGURE 7.17

Selecting a range of cells for a function.

As with the other applications in the OpenOffice.org suite, you can use the toolbar to format the spreadsheet. In addition to the usual text-formatting buttons, you'll find some special functions for formatting spreadsheets, such as border styles, number of decimal places, background color, and text direction.

To sort a range of cells, simply select them and then choose Data, Sort. You can set up to three sort keys, each in descending precedence.

In addition to simply calculating values, Calc has a wizard to visualize your data through a variety of charts (see Figure 7.18). You can access this wizard by clicking the Insert Chart button on the toolbar or by choosing Insert, Chart. The wizard provides both 2D and 3D line, area, bar, and pie charts. It also has specialized charts, such as XY scatter plots, "candlestick" stock charts, and a "net" chart.

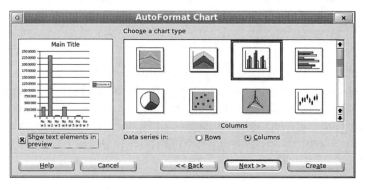

FIGURE 7.18
Charting wizard.

You can save your spreadsheet in native OpenOffice.org Calc format, Excel format, or a common data interchange format such as Comma Separated Values (CSV). You can also export the spreadsheet as XHTML or PDF.

Having Fun

The Eee PC comes well stocked with entertainment software and games. This section takes a look at some of these, in particular applications that you can use to view and organize your photographs and play music.

Organizing Your Pictures with the Photo Manager

The photo manager is the open source image browser and organizer Gwenview. It also has some basic image manipulation functions, but is in no way a replacement for something such as GIMP (see Chapter 9, "Must-Have Applications"). You can think of Gwenview as a file browser optimized for viewing and manipulating graphics files.

You can launch Gwenview from the Play tab in Easy Mode by clicking the Photo Manager icon. In Full Desktop, choose Launch, Applications, Graphics, Gwenview. It opens as a multipart browser window, as shown in Figure 7.19. The upper-left pane is a file tree navigation pane. The right pane shows thumbnails of the image files in the folder selected in the tree. The slider above the thumbnails pane sets the size of the thumbnails, which is really handy for the Eee PC's built-in display. The icons to the left of the slider enable you to choose whether to show only file details or to have the file detail information appear to the right or under the thumbnail.

In the drop-down list to the right of the slider, you can select to view all files, only image files, or only video files. Clicking the More button provides filters for filename or data ranges. You can use these to restrict what's shown in the thumbnails pane. By the way, you can also browse within ZIP files, tarballs (a group of files consolidated into a single file with the Linux tar command), or across the network file system.

The lower-left pane is a preview pane. This reflects a larger, though not full-sized, view of the image currently selected in the thumbnails pane. There are controls to zoom in or out, and to autofit the image to the pane. You can also rotate the image right or left. The right- and left-pointing blue arrows load the next or previous image, respectively, in the thumbnails pane, while the circle icon reloads the image (if it has been modified).

Gwenview provides a handy way of organizing images. You can copy, move, or link them via a right-click menu, as shown in Figure 7.19.

The right-click menu also provides a way to load the images into other tools, via the External Tools submenu. You can select KolourPaint (a very basic paint program) or GIMP (if it's installed). You can also load the image into Konqueror, though, given that its function would be as a file browser, there seems little reason to do this because Gwenview serves as a file browser. The External Tools submenu also provides controls to set the image as the current wallpaper.

note If you double-click an image, it fills the Gwenview screen. This is a very handy way to view images on the small screen. Press the Esc key to return to the Gwenview interface.

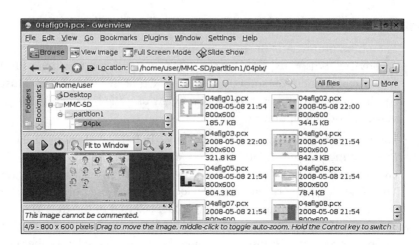

FIGURE 7.19

Gwenview, with the file commands right-click menu.

The Batch Processing submenu under the Plug-Ins menu provides tools to apply various image filters and effects to a set of images. This is a handy way to convert images to a particular format or to sharpen a set of photos. There are a number of image effects provided, ranging from charcoal drawings to embossing.

Playing Tunes with Music Manager

Music Manager is actually the open source player Amarok, which can play CDs and most audio files, including files from the iPod, and can be set as your default streaming player in Firefox. If you have installed K3b (see Chapter 9), you can also burn audio CDs via its K3b plug-in.

From Easy Mode, you can launch Music Manager from the Play tab by clicking the Music Manager icon. From Full Desktop, choose Launch, Applications, Multimedia, Music Manager.

The Music Manager interface has tabs along its left side for a connected Media Device (such as an iPod), Files, Playlists, Collection, and Context, as shown in Figure 7.20. Of these tabs, the Collection and Context tabs are a little different from what you find in the average music player. The Collection tab lists the set of music that Music Manager has found. To set the parts of the file system that it should check, choose Settings, Configure Music Manager. To get Music Manager to build its collections, choose Tools, Rescan Collection.

FIGURE 7.20

Music Manager interface.

The Context tab includes its own tabs to provide information about what played (which is marvelous when listening to streaming audio), information about the artist, and even the lyrics (if available). To get lyrics, you must click the Lyrics script under the Lyrics tab.

When you plug in a device, such as an iPod, Music Manager scans for installed music and shows you the library (see Figure 7.21). You can play it or copy it.

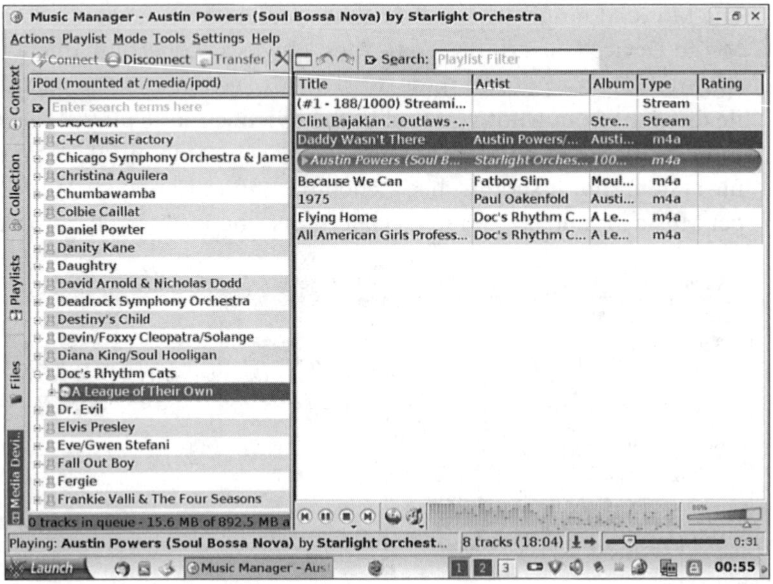

FIGURE 7.21
Music Manager working with an iPod.

If you want to configure Firefox to use Music Manager, open Firefox and
choose Edit, Preferences. Under the Content tab, click the Manage button
under File Types. Scroll down to M3U and click it. Click the Change Action
button. Select Open Them with This Application and browse to select
/usr/bin/amarok.

Playing Multimedia with Media Player

Media Player (SMPlayer) is actually the graphical interface for MPlayer, which
is the plug-in that plays video files inside Firefox. SMPlayer has such features
as configurable subtitles. It would not play DVDs successfully on my Eee PC,
however, until I installed K3b. See Chapter 9 for more information about K3b.
It will not, by default, play DVD movies. However, this is easily fixed by
installing the libdvdcss2. Installing this library requires the additional repositories mentioned in Chapter 8, "Getting More Linux Applications." If you
have these repositories listed in your sources.list file, you can easily install this
library from a terminal window. You can launch a terminal window from
Easy Mode with Ctrl-Alt-T or by typing Konsole in the Launch, Run Command
field in the KDE. To install the library, type the following commands:

```
> sudo apt-get update
> sudo apt-get install libdvdcss2
```

In Easy Mode, you start Media Player from the Play tab. In Full Desktop, choose Launch, Applications, Multimedia, SMPlayer.

SMPlayer can play both video and audio files, as well as video DVDs and audio CDs. When playing a DVD, it has a tendency to pick up the director's narration by default. You can fix that by choosing Audio, Filters and selecting one of the filters. This stops the extra narration.

SMPlayer can turn on subtitles for different languages (see Figure 7.22), but seems to have difficulty switching to different language tracks when playing a DVD. Also, in full-screen mode it tends to skip tracks.

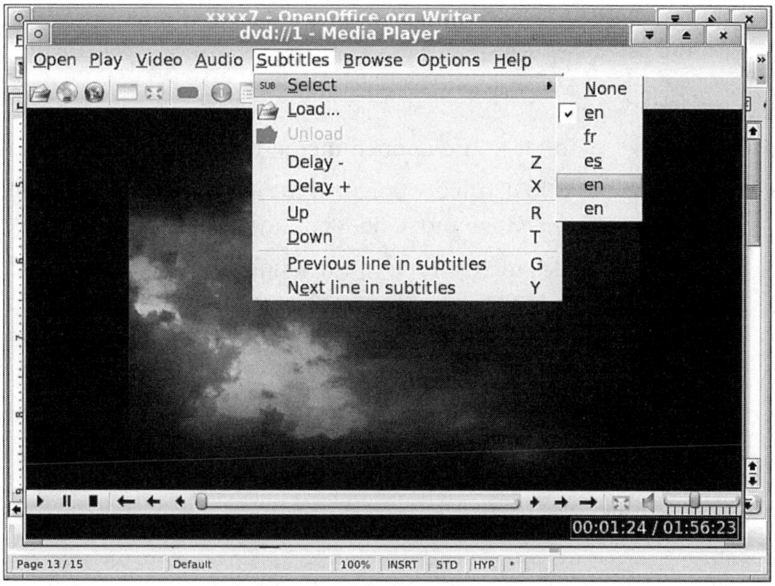

FIGURE 7.22

Selecting subtitles for a DVD in SMPlayer.

Having said all of that, SMPlayer does play DVDs on the Eee PC tolerably well.

Learning

The Eee PC ships with a set of educational packages that include a typing programs, a number of math and spelling programs, a periodic table, and even a wonderful virtual planetarium. The quality of these applications is quite good and should appeal to a wide age range.

The following sections provide a sampling of some of these programs: the typing tutor, the fraction tutor, and the planetarium. If you have school-age children that either own or use an Eee PC, you should take the time to explore the entire set of learning applications. Even if you don't, the planetarium is a lot of fun for adults as well.

Learning to Type with Tux Type

Tux Type is the built-in typing tutor, and is a very solid typing-practice program. You can launch it from Easy Mode by clicking the Learn tab, then the Language subtab, and finally the Typing icon. Strangely, Tux Type was omitted from Full Desktop. However, from a command prompt, you can run it with the following command:

```
> tuxtype &
```

If you want to add it to the Launch menu, the full path is /usr/games/tuxtype.

Tux Type is not a KDE application, but rather an X Window System application. Therefore, the video mode does change when you run it.

The practice modes in Tux Type run through fingering drills on the keyboard. The screen shows how to orient your fingers and what rows to place them on. It then highlights each finger to show what to type. It's quite clever and provides a good set of drills.

In addition to the drills, Tux Type also includes a few games in which words fall from the top of the screen. Students rack up points by typing the words before they reach the bottom. There are controls that adjust the difficulty level as well, so that the games can keep pace with a student's increasing level of skill.

Learning Fractions with Fraction Tutor

Fraction Tutor is actually an open source application called KBruch. You can launch it from Easy Mode by clicking the Learn tab, the Mathematics subtab, and then the Fraction Tutorial icon. From Full Desktop, choose Launch, Applications, Education, Mathematics, Fraction tutor.

In its basic task mode, shown in Figure 7.23, Fraction Tutor presents a set of tasks in fraction arithmetic. It keeps track of correct and incorrect answers as you work through the problems, and you can reset this by clicking Reset.

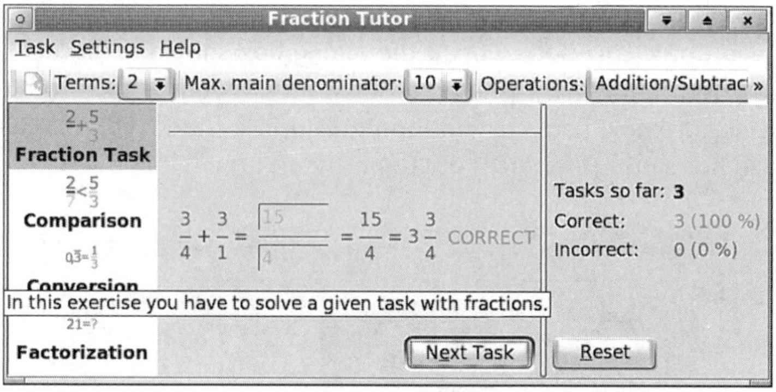

FIGURE 7.23

Fraction Tutor in its basic task mode.

In Comparison mode (click Comparison on the left), you are asked to compare two fractional values and choose which is greater. The choice is made by clicking the greater than or less than operator between the fractions to toggle it between the two.

In Conversion mode (click Conversion), you are presented with a decimal value that you must convert into a fraction. In Factorization mode, you are given a value for which you must list all the prime factors. Thus, 16 is shown as $2 \times 2 \times 2 \times 2$. As in the other modes, Fraction Tutor keeps track of right and wrong answers, and it can be reset.

You can set preferences through Settings, Configure KBruch. You can change the fonts used and the colors.

Learning the Sky Through Desktop Planetarium

Desktop Planetarium is the KStars application. The following is quoted from the KStars website (http://edu.kde.org/kstars/):

KStars is a Desktop Planetarium for KDE. It provides an accurate graphical simulation of the night sky, from any location on Earth, at any date and time. The display includes 130,000 stars, 13,000 deep-sky objects, all 8 planets, the Sun and Moon, and thousands of comets and asteroids.

That's pretty impressive. To launch it in Easy Mode, click the Learn tab, Science subtab, and the Planetarium icon. In Full Desktop, choose Launch, Applications, Education, Science, Desktop Planetarium. On a 701 screen, you'll need to use the Alt-drag method of moving the oversized windows around to reach some of the controls.

First off, you need to set your location. To do so, choose Settings, Set Geographic Location to open the dialog box shown in Figure 7.24. You can set your location by city, province, or country. If you happen to have a GPS device or know your current longitude and latitude, you can set that as well. It also has settings for local daylight saving time (DST) rules.

FIGURE 7.24

Setting the location in KStars.

You can focus the cursor on any star in the display and, if it has a name, KStars pops up the name like a tool tip (see Figure 7.25). You can also drag and move the sky around, although this messes up the time synchronization a bit. There are buttons along the button bar to toggle the display of various items, ranging from the location of the Milky Way to whether constellation names are shown.

Under the Pointing menu, you can change the direction in which your "looking" at the night sky to any of the compass points or zenith (straight up). You can also search for a particular object (from a drop-down list with search) and the planetarium display will rotate to center on it. You access the object search function through Pointing, Find Object.

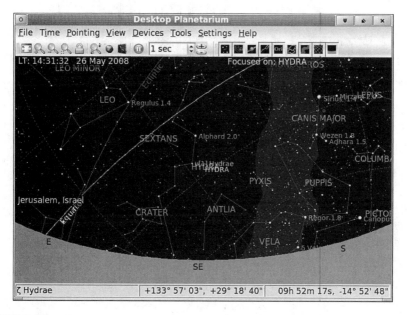

FIGURE 7.25

The sky, viewed through KStars, with the current focus on Hydra.

The Tools menu has a number of very cool features. What's Up Tonight lists points of interest to observe at your location that night, including stars, planets, comets, asteroids, nebulae, and galaxies. You can set the planetarium to focus on the object once you've selected it. The Solar System Viewer is also kind of interesting, as it shows the current positions of the various planets along the plane of the ecliptic (see Figure 7.26).

Perhaps the most interesting feature of the Desktop Planetarium is its ability to control actual equipment. If you have a telescope with a drive, and it's in the list of supported hardware, you can control the drive via KStars. Given the size and portability of the Eee PC, it should make an ideal control unit for a telescope.

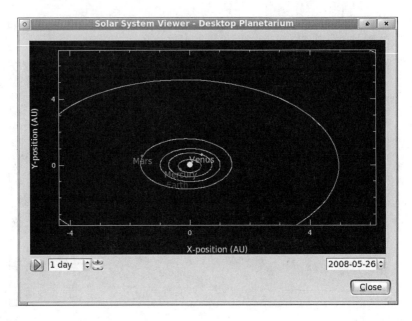

FIGURE 7.26
Current position of the planets.

Summary

In this chapter, you got an overview of some of the pre-installed applications in the Eee PC. This is probably one of the Eee PC's greatest strengths. It already has most of the applications people need to do any basic computing task. You should really take the time to explore the rest of the installed applications, as the computer has too many to cover in a single chapter.

You also got instructions for adding the ability to play DVDs in the multimedial player: SMplayer. This is another strength of the Eee PC and of Linux in general, as many of the additional drivers, libraries, and applications that you might need can be easily installed via the internet and the built-in package management tools.

Getting More Linux Applications

Almost all of the software you'll use in Xandros Linux is "open source" software whose source code is open to everyone and normally supported by volunteer efforts. Occasionally, as is the case with such applications as the Alfresco Content Management System, the code is open source but is mostly maintained and developed by a commercial enterprise. Open source software is always free; however, sometimes commercial support is available for a fee (Alfresco uses this model). By the way, I'm not recommending that you run Alfresco on an Eee PC; that's just an example. I must, however, admit that the idea of running a complete content management system on something that small is intriguing....

There are some closed source software applications that are free (or free with restrictions). Programs such as the XnView graphics viewer/converter and the XMLmind XML editor are examples of free, closed source applications. Closed source commercial applications are built and sold by commercial enterprises. These have their own installers or specific installation instructions.

Another big difference is external libraries. Most Windows software includes private libraries that are installed with the application. This makes for rather large installations and takes up quite a bit of disk space, because multiple programs may have their own copies of the same libraries. Linux applications that you download and install are just the executable files; however, these executables also depend on shared libraries that are installed as separate entities. Finding, downloading, and manually resolving the dependencies on shared libraries can be an absolute nightmare because you also have to keep track of the versions of the executables and the libraries on which they depend.

Adding to the complexity of keeping track of the library dependencies is the number of distributions ("distros") of Linux available, each of which may have many versions of executables and libraries. One final twist: at any given point, both stable and experimental versions of libraries and executables may be available.

Fortunately, in the Linux world, software for various distributions are gathered into collections called repositories. Even more fortunately for you, software specifically intended for the Eee PC is also gathered into repositories.

Repositories contain both applications (bundled into "packages," which also list dependencies on libraries, descriptions of the software, version numbers, etc.) and libraries. The installation of packages is handled by package managers.

Using a Package Manager

The genius of package managers is that they connect to repositories and keep track of packages and their dependencies for you. They download and install not only the executable files but also the libraries on which they depend, keeping track of what versions of each have been installed. As repositories are modified, the package managers can refresh their indexes of each repository's package contents. They can also delete applications and remove dependent libraries. When things go wrong, they can (to a certain extent) attempt to repair things as well. You can even search through the various repositories to which the package manager is pointed.

Both Easy Mode and the Full Desktop (KDE) have their own package managers, and they have very different interfaces. The following sections cover these in detail.

Using the Easy Mode Package Manager

In Easy Mode, the package manager is the Update Software application on the Settings tab. It's designed to manage only the packages that ship with the Eee PC, and does not function as a general-purpose package manager. Still, it's not without its virtues. It provides information about available upgrades, such as the upgrade for Skype. It also lets you know if there are upgrades to the Eee PC's BIOS.

Using the Easy Mode package manager can be a little frustrating in that it provides very little feedback about what it's doing. This is especially true the first time that you run it, as it must "refresh" its database of the repositories it knows about. This can take several minutes.

The interface for the Easy Mode Package Manager is very similar to the interface for Easy Mode itself. The various packages are categorized under Internet, Work, Learn, Play, and Settings tabs. Each tab shows a set of packages that can be updated. All you do to update a package is to click the related Install button. Occasionally, a Remove button will appear after installation. Clicking Remove deletes the installation files and therefore releases some storage space.

The bios updates are on the Settings tab. These are a little tricky as they will shut down the system and restart it to load a bios update. During an update, you'll see almost no feedback and the screen may go black for several minutes. Be patient and don't intervene. Interrupting a bios update can make your Eee PC unusable.

Using the Synaptic Package Manager and the apt-get Command

In Full Desktop Mode, you can access packages either via the Synaptic Package Manager or through the `apt-get` command- line utility. Both are package managers and both work from the same set of repositories. The chief difference is that Synaptic has a graphic interface and `apt-get` is strictly a command-line tool.

Before you can install packages with either of these package managers, you must first point them package managers at the package repositories via their Internet URL and then define some additional information about the repositories.

The package manager can then open the repository and download the metadata and create an index of the software it contains. The package manager won't actually download any of the software until you request the package, and then it'll download only if it can succeed in downloading all of the dependencies as well (or, at least that's the theory).

For the Eee PC, unless you're a Linux power user, you'll probably want to stick to the repositories that are recommended through the major Eee PC web sites. The next most reliable repositories are specifically for the current release of

Xandros. You can also use Debian repositories, but this is riskier. Although Xandros was derived from Debian, they aren't quite the same any more.

Before you actually install software, you should make sure that you can restore your Xandros image back to its pristine state using the DVD-ROM that came with the computer. Refer Chapter 12, "Linux Distributions" for a complete description of how to do that. Being prepared to reinstall means that if something goes tragically wrong when installing an application—and your Eee PC becomes a cute, 2-lb block of dead plastic—you can restore it to life.

Picking Repositories That Work with the Eee PC

The Eee PC package manager knows about two repositories by default, which isn't much:

- deb http://update.eeepc.asus.com/p701/ p701 main
- deb http://update.eeepc.asus.com/p701/en/ p701 main

Obviously, you'll want to add to that, but be careful. Not all repositories contain software that's compatible, and not all repsoitories are trustworthy. Installing software on your computer is a security risk.

The following list is a pretty good starting point that provides a wide range of useful applications, and is recommended on EeeUser.com (a large and active Eee PC user community, at http://www.eeeuser.com/):

- deb http://xnv4.xandros.com/xs2.0/upkg-srv2/ etch main contrib non-free
- deb http://dccamirror.xandros.com/dccri/ dccri-3.0 main
- deb http://www.geekconnection.org/ xandros4 main
- deb http://download.tuxfamily.org/eeepcrepos/ p701 main

The following sections explain just how to point to these repositories and set the pinning directives. *Pinning* is a way of assigning preferences for which repositories and versions are used. This is covered in detail in the section, "Using the apt Command-Line Package Manager." The pinning order I'll show is the recommendation of EeeUser.com, and provides a little extra insurance that things won't go utterly "in the weeds." I've used this set of repositories and pinning order for quite a while, without a problem. Naturally, nothing is a sure thing, but these repositories seem to work very well.

Note that in the following sections, the discussion may go back and forth a bit between the Synaptic Package Manager and the apt-get command. This is because they are really just two ways to do the same thing. The both access the same database (really just a file) of repositories. So, if you add a repository via Synaptic, apt-get will see it as well.

Using the Synaptic Package Manager

Having a set of repositories is just the beginning; you need to have a way of installing and managing software. The Synaptic Package Manager provides an easy-to-use, GUI-based tool that you can use to install, update, or remove applications as well as point to new repositories. There are two ways to run the Synaptic Package Manager:

- From the Full Desktop, choose Launch, Applications, System, Synaptic Package Manager, as shown in Figure 8.1.

- From the command line, enter

  ```
  > sudo Synaptic
  ```

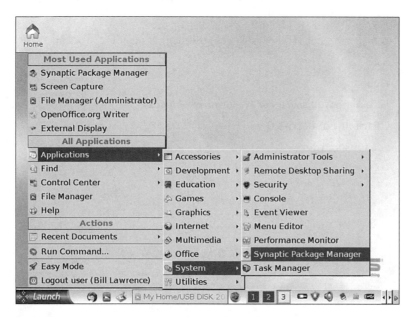

FIGURE 8.1

The Synaptic Package Manager.

Loading Repositories

The first order of business in using Synaptic is to point it at the various repositories you're going to use. To do that, choose Settings, Repositories and click the New button to open the Repositories dialog box, shown in Figure 8.2. A few definitions are required at this point so that you understand the fields at the bottom of the dialog box:

- **URI:** The universal resource identifier, which is the web address of the repository.

- **Distribution:** The Debian distribution name. As of the writing of this book, the most up-to-date stable distribution is 4.0, which is called Etch. You'll also encounter older distributions, such as Sarge (3.1) and Woody (3.0). The current unstable distribution is called Sid. Unless you don't mind re-imaging your Eee PC, it's probably a good idea to leave Sid alone.

- **Sections:** Distributions may contain sections marked `main`, `contrib`, and `non-free`. Both `main` and `contrib` are free to use for both commercial and noncommercial use, while `non-free` usually has some restrictions (such as not free for commercial use).

So, referring to the list of repositories, you would enter the following (see Figure 8.2):

`deb http://dccamirror.xandros.com/dccri/ dccri-3.0 main`

as:

Deb

URI: `http://dccamirror.xandros.com/dccri/`

Distribution: dccri-3.0

Sections(s): main

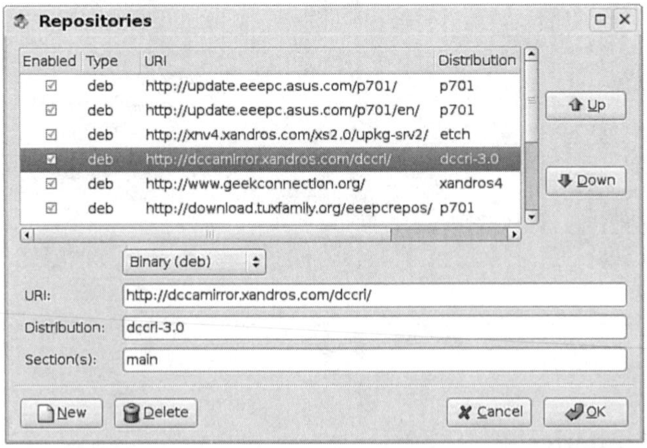

FIGURE 8.2

Entering a repository.

After you add the repositories, click the Reload button to build the database of available packages. This will take several minutes. Don't panic if you see some security errors; this is common. These are shown as GPG errors, and simply mean that there was no way of verifying these repositories via a public key.

However, if you get an "Unable to parse package file…" error, you probably have a typo in your entry for that repository. Double check that entry. You can to that through Settings, Repositories and then clicking the entry that had the error. You can now edit that entry.

Finding and Loading Packages

Before you can install a package, you must find it. Fortunately, package managers have functions to help yo locate the sort of packages you're looking for, whether it's a chess game or a GPS navigational program. Once you've found the package, or packages, you want all you need to do is "mark" them for installation and click Apply. Then the package manager carries out the actual installation.

Installing a package is actually a multistep process for the package manager. First, it makes sure that it can find and download all of the associated applications and libraries that support the package you want. These are called "dependencies" and are additional packages to the one that you requested. The package manager makes sure that it can resolve all the dependencies and get everything it needs before it goes on.

Next, the package manager downloads the package you requested and all of the supporting packages.

Finally, the package manager installs the software contained in the packages. In most cases, you will find the new software neatly installed in the KDE Launch menu. If you're doing this from Easy Mode, resign yourself to either the drudgery of building new icons and adding them to the Easy Mode interface (see Chapter 4, "Customizing Easy Mode") or to running your new applications directly from the command line.

Finding Packages to Install

The easiest way to find a package is by searching for a keyword (contained in that metadata). The Synaptic Package Manager includes a Search utility that you can use to search for keywords in the titles and descriptions of packages.

> **note** There's something not quite right about the Search function in the Eee PC implementation of Synaptic. Using it can cause subsequent installs to fail with the error message shown in Figure 8.3. This is easy to fix by choosing Edit, Fix Broken Packages. Stranger still, you will probably have to run this twice in a row before things are truly fixed. If the problem recurs—and it will if you use Search—you now know the drill. I go through this after every search; otherwise, Synaptic won't install the selected packages.

FIGURE 8.3

The infamous "Unable to parse..." error.

To search the repositories for packages, click the Search button on the toolbar. In the Find dialog box (see Figure 8.4), enter a search string, such as "HTML," and choose a value in the Look In drop-down list to select where to look. Choosing Name simply searches through the names of the packages, but Description and Name searches both. Searching the descriptions is usually a much richer source for "hits" because the name may not be very descriptive. For example, searching for "ship" in the name produces very few hits, but by searching in the description as well, a number of games with the word "ship" in the description are identified. The same goes for "HTML." Very few people name their web editor application "HTML," but most put that in the description.

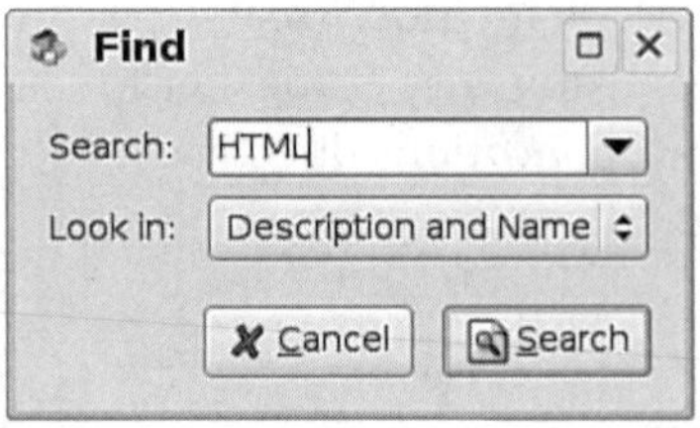

FIGURE 8.4

Searching for a package.

After you select where to look and what to look for, click the Search button to send Synaptic searching through the repository metadata in its database. When it finishes, it places your search term in the list at the left of the window. Click a search term to load all the packages that match your criteria in the list on the right. You can then scroll through the list until you find what you want.

If you know what you're looking for, a quick way to find it is to select All in the left pane and then click any package in the list to the right. Once a package is selected, you can simply begin typing the name of the package and the list will begin matching as you type. Usually, you only need to type a few characters before you get a match. Using this method does not cause the Synaptic error messages when you try to load the package, so in some ways it's a better way to work than using Search.

Installing Packages

Once you've found what you're looking for, right-click the entry and select Mark for Installation. You may get a warning dialog box that the software can't be authenticated. Heed these warnings, because software that can't be authenticated might contain malicious code. This is where you must consider how trustworthy the source is. If you think it is trustworthy, go ahead and click the Mark button. (Actually, you'll get this message a lot. You just learn to live with it.) Click the Apply button to start the installation.

If the package manager can't resolve all of the dependencies, you won't be able to mark a package for installation. You'll need to expand your list of repositories, which increases your risk, or find another package. If you can mark it for installation, which is the usual case, click the Apply button.

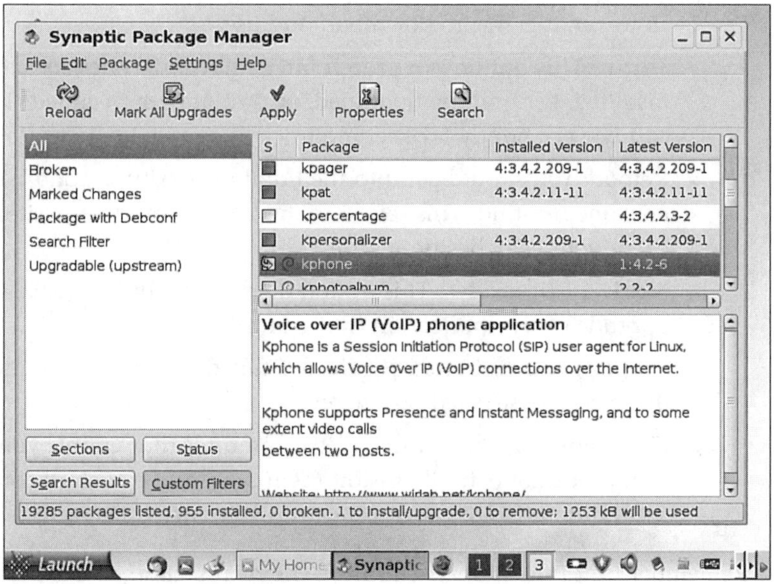

FIGURE 8.5

A package marked for installation.

Next, you'll see the Summary dialog box, which is an information screen about the package. It may contain another warning such as "the package cannot be authenticated," as well as information about the number of packages that will be upgraded as part of the process. If you click the Show Details button in the Summary dialog box, you can see exactly which version will be installed.

On a 701, you'll need to use the Alt-drag technique to move the window up so that you can click the Apply button on the Summary dialog box.

You should see the progress of the package download and installation (and if you're really bored, you can select to watch as individual files are pulled down or the installation script runs). After your package is installed, the installed application may appear in your Launch menu. Odds are that it will, but be prepared to play hide-and-seek with the executable file. So that you know how to handle this if it arises, I'll cover adding an application to the menu manually in the following section.

Before you learn about the apt-get interface for managing packages, there are a few other things you should know about the Synaptic Package Manager:

- **Sections:** Clicking this button shows an index of sorts, with broad package categories. For example, if you select Cross Platform (non-free), you'll find the Google graphics application Picasa. It's under non-free because it's not open source but rather a Google product. However, it is free to download and use.

- **Status:** This button has search filters that show packages that are installed, that can be upgraded, or that are not installed. The filters can be very handy for keeping track of available upgrades.

- **Reload:** You should get into the habit of clicking Reload before you go package hunting. This refreshes the indexes of the repositories and keeps your searches up-to-date.

- **Mark All Upgrades:** This button does just what it says, and prepares to upgrade every application that can be upgraded.

- **Properties:** This button provides detailed version information about the currently selected package.

- **File menu:** This menu includes commands that enable you to mark things but not actually install them now, and a History command that shows you a history of package manager activities by date.

Remember that I mentioned pinning? The next section covers the apt-get package manager, but it also covers pinning. This is just as appropriate for using Synaptic and, before you go wild downloading packages, take a look at the pinning instructions.

Using the apt-get Command-Line Package Manager

`apt-get` is a command-line package manager that is quite easy and efficient to use. You can launch it from any xterm command line, so by pressing Ctrl+Alt+T, you can fire up an xterm window in Easy Mode and pull down packages with `apt`. The easiest way in Full Desktop to launch a terminal-emulator window is to enter the following at the Launch, Run Command prompt:

```
Konsole
```

You can find the vast, canonical document that covers all the intricacies of `apt-get` and the other `apt` commands at http://www.debian.org/doc/manuals/apt-howto/. This is the "How To" document maintained by Debian.org.

What follows is a "quick reference" that covers the important details that you need to know to effectively use the `apt` commands. Before you dive into the command-line arguments, recall that you need to add the appropriate package repositories and set the order for referencing these (pinning). To do this, you need to edit some configuration files. If you're not adept at any of the typical UNIX-type editors, you can always use Kwrite. Kwrite has a very simple interface, reminiscent of Windows Notepad. Having grown up in the world of UNIX, I prefer XCEmacs. The point is that pretty much any text editor will do. Don't use OpenOffice.org Writer, however, because saving the file as something other than text is quite easy in Writer, making the configuration files unavailable to `apt-get` until this is fixed.

Working with the Package Manager Configuration Files

The configuration files in question are

- /etc/apt/sources.list, which contains the list of repositories.
- /etc/apt/preferences, which contains the "pinning" list, or order of preference for searching repositories.

So, the first order of business is to add the repositories. You need to create (or edit) the file via `sudo` to have write permissions, so issue the following command from an xterm window or from Konsole:

```
> sudo kwrite /etc/apt/sources.list
```

Enter the list of URIs, exactly as shown in the list of packages in the "Picking Repositories That Work with the EEE PC" section earlier in this chapter. When you're finished, choose File, Save and then select Exit. Next, you need to set the pinning order. First, open the preferences file with `kwrite`:

```
> sudo kwrite /etc/apt/preferences
```

Enter the following:

```
Package: *
Pin: origin update.eeepc.asus.com
Pin-Priority: 950

Package: *
Pin: origin
Pin-Priority: 925

Package: *
Pin: origin xnv4.xandros.com
Pin-Priority: 900

Package: *
Pin: origin dccamirror.xandros.com
Pin-Priority: 850

Package: *
Pin: origin www.geekconnection.org
Pin-Priority: 750

Package: *
Pin: release a=stable
Pin-Priority: 700

Package: *
Pin: release a=testing
Pin-Priority: 650

Package: *
Pin: release a=unstable
Pin-Priority: 600
```

The actual values for these directives are in fact important and somewhat arcane. Note that all the Pin-Priority values are less than 990 but more than 600. Numbers in this range mean that the designated package version (the Package: line) will be installed, unless there is a version available from the target release or if the current installation is more recent. The wildcard * means that any package version will be installed if it's available. The higher the Pin-Priority value, the more weight each of the repositories, designated by the Pin:

origin line, have. So, update.eeepc.asus.com has top priority for new releases, followed by any packages in local repositories, then xnv4.xandros.com, and so on. The second entry, which has the Package: set to origin, simply indicates to check local repositories (it means literally the origin is unknown).

The Pin: release lines give priority to stable, then testing, and then unstable releases.

A few more tidbits about pinning syntax:

- Pin-Priority numbers greater than 1000 install the designated package version even if it requires downgrading the current package. You can use this to set a particular version for a particular package that won't ever change.

- Numbers between 990 and 1000 install the designated package, even if it comes from a release that's not the target release, unless the current installation is more recent.

- Numbers between 500 and 990 install the designated package unless there is a version available that belongs to the target release or the current installation is more recent.

- Numbers between 100 and 499 install the designated version unless there is a version available from another repository or the current installation is more recent.

- Numbers between 0 and 99 install the designated version only if there isn't any version installed.

- Numbers less than 0 prevent the designated version from being installed.

Once again, when finished, choose File, Save and then select Exit. Now, you've completed the setup and pinning and are ready to use apt. You need to have apt scan the repositories and build the index, by using the following command:

```
> sudo apt-get update
```

apt-get will spew a set of messages about its progress as it traverses the various repositories. It'll also alert you to potential security problems, such as no public keys available to authenticate a repository. This is a polite way of saying that it can't verify how genuine a given repository is, as it has no public key.

Now you're ready to install something. Suppose that you want to install the solitaire game ace-of-penguins. You would issue the following command:

```
> sudo apt-get install ace-of-penguins
```

If `apt-get` can't authenticate the source of the package, which is likely, it will stop and ask the following:

```
WARNING: The following packages cannot be authenticated!
    ace-of-penguins
Install these packages without verification [y/N]?
```

Enter Y on the command line to continue with the installation. `apt-get` will continue on its way and let you know that the installation succeeded.

The following are a few more cool things you can do with `apt-get`:

- Each time you install a package, `apt-get` stuffs the files it needs in a local repository within the /var/cache/apt/archives directory. Given that disk space is at a premium, you probably don't want files to accumulate in that archive. So, you can clean them out with the following command:

  ```
  > sudo apt-get clean
  ```

- It is possible that some package files may, over time, no longer be available from the designated repositories. If that's a concern, you can clean out only those files that can still be downloaded by entering the following:

  ```
  > sudo apt-get autoclean
  ```

- You can upgrade your applications by using the following command:

  ```
  > sudo apt-get upgrade
  ```

- If you want to remove an application, say for instance, ace-of-penguins, use the following command:

  ```
  > sudo apt-get remove ace-of-penguins
  ```

Adding Packages to the KDE Menu

Usually, when you install a new package, it shows up right where you might expect in the KDE menu.). For example, if you install the VLC media player, it immediately shows up under Launch, Applications, Multimedia. Sometimes, a package shows up somewhere else in the menu structure. However, occasionally, it doesn't show up anywhere. So, what to do? If you want to use it at all, you must at least ensure that you know what it's called and that it's in one of the directories in which Xandros currently looks for executable files. If you want it to work from the menu, you have to manually construct a menu entry.

Unfortunately, finding the installed application can be quite challenging. There are a couple of ways of finding the package.

■ You can use Synaptic to tell you where the application was installed.

■ You can hunt for it with the package using the which command.

Finding a Newly Installed Application with Synaptic

To find an installed file:

1. In the Synaptic Package Manager, click the Status button.

2. Click Installed in the Filters list.

3. Locate the package in the Package list.

4. Right-click the package and choose Properties.

5. Click the Installed Files tab, shown in Figure 8.6.

Look for entries such as /usr/bin or /usr/bin/*package_name* (where *package_name* is the name of the package).

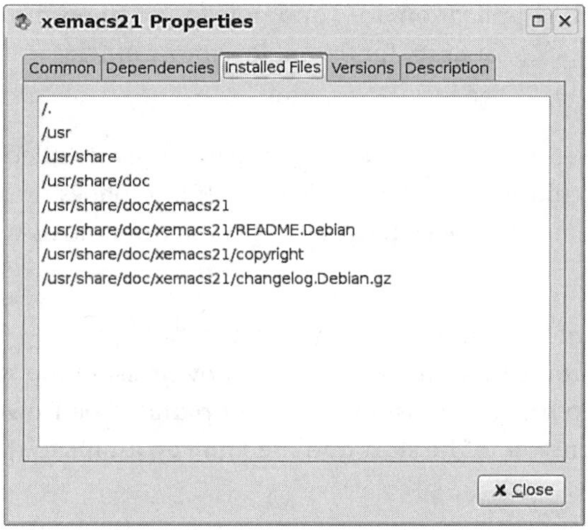

FIGURE 8.6
The Installed Files list for a package.

Finding a Newly Installed Application with the which Command

You can also try to find a package through the command line. The Linux which command will identify the location if it finds the file you are querying. For example, if I've installed the gpsd package and I want to find it, I can use which to tell me where it is:

```
> which gpsd
/use/bin/gpsd
```

Of course, that only works if gpsd is installed somewhere that's defined by the PATH environment variable. If you want to know what your PATH setting currently is, use the following command to pipe it through grep and search for the string PATH. (Chapter 11 discusses Linux commands and environment variables in more detail.)

```
> env | grep PATH
PATH=/usr/local/bin:/usr/bin:/bin:/usr/games
```

This path is the default Xandros PATH setting on the Eee PC.

Finding Instructions for Applications That You've Installed

Before you can add an application to the Launch menu, you must understand what, if any, command line switches are required. To do that, you'll need instructions for the application. Normally, a package will install some sort of instructions along with the application. You can almost always expect at least a man page. *Man pages* are command reference pages that provide a synopsis of what the application does and how to use the command switches. To get the man page for gpsd, for example, simply enter:

```
man gpsd
```

Info pages, if they are available, provide more detailed information and are akin to a manual for the application. If info pages aren't available, the man page will usually be displayed. To get the info pages, type the following:

```
info gpsd
```

In both info and man pages, you can exit by pressing Q (the case doesn't matter). You can jump down a screen by pressing the spacebar. Also, you can browse up and down using the Page Up and Page Down keys. The Home key will return you to the start and the End key jumps to the end of the man or info page.

You can also search the various Eee PC forums and the homepage for the application for more information. Other Eee PC users may have encountered the same problem in dealing with a wayward application and may be able to provide some clues.

If you find your package and instructions, running it from the command line should be simple. If the package isn't in a directory defined by the PATH environment variable, remember to include the absolute path to the executable file, as well as any handy command-line switches you might need (from the information you found via man or info pages).

Adding a Package to the Launch Menu

Once you've found the package and understand what command-line switches (if any) you might want to include, you can add it to the Full Desktop Launch menu. It's a good idea to pull up a command line and try running if from there first.

To add something to the Launch menu:

1. Open the Menu Editor (Launch, Applications, System, Menu Editor).

2. Expand the Applications tree (click +) and decide exactly which category best fits the application you've installed. This example uses ace_taipei (which is the slightly nonobvious name for one of the Ace of Penguins games) and adds it under the Games category.

3. Expand the Games folder.

4. Right-click the Games category and choose New Item, as shown in Figure 8.7.

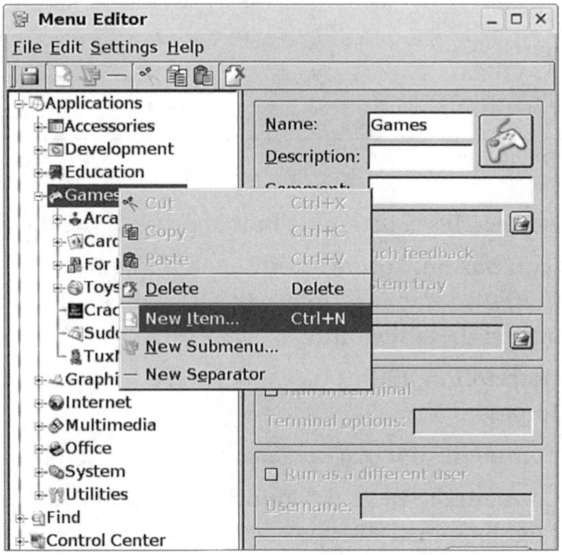

FIGURE 8.7

Adding a new menu item.

5. In the right pane of the Menu Editor window (see Figure 8.8), for the Name, use something not too long yet more descriptive than just the name. For ace_taipei, I chose "Mah-Jong" as the name. The other options available in the right pane are described after this list.

6. When you've finished filling out the pane, click File, Save to have your changes take effect.

The following list explains the various Menu Editor fields and check boxes shown in the right pane of Figure 8.8.

FIGURE 8.8

Setting up a new menu item.

- **Name:** This is the name that appears in the menu itself.
- **Icon button:** Located next to the Name field. Click to select an icon from the set to associate with this command in the menu and, option-ally, in the system tray.
- **Description:** In this case, I described it as really being Ace of Penguins Taipei.
- **Comment:** You can add a comment if you like.
- **Command:** This is the launch command (i.e., the command you'd use from to launch the applications from the command line) for the appli-cation, including any command-line arguments.
- **Enable Launch Feedback:** When selected, KDE will use the spinning hourglass to indicate that application is loading.
- **Place in System TrayAce:** Check this box if you want to launch this application from the system tray. The icon associated with the applica-tion will appear in the system tray when the application is active.
- **Work Path:** This is the directory from which the application will be launched. In some cases, this becomes the default directory for working files, providing a handy way of setting a default directory.

- **Run in Terminal:** This creates a terminal window (console) for programs that require one. Check the application instructions for any relevant terminal options to enter.

- **Run as a Different User:** Add a different username here if you wish to run the program as someone else on the system.

- **Current Shortcut Key:** Click the button and then press the key combination you wish to associate with the application.

There are a few more things you can do with the Menu Editor, such as build new categories for the Launch menu and add separators between lists of applications. To create a new category, click the entry in the tree (such as Applications) under which you wish to add a new category. Next, choose File, Submenu. Enter the name for the new category, and then click OK. The new category (submenu) will appear at the top of the set of others, which is really not a problem because you can drag it to any position in the list. The separator (File, New) is just a visual separation line that appears in the menu entry.

Of course, if you can add something to the Launch menu, you can also delete it. This is trivial: select it, right-click, and choose Delete from the shortcut menu.

Installing Software the Old-Fashioned Way

Suppose that you want to load a Linux program that has no repositories. What then? You can install software manually via a DEB file. For example, the Opera browser, which some folks prefer to Firefox, is provided this way. To download Opera:

1. Create a directory, perhaps on your MMC-SD drive.

2. Launch Firefox from the Firefox icon on the panel.

3. Navigate to www.opera.com via Firefox. The website will detect that you're running Linux and offer a green Free Download button that will take you to the Download page.

4. Select Debian from the list (see Figure 8.9), not Xandros (the Xandros version is missing some files).

5. Pick the Debian 4.0 (Etch) version.

6. Download the file to the directory you previously created.

   As described next, you can install the software from either the Administrative File Manager or the command line. You must use the Administrative version of the File Manager, because it has sufficient privileges to install software.

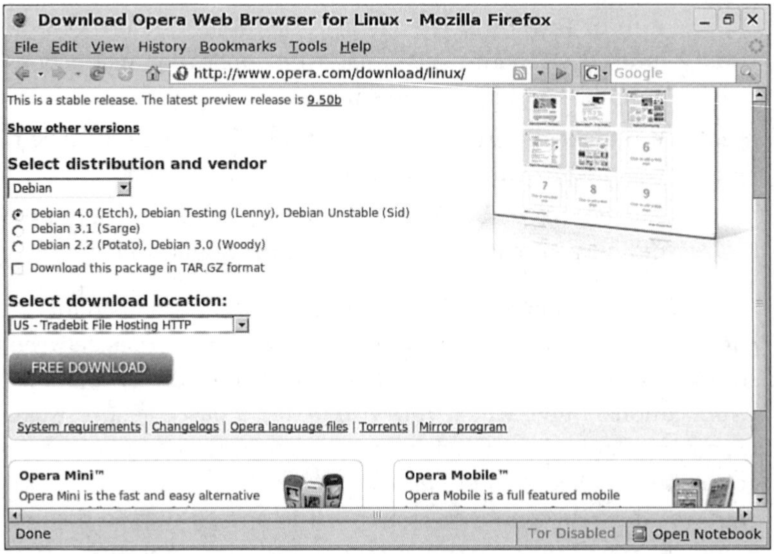

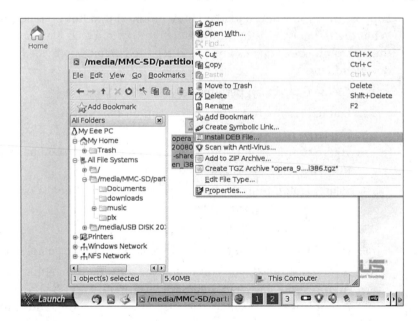

FIGURE 8.9

Selecting the Debian Opera version.

7. Navigate the Administrative File Manager to the scratch directory and locate the DEB file. Right-click the file and choose Install DEB File (see Figure 8.10). That's all there is to it.

FIGURE 8.10

Installing the DEB file.

Installing via the command line is almost as easy. Launch a command-line window and enter the following command:

```
> sudo dpkg -i /path/to/your_new_package.deb
```

The `dpkg` command is a lower-level package manager than Synaptic or `apt-get`, and is perfect for installing DEB files. The `-i` switch simply tells it to install the package. You must provide the path to the package and the name of the package file as an argument to the command. You must, of course, use `sudo` to have sufficient privileges to install the file. Press Enter, and `dpkg` will do the rest.

To test the installation, enter the following at the command line:

```
> which new_executable
```

`new_executable` is the name of the file to run the application. For example, if you used the opera file, then the command would return the following:

```
> which opera
  /usr/bin/opera
```

The real test is in running it. From the command line, enter the name of the executable. If it runs, then all is well. By invoking the executable by its name alone, if something goes wrong, you can quickly kill it by pressing Ctrl+C in the terminal window. You can now either install an entry in the menu for the application, as you did earlier in the chapter, or run it followed by a space and an & to make it independent of the terminal window. For example:

```
> opera &
```

Managing Installed Packages

Now that you've installed the package, how do you manage it? Well, because you properly installed it, Synaptic will locate it if you click the Reload button to reload the repositories. Try it, and you'll find your new package marked with the familiar green box showing that it's installed.

The same is true of the command-line utilities. For example, update the package cache by using the following command:

```
> sudo apt-get update
```

Next, check on the status of your package. To check on the opera package, you would issue this command:

```
> apt-cache showpkg opera
```

The `apt-cache showpkg` command lists information about the opera package *if* it's in the cache.

Because it is in the cache, the command returns all sorts of exciting information about the package, such as its version and so forth. Note that `apt-cache` didn't require `sudo`, because you weren't really changing anything with the command, just getting a report.

Summary

This was an important chapter, as it covered how to get additional applications for your Eee PC. You learned not only about packages and package repositories, but also about the various package mangers provided by Xandros. You also learned about the fairly esoteric, but essential concept of pinning.

Along the way, you also learned about Linux application and command documentation: man pages and info files. So, now you can look up what you need to know about any command or applications.

Must-Have Utilities

This chapter introduces a set of applications that I couldn't do without:

- **GIMP:** A high-end graphics processor, similar to Adobe Photoshop.
- **Inkscape:** A vector-based illustration program, similar to Adobe Illustrator. Inkscape is built to create SVG graphics files.
- **VLC media player:** A very versatile, simple-to-use media player.
- **Tor and Privoxy:** A combination of applications that, when used together, can help make web surfing anonymous.
- **KompoZer:** A powerful web page and CSS editor.
- **BitTornado:** A BitTorrent client. BitTorrent provides a more efficient way to download very large files (such as the installation ISO files for other versions of Linux).
- **K3b:** A versatile CD and DVD writer.

Admittedly, as a writer, I'm biased toward the communications side of things. However, I tried to provide enough of a mix of useful applications that you'll find a few things you like.

The end of the chapter introduces a few applications that I'd really like to use that don't work under Xandros. These applications do work under other Linux versions on the Eee PC (and, in one case, under Windows), and I'll talk about that as well.

By the way, you need to be in Full Desktop to load these applications, because you'll be using the package mangers to get them. Also, these applications load by default into the Full Desktop Launch menus under Applications.

GIMP

GIMP (GNU Image and Manipulation Processor) is an open source application that is similar to Adobe Photoshop, with many of the same capabilities. It enables you to create bitmapped art or edit and retouch photography. The photography in this book was cropped and edited using GIMP. GIMP can handle such esoteric tasks as correcting "keystoning" in photograph color correction. You can crop photos, clone images, apply all sorts of filters...in short, do just about everything you'd want to do in a digital darkroom.

What makes GIMP especially handy on the Eee PC is the Eee PC's portability. If you're a serious photographer, you can actually toss the Eee PC in your camera bag. While the screen space is limited on the Eee PC, it does provide all of the power you need to edit and fix photos on-site and have them ready for upload when you can get to an Internet connection.

Think of GIMP as a bigger toolbox than the built-in Photo Manager application (Gwenview). Photo Manager is great for the simple, day-to-day photo processing and organizing tasks. However, if you really want to edit or retouch a photo, you'll need GIMP. Also, if you're a Photoshop fan, you'll love GIMP. Figure 9.1 shows a photo being cropped in GIMP.

GIMP, the brainchild of Spencer Kimball and Peter Mattis, is extremely powerful in its own right, but also has many plug-ins. For example, you can install plug-ins for extra brushes, or to manipulate SVG (Scalable Vector Graphic) images, or even to create animations. Even the Help tool is a plug-in (which makes sense, to save space, because you need to load only the Help version specific to your language).

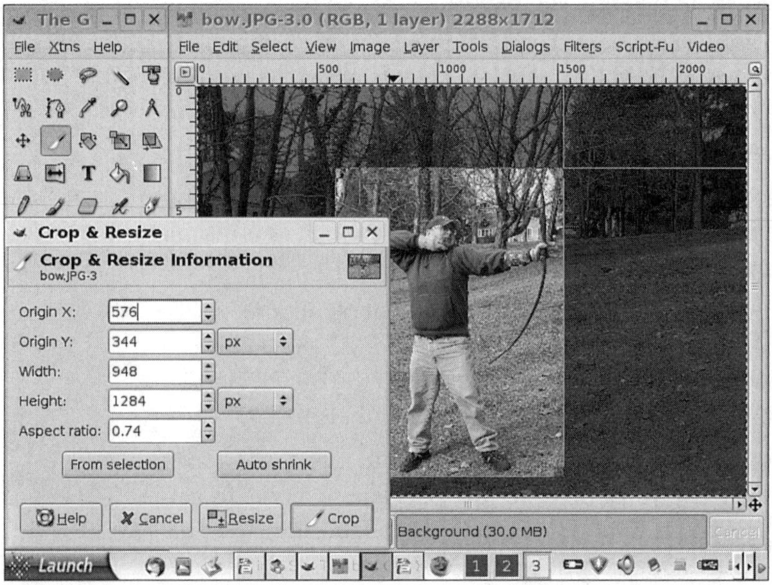

FIGURE 9.1

Cropping a photo in GIMP.

The package repositories listed in Chapter 8, "Getting More Linux Applications," have all the information that you need to load GIMP and many of its plug-ins. So, loading GIMP is a bit like filling out a shopping list. Simply look for GIMP in the Synaptic Package Manager, and check out the various other packages that begin with gimp (see Figure 9.2). GIMP automatically installs into the Launch menu under Graphics.

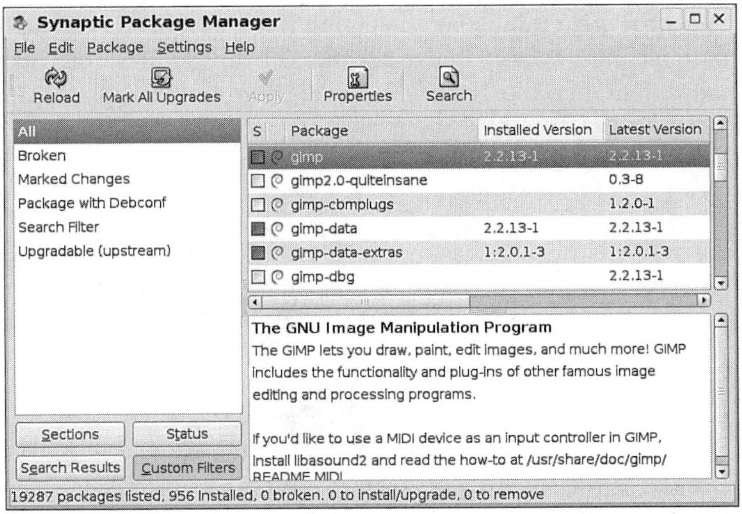

FIGURE 9.2
Selecting GIMP in the Synaptic Package Manager.

GIMP runs flawlessly on the Eee PC, though you'll need to use the Alt-drag mouse technique to drag the oversized setup windows up a bit when the program is first run. The controls extend below the screen. Once GIMP is running, you'll probably want to drag the two GIMP control windows wider and make them shorter to fit the smaller screen size. Keep in mind that space is limited on the Eee PC and that photos can be quite large. Naturally, having more memory will help if you have a lot of larger photographs. To learn more about GIMP, peruse the tutorials, and so forth at http://www.gimp.org.

Inkscape

Inkscape is an illustration package, and you are probably asking, "Why do I need another illustration package when I have OpenOffice.org Draw?" Well, Inkscape can do things that OpenOffice.org Draw can't. Inkscape was designed to work from the ground up with an XML graphics format called Scalable Vector Graphics (SVG). SVG can display in web browsers and even Microsoft Internet Explorer if you have the SVG plug-in installed.

Like Adobe Illustrator, Inkscape has Bezier-curve drawing tools, freehand tools, tools for drawing geometric shapes, and even an eyedropper tool for transferring color from one thing to another. It also has some nonstandard tools, such as a really interesting spiral/arc tool and a calligraphic freehand tool. If you know how to use Illustrator or Draw, it won't take you long to learn Inkscape. However, if you do get stumped, http://www.inkscape.org has FAQs and documentation.

The other great thing about SVG is that it's an XML-based graphics file format, meaning that you have another way to edit files. You can call up your drawing in a built-in XML editor and edit it. For example, Figure 9.3 shows a rectangle from the drawing in the XML editor.

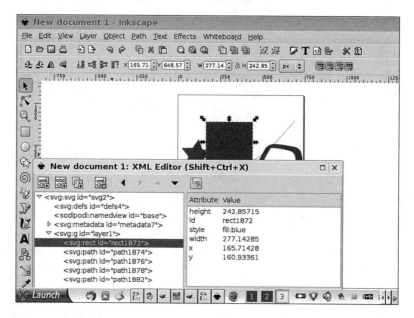

FIGURE 9.3
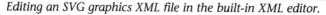
Editing an SVG graphics XML file in the built-in XML editor.

You can also tap the resources of the SVG clip art files at http://www.openclipart.org if you don't want to draw something yourself. These aren't terribly extensive, but they're nicely executed and (best of all) completely free. They also serve as interesting examples you can study to learn techniques.

You can install Inkscape via the Synaptic Package Manager using the repositories listed in Chapter 8. It also runs flawlessly on the Eee PC hardware, although you might want to consider an external monitor if you'll be using Inkscape a lot. Inkscape also automatically installs into the Launch menu, under Graphics.

VLC Media Player

For some file formats, VLC media player works better than the built-in SMPlayer application (which is actually the graphical interface for MPlayer). For example, VLC can play some video formats that SMPlayer can't handle. It's nice to have both media players, especially because VLC is very light-weight. As I pen these words, I'm listening to streaming audio on the Eee PC via Radio Rivendell. Yes, I could also use Music Manager, but VLC is so compact and easy to use that I just prefer it.

Firefox, by the way, was set by default to use VLC as the default player for some audio formats, but this was modified on the Eee PC. You can fix that by going to Firefox Preferences (under Edit), clicking the Content tab, clicking the Manage button under Filetypes, and resetting this back to the VLC default in the Change Action dialog box (see Figure 9.4).

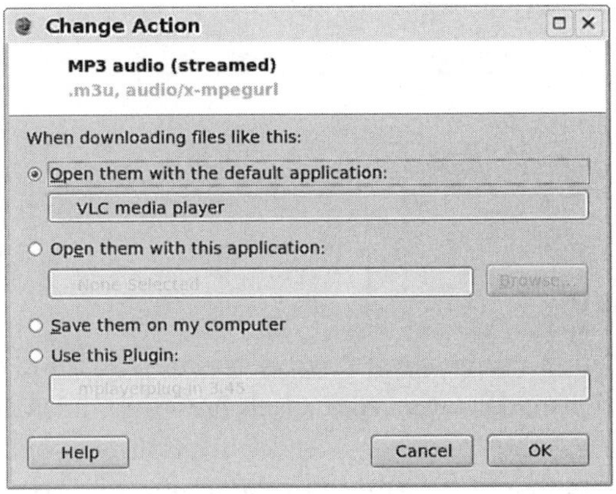

FIGURE 9.4

Resetting the audio defaults in Firefox.

One great thing about VLC is that it has a very easy-to-use audio equalizer you can access through Audio, Presets. The equalizer has lots of nice presets, ranging from Classical to Techno (see Figure 9.5). It really seems to excel when you are listening to or watching streaming media. Its visualizations are pretty ho-hum, but you can't have everything.

VLC also loads easily via the Synaptic Package Manager from the repositories listed in Chapter 8. It automatically installs itself in the Multimedia section of the Launch menu. You can get more information about VLC at http://www.videolan.org/vlc/.

FIGURE 9.5

VLC media player's audio equalizer.

Tor and Privoxy

Tor (The Onion Router) and Privoxy combine to build an environment that purports to provide autonomous web browsing. Basically, Tor is a large set of Internet relays that bounce your web communications around until they're nearly impossible to trace back to the originating computer. As such, Tor slows things down a bit (okay, maybe more than just a bit, although it's tolerable). Its website is http://www.torproject.org.

The best explanation of Privoxy comes from its website (http://www.privoxy.org): "Privoxy is a non-caching web proxy with advanced filtering capabilities for enhancing privacy, modifying web page data, managing HTTP cookies, controlling access, and removing ads, banners, pop-ups and other obnoxious Internet junk." In a nutshell, Privoxy enhances security and enforces privacy.

Using Tor and Privoxy together can be a simple choice to not have one's Internet browsing tracked or it can be deadly serious business if you live in a country that frowns on free speech or freedom of information. I cannot vouch for how good the anonymity or privacy is that's provided by these packages, but I do know many folks use them.

You can install these packages via the Synaptic Package Manager from the repositories listed in Chapter 8, and installation is straightforward. However, you must configure Privoxy to have it work properly. The configuration file in question is config, and it lies in the /etc/privoxy/ directory. Open the config file by either browsing to it via the Administrative File Manager or using the command line (don't forget `sudo`). You can use the default text editor from the Administrative File Manager. Find this line:

```
listen-address   127.0.0.1:8118
```

and add the following line after it:

```
forward-socks4a / localhost:9050 .
```

Save the file and you're done. You'll need to start Tor and Privoxy from an xterm window or Konsole command line. The syntax is

```
> sudo /etc/init.d/tor start
> sudo /etc/init.d/privoxy start
```

Instead of the `start` argument, you can use `stop` (to stop the process) or `restart` (to stop and start the process) in the commands. You can create a simple shell script to do this if you like. (Chapter 11, "Introduction to the Linux Command Line," explains scripts and autostarting them.)

Now that you know how to install and run Tor and Privoxy, you need a way for a browser to use them. The simplest add-on to Firefox is called Torbutton, found at https://addons.mozilla.org/en-US/firefox/addon/2275. To install it, simply click the green Add to Firefox button on that web page. Once it is installed, you'll see a dandy little button at the bottom of the Firefox window that says Tor Disabled. If Tor and Privoxy are currently running, simply click the button (it will change to Tor Enabled).

The next trick is to determine that it's really running. Fortunately, the Tor folks provide a web page to test this: http://check.torproject.org. If it's working, you'll see something like the web page shown in Figure 9.6.

Tor and Privoxy are kind of fun to play with. For example, when enabled, if you navigate via Firefox to Google, you're never sure in what language the Google page will greet you, because that depends on the last relay in the set. Also, sometimes Google will detect that it's a known Tor relay and will balk by throwing up a Captcha screen. This is Google's attempt to foil automated tomfoolery via programs that use Tor. You'll also find that Wikipedia may block you, because some nefarious types have vandalized the entries under cover of the Tor relays.

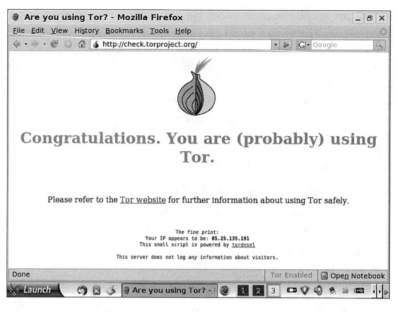

FIGURE 9.6

Apparently, Tor is working.

KompoZer

KompoZer is a complete, integrated website, HTML, and JavaScript development application. It's an outgrowth—well, actually a bug-fix version—of the popular Nvu editor. KompoZer is a marvelous environment for web-page development, with FTP upload capability, a full JavaScript console, and a cascading style sheets (CSS) editor.

If you're not the greatest web wizard of all time, KompoZer is for you. It has lots of wizards and helpful dialog boxes, and can insert HTML tags via menus. It can also validate your HTML and clean up your HTML to make the code more readable. Figure 9.7 shows an HTML file loaded into KompoZer, showing the HTML source. You can get more information about the program from http://kompozer.sourceforge.net. (SourceForge.net is one of the largest repositories of open source code on the Internet.)

You can easily load KompoZer via the Synaptic Package Manager using the repositories listed in Chapter 8. It automatically installs a menu entry under Launch, Applications, Development.

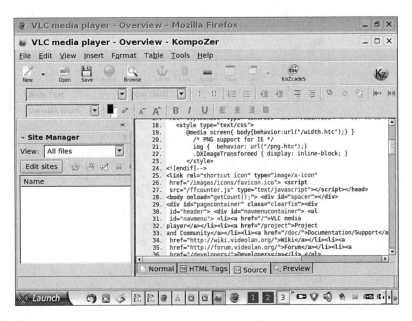

FIGURE 9.7

KompoZer in action.

BitTornado

Getting Linux distros and so forth for the Eee PC is best done via BitTorrent, a peer-to-peer file-sharing technology that is popular for downloading really big files, such as the ISO CD image files for Linux distros. You'll want to use BitTorrent if you'll be downloading such big files, which means you need a BitTorrent client. BitTornado (http://www.bittornado.com) is just such a client. It provides an easy-to-use GUI to download "torrent files," the peer-to-peer method used by BitTorrent. Torrent files may be found on BitTorrent catalog sites, which are searchable, such as http://www.torrentz.com. There are other easily installable clients, such as Vuze (formerly known as Azureus), but BitTornado is very easy to use.

BitTornado is another easy install via the Synaptic Package Manager using the repositories listed in Chapter 8, and the installation provides a Launch menu entry under Internet. Actually, the toughest part of using BitTornado, or any other BitTorrent client, is getting your ports open on your router's firewall. If you don't, download speeds are excruciatingly slow. The dead giveaway that Tor is having firewall challenges is a big yellow circle on the upper right of the interface. If you see that, it's time to go to your router documentation and find out how to get the ports open. Figure 9.8 shows the various status lights that BitTornado can provide.

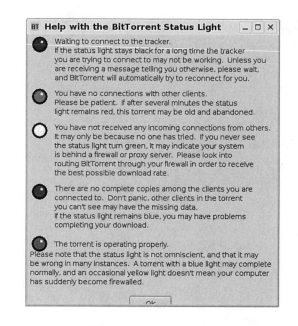

FIGURE 9.8

The BitTornado status lights, which let you know if you've got a firewall issue.

You can get some real assistance with configuring your router's firewall from a company called Port Forward. It maintains a series of instructions for getting BitTorrent and your router to cooperate, at http://portforward.com/english/ applications/port_forwarding/Torrent/Torrentindex.htm. Also, the following forum is a good resource: http://forums.afterdawn.com.

K3b

If you plan on hooking a DVD writer to your Eee PC, you'll really appreciate K3b (http://www.k3b.org/). Xandros mounts and reads data CDs and DVDs just fine, but won't format or write them. However, the Eee PC will format and write data CDs and DVDs with K3b.

This absolute gem of a program is available via the Synaptic Package Manager (see Figure 9.9) using the repositories listed in Chapter 8. Figure 9.9 shows the trick in loading it: You must mark K3B-1.0 for installation, not K3B. It is installed under Launch, Applications, Multimedia.

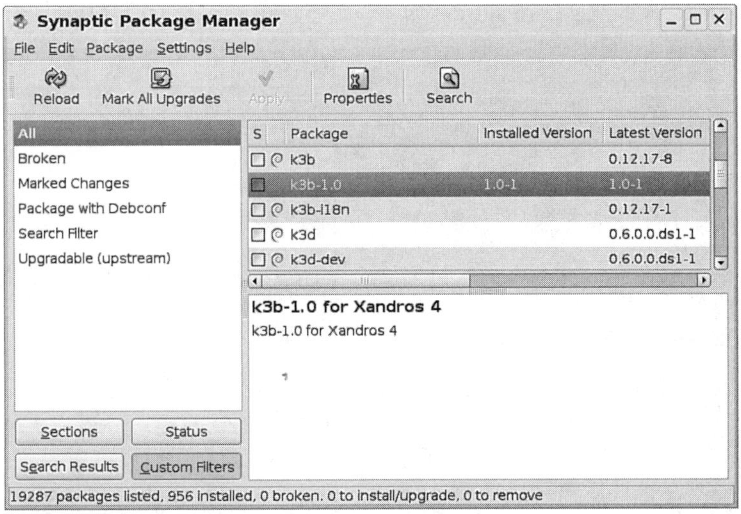

FIGURE 9.9

Installing K3b from Synaptic.

When you launch K3B, you'll see a few nuisance dialog boxes and messages. One will ask if you wish to integrate K3B functionality with the Konqueror file manager/browser. If you use Konqueror instead of the Xandros File Manager, this is a nice convenience feature. Another may complain that the cdrecord function is running without root privileges. This is OK, just close the dialog box.

K3b provides a file-manager–like interface that's a snap to use. It has large buttons on the main screen for creating new audio and data CD projects, as well as data DVDs. It also has a one-button solution for copying CDs.

K3b can also rip audio CDs, and it does a marvelous job at that. In addition, it can rip a video DVD, although space becomes a trifle challenging in the Eee PC environment.

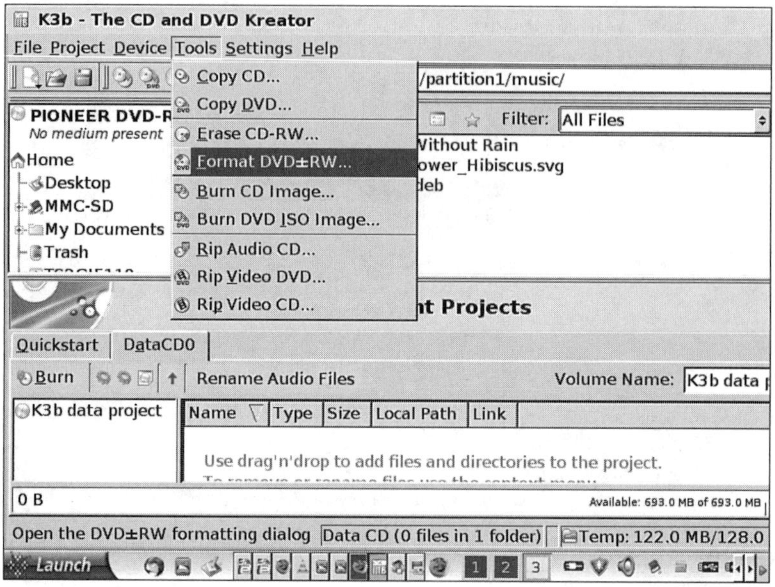

FIGURE 9.10

K3b formatting a data DVD.

Stuff That Doesn't Work Under Xandros

Two programs that I really wish worked easily under Xandros are TrueCrypt and Scribus.

TrueCrypt

TrueCrypt is, I think, an essential application for a machine as portable (and therefore as easily stolen) as the Eee PC. TrueCrypt provides military-grade data encryption capabilities and can either create encrypted partitions on a flash drive or memory card or (if you have the latest version) encrypt a file system.

If you have confidential or sensitive information on your Eee PC, it would be great to protect it with TrueCrypt. Unfortunately, very few people have gotten it to work on the Eee PC. (There is a solution provided by a gentleman in Hungary who has a precompiled version that appears to work. However, many folks feel a little uneasy about accepting an encryption program compiled by another private individual.) TrueCrypt does work under some other Linux distros and under Windows.

Scribus

Scribus is a personal favorite of mine: it's a full-blown desktop publishing program for Linux. Scribus has roughly the same page layout power as the last edition of Adobe PageMaker. Scribus is not yet on par with Adobe InDesign or Quark Express, but it's catching up fast. Added to the trio of OpenOffice.org Writer, Inkscape, and GIMP, Scribus would complete a true desktop publishing suite of tools running on the Eee PC.

Again, one can get Scribus running under other distros and Windows. But it sure would be cool if it would work on the Eee PC version of Xandros.

Summary

This chapter presents a few "best-of-breed" applications that you can install on the Eee PC. These applications can make using your Eee PC even more fun. One word of caution: consider how much disk space you have available if you are thinking of loading them all.

Introducing Google Applications

Asus thought enough of the usefulness of Google Docs and iGoogle that they provided icons for these on the Easy Mode Internet tab. You might be asking yourself, "Why bother with Google applications, given that, despite its diminutive size, the Eee PC is actually a very capable computer with the whole OpenOffice.org suite built-in?" The answer is that the combination of Google applications and OpenOffice.org tools provides a powerful collaboration center you can use to work with other people in your organization or around the globe.

Google Docs and iGoogle also provide ways to expand your storage to network locations. You can upload OpenOffice files directly to Google Docs shared spaces. Through a Firefox add-in, you can also use Gmail as an extension of your file storage space.

While the examples shown in this chapter use Xandros Linux, there's really nothing here that has operating system dependencies. You can do this just as easily under Windows or other Linux distributions. The Gspace plug-in shown later is specific to Firefox, so if you're running Windows and want to use Gspace, you'll need to install Firefox.

The following are a few of the things that you can do with Google Docs and iGoogle:

- Google provides you with a configurable home page that has access to Gmail, Google Calendar, and Google Docs.

- The iGoogle home page is actually a clever RSS feed aggregator. So, if you'd rather not clutter up your precious storage resources with RSS feeds, you can simply add them to your home page.

- You can collaborate with an entire team of people via the private edition of Google Docs and Spreadsheets. Used in conjunction with OpenOffice.org, you now have a focal point for offline storage and collaboration. You can share your documents, spreadsheets, and presentations with others; however, you can also work jointly with others on the documents. Google provides not only storage, and a history of changes, it also keeps each version of your document. You can also set who can see the files and who can edit them.

- Gmail, which you can get with an iGoogle account or as standalone webmail, is perhaps the most powerful, innovative, and useful webmail system ever created. It has up to 100MB of *free* online mail storage, with faster and better sorting than you can achieve with Thunderbird on your Eee PC.

In this chapter, you'll learn why Asus thought so highly of the Google applications, and how to leverage them to extend the Eee PC's capabilities. You'll discover how to collaborate and communicate with others around the globe using your Eee PC, as well as how to run Google applications when disconnected from the Internet.

Setting Up an iGoogle Account

Before you can use the more-advanced iGoogle features described in this chapter, you must have an iGoogle account.

From Easy Mode, click the iGoogle icon on the Internet tab. If you're in the Full Desktop, launch Firefox from the panel and in the browser, navigate to http://www.google.com/ig. Click the Sign In link in the upper-right corner. On the Personalize Your Homepage web page (see Figure 10.1), click the Create an Account Now link to start the process of building an account.

FIGURE 10.1

Click the Create an Account Now link.

In the Create a Google Account - iGoogle window, shown in Figure 10.2, Google requires that you provide the following information:

- **Your Current Email Address:** Enter a valid email address.

- **Choose a password:** To make it "strong," make it reasonably long and a mix of upper- and lowercase letters, numbers, and special characters (#, $, and so forth).

- **Re-enter Password:** Make sure to re-enter the password in the second field to confirm it.

- **Remember Me on This Computer:** Enabling this check box probably isn't too much of a security threat, but is the convenience really worth sacrificing the added security of forcing a sign-in?

- **Enable Web History:** Enabling the Web History feature is a convenience if you're doing research, but probably more of an invasion of privacy if you aren't.

- **Location:** Enter your location or country.

- **Word Verification:** Enter the warped-looking series of characters you see in the picture. This is a verification step to stop programs, often with nefarious intent, from setting up accounts. Only a person can decipher the bent characters correctly (or at least that's the theory).

- **Terms of Service:** Read the license agreement. No one ever does that. How do you know you haven't just signed away the title to your car?

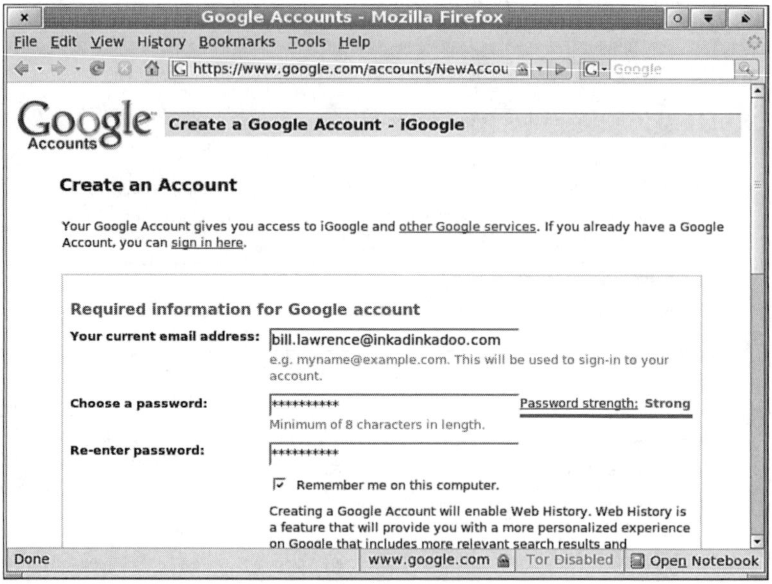

FIGURE 10.2

Required information to set up your iGoogle account.

That's it...you're ready to go.

Setting Up Your iGoogle Home Page

After you are on your iGoogle setup page, your next task is to set the initial preferences for your home page. Anything you select at his point can be easily changed later. You are asked to check boxes to choose your interests. This sets up the tabs on your home page quickly. However, you'll definitely get a Google slant on the information that appears on tabs such as Politics. If you don't want Google picking the sources of information for you, don't check any boxes; tabs are easy to build.

You can select an overall theme for your home page, which changes to reflect day and night. There are only five themes available in the initial preferences. Figures 10.3 and 10.4 show the setup page and final iGoogle home page.

FIGURE 10.3

The iGoogle preferences setup page.

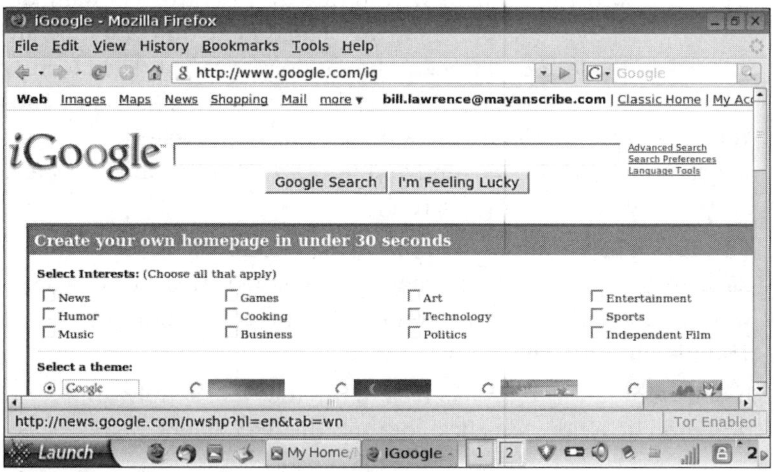

FIGURE 10.4

The final iGoogle home page.

Having your own tabs is the first big advantage of using iGoogle. The tabs provide a way of segregating information by type. The contents of the tabs are RSS feeds that you can select from the list that Google maintains, which is quite extensive. It has millions of feeds already loaded, so that you can just do a search. To add a tab, click Add a Tab. If you don't clear the "I'm feeling lucky" option, Google will add feeds to your new tab based on the tab's name.

To add your own RSS feeds to the tab, simply click Add Stuff. You can search through the list of feeds by entering the name of the feed into the Search for Gadgets field. Simple enough, but what if you come up blank?

note See Chapter 3, "Configuring Internet Applications," for a basic description of RSS feeds.

Suppose for a moment that you're addicted to electronic toys, and you just have to keep up on the latest and greatest offerings. Engadget.com is the best way to do this, but when you search for feeds, you get Engadget only in Spanish...and you're Spanish is just a little "rusty."

Open a separate tab in Firefox and hop over to http://www.engadget.com. Click the RSS Feed button below the Search field, and you'll be greeted with a preview of the feed and the familiar Subscribe to This Field Using drop-down list box (see Figure 10.5). Select Google from the list and click Subscribe Now. You'll get a choice to add the RSS feed to your Google Homepage or Google Reader. Click Homepage, and you now have an Engadget RSS feed in the currently active tab (see Figure 10.6).

This is in many ways better than using a local RSS reader. When you log into iGoogle, your feeds are automatically updated. This cuts down on both network traffic and your local storage. It's also easier than setting this up in Thunderbird (described in Chapter 3).

If you want to move an RSS feed to another tab, simply drag it to the new tab and drop it. When you click your tab the feed will be there.

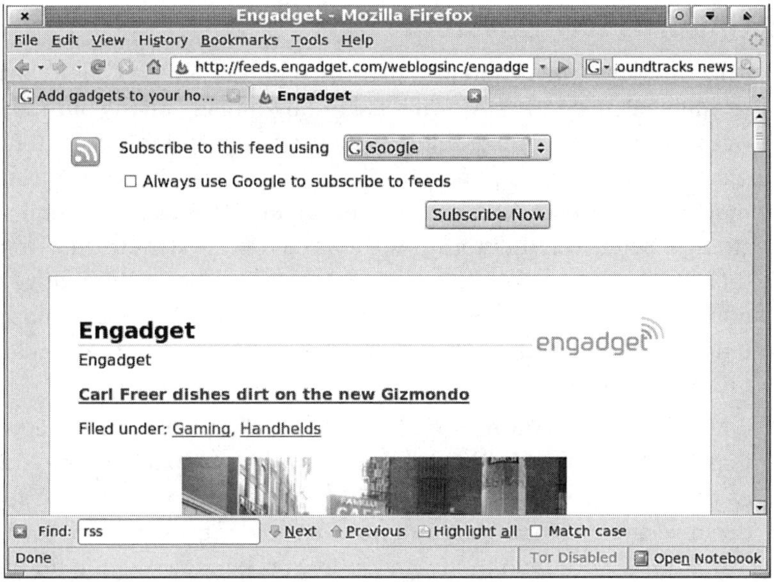

FIGURE 10.5
Adding the Engadget RSS feed...

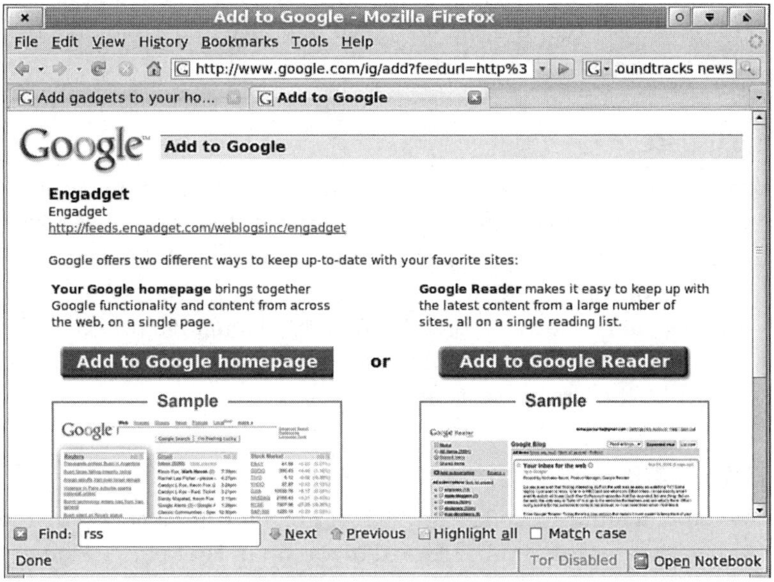

FIGURE 10.6
...and placing it on your iGoogle home page.

Using Gmail as a File System

Chapter 3 described configuring Thunderbird to talk to Gmail, including how to enable POP3 and IMAP. This essentially makes Gmail your mail server and webmail program. Also, Gmail is, by itself, a great mail system. But there's another trick you can play with Gmail that's really handy for a space-limited machine like the Eee PC: you can use up to 4.1GB of your Gmail space for file storage. Better yet, the storage appears as a file system within Firefox. Later in this chapter, I'll explain how to use Google Docs for collaborative file space, and the big difference there is that it can be shared. This file space is private, but can hold anything (whereas the Google Docs version can hold only certain file types).

The magic for this particular file storage trick comes from something called Gspace. Under more robust Linux installations, Gspace can be easily installed as part of the file system and mounted. However, on the Eee PC's stripped-down version of Xandros, that's not easy to do (trust me, I've tried). I'd been using the Gspace plug-in for Firefox from a Windows laptop for quite a while, so I got the bright idea of trying it on the Eee PC. It works equally well with Firefox and Xandros. The only drawback to using this with Xandros (or any operating system) is that it isn't directly mounted as part of the file system, so you must use the Firefox plug-in to upload, download, and manage files. However, Gspace has a well-designed interface that's a lot like the fancier GUI tools for working with FTP sites.

Installing Gspace

After you set up your iGoogle account, you have a Gmail account and password. That's all you'll need to set up Gspace. To install the Gspace plug-in, open Firefox (either through the Internet tab in Easy Mode or via Launch, Applications, Internet, Firefox Web Browser in Full Desktop). Navigate to https://addons.mozilla.org/en-US/firefox/addon/1593 and click the green Add to Firefox button. After installing the plug-in and restarting Firefox, you'll find Gspace in the Firefox Tools menu.

Setting Up Gspace

When you launch Gspace for the first time, if you have pop-up blocking on, you'll discover that it has blocked a pop-up in Firefox (see Figure 10.7). This is just a help wizard that's provided for installation, but you can easily install the account information manually. If you want to see any other helpful pop-ups that show up, click the pop-ups bar that appears toward the top of Firefox and allow pop-ups from the Gspace site.

FIGURE 10.7

The opening view of Gspace, with an alert promising the help wizard will follow.

To set up Gspace, click the Manage Accounts button to open the Gspace Account Manager window shown in Figure 10.8. For the Gmail ID, enter your entire Gmail email address. Enter your iGoogle password as the password. Enabling Remember Password is a nice convenience, but the password will be stored on your Eee PC, so if you're concerned about security, leave this unchecked and simply log in each time. Click the Close button to enable the Account.

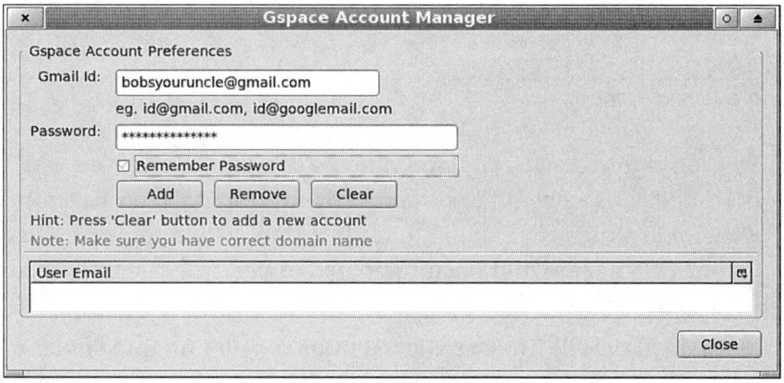

FIGURE 10.8

Setting up Gspace manually.

Using Gspace

Once your account information is set up, just click the blank field to the right of Manage Accounts and select your Gmail account. Click the Login button, and Gspace should connect to your account (see Figure 10.9).

You can user the My Computer file browser on the left to browse through the Eee PC file system and the My Gspace file browser on the right to work with the virtual file system built on Gmail. To upload files, select them on left and then click the right-pointing arrow. The Transfers pane, at the bottom of the Gspace window, shows the progress of the uploaded files.

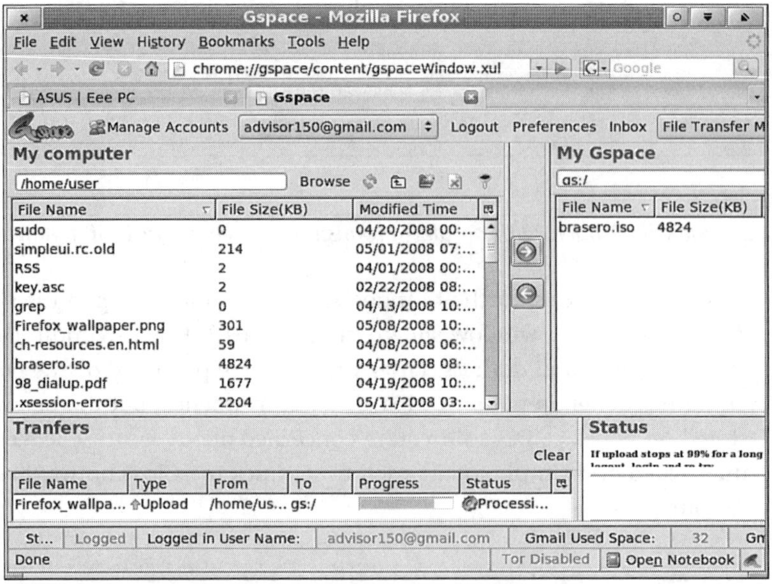

FIGURE 10.9

Uploading a file via Gspace.

You can right-click the files to launch a shortcut menu from which you can download files, copy and paste, make files read only, and even build directories to add structure to the virtual file system. Once you've created directories, you can click them and open them just as you would handle directories on your local file system.

If you click the File Transfer Mode button, you'll find three other modes of operation: Photo, Drive, and Player. While they sound promising, they don't appear to work. I've had the Photo mode functional from time to time, but Player mode doesn't seem to work at all. However, File Transfer mode seems quite reliable and does provide additional file storage on the Internet for most file types. There is a list of "harmful" file types under Preferences that you can designate, including executable files and other file types known to be virus risks.

Combining Google Docs and OpenOffice.org

Google Docs provides three basic office tools: a word processor, a spreadsheet tool, and a presentation tool (similar to PowerPoint or OpenOffice.org Impress). These are very basic tools, without the power and sophistication of

OpenOffice.org. However, they are functional and, most importantly, share file compatibility directly with OpenOffice.org Writer and OpenOffice.org Calc. If you save Impress files in PowerPoint format, you can transfer them to the Google Docs presentation tool as well.

There are some limitations in moving files between OpenOffice and Google Docs. For example, if you create a document with more than basic formatting in OpenOffice.org Writer, you'll lose much of that in the translation. Google Docs actually translates the files to HTML and then provides you with a rather sophisticated, word-processor-like HTML editing environment for online documents. When you download the documents, it translates them back into the format you request. So, in theory, you can "round-trip" from OpenOffice.org Writer to Google Docs and back. However, the typography and spacing will change with every translation. These are not major changes, but they are obvious. Figures 10.10 and 10.11 show the same text file in OpenOffice.org and Google Docs, respectively. The document is functionally the same, but its appearance is different.

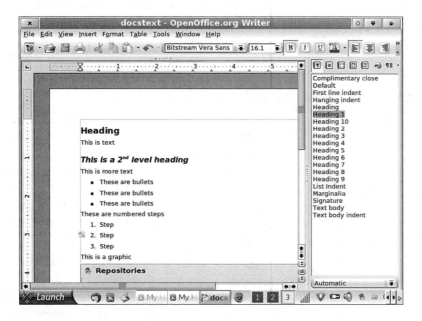

FIGURE 10.10

A document in OpenOffice.org Writer.

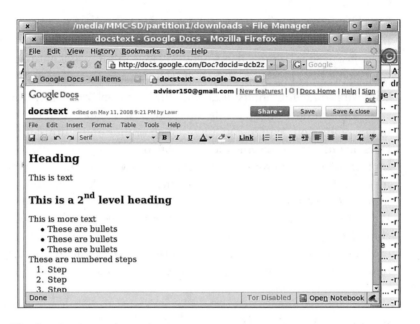

FIGURE 10.11

The same document in Google Docs. Well, not quite the same....

Reasons to Use Google Docs with Open Office

So, why bother with this if it's going to change your documents? Suppose that you must work with other folks who aren't within your network and in fact are halfway around the world. Suppose further that they not only must review and make comments on the parts of the document that you write, but also contribute major sections to the document. Or perhaps you'll be collaborating on a large financial spreadsheet, or a presentation, spreadsheet, and set of documents for a proposal that you'll be presenting to a client. How can you all work together when you're outside of the network?

Sure, you can email things back and forth, and that's done all the time. It's also terribly inefficient and provides almost infinite opportunity for error. After several versions have been sent around, exactly who has the most up-to-date version? If you get separate documents from eight or ten people and they all have comments, reconciling everything can be a daunting task. Worse, what if there are conflicting changes? I've spent many a nightmarish evening trying to pull together up to 15 separate versions of a contract proposal that had a looming deadline.

To solve these sorts of problems, organizations often employ a content management system such as Alfresco (open source) or Microsoft SharePoint to handle document storage, revisions, and collaborative editing and review of a single document. This is a vital tool, because having everyone working on one copy of the document means that they can all see the changes and that everything is always combined. It's also possible to provide secure, outside access to such systems via a virtual private network (VPN) or secure portals. However, this takes time to set up and may be beyond the capabilities or resources you have.

Enter Google Docs. You can build documents with your OpenOffice.org applications, upload them, and then collaborate with as many folks as you like with a modicum of security via the system Google already has set up. Because you've set up an iGoogle account, you have access to all of this for the low, low price of nothing.

Consider another scenario. Suppose you're working on a book and want to be able to "check in" versions as they are edited and modified. Again, you'd need something like a content management system, or at least a source-code control system such as programmers use (perhaps, for instance, CVS or SVN in the Linux/Unix world, or Visual SourceSafe in the Microsoft world). You'd also need a system to run this on and a way to provide access for you and the editor. You probably don't want to burden the tiny file system on the Eee PC with such a repository. Once again, Google Docs already provides this functionality, including the ability to go back to any previous version of a document or even compare versions.

Recently, Google added a new capability that cuts out the dependency on OpenOffice.org entirely. You can, by installing the Google Gears plug-in in Firefox, edit your documents offline (that is, not connected to the Internet). Moreover, Google Docs will synchronize your offline versions with the online versions. Best yet, this works equally well from either Simple Mode or Full Desktop.

Setting Up Google Docs

Actually, Google Docs is mostly set up for you the minute that you complete your iGoogle account signup. To access Google Docs, simply navigate to http://docs.google.com. Your login credentials from iGoogle (if you're already logged in there) will carry over. If you aren't logged in to iGoogle, you'll be able to log in to Google Docs at that point.

Working with the Google Docs File System

The initial Google Docs page shows you the current files and file structures in your Google Docs file system. Figure 10.12 shows a few files already uploaded or created directly through Google Docs, to give you an idea of what the interface is actually like. Click the New menu and you can create a new document, spreadsheet, presentation, or folder. Creating folders allows you to impose additional order on the Google Docs file system.

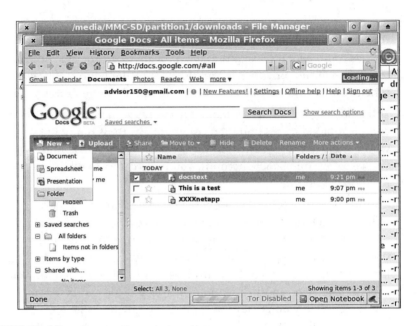

FIGURE 10.12

Creating a new document in Google Docs.

Like the file system for Gspace, you can't mount the Google Docs file system directly. Instead, you must use the upload and download functions in the Google Docs pages to move files back and forth from the Eee PC to Google Docs. To upload a single file, just click the Upload button. Also, note the email address farther down on the Upload page. If you send emails to that address, the contents will be captured as Google Docs files. This also provides a dandy way to send multiple documents. Just attach a set of OpenOffice.org Writer documents. This doesn't work for spreadsheets and PDF files, unfortunately.

Working with Documents in Google Docs

To open a document, simply click it in the file list and Firefox will open it in a separate tab. You can choose to save the file (although Google Docs autosaves often) or you can Save and Close. If you want to abandon changes and close the document, click the Close button for the tab.

Google Docs is pretty much driven by styles, and the styles are pretty much driven by its native file format: HTML. So if you look in the Format menu, you'll see a set of styles that corresponds to HTML tags. The formatting controls reflect HTML capabilities as well, with numbered and bulleted lists, font changes, and so forth. Pretty much anything you can do on a web page you can do in Google Docs. This includes placing figures in your documents.

Google Docs itself, while a basic word processor, does have some advanced editing features such as comments and a spelling checker (you can select the language). You can, if you know how to set up cascading style sheets (CSS) and are willing to invest the time, get some very nice formatting results out of Google Docs using custom style sheets. This, too, makes sense, given its dependency on HTML. Simply choose Edit, Edit CSS and create your own style sheet. You can then apply these styles to the text.

If you're comfortable editing in HTML, you can choose Edit, Edit HTML to get a view of the raw HTML that's similar to what you'd see in any text editor (see Figure 10.13). This can be a handy way to fix tricky formatting problems; however, you won't want to be switching back and forth from formatted text to HTML in long documents. It simply takes too long.

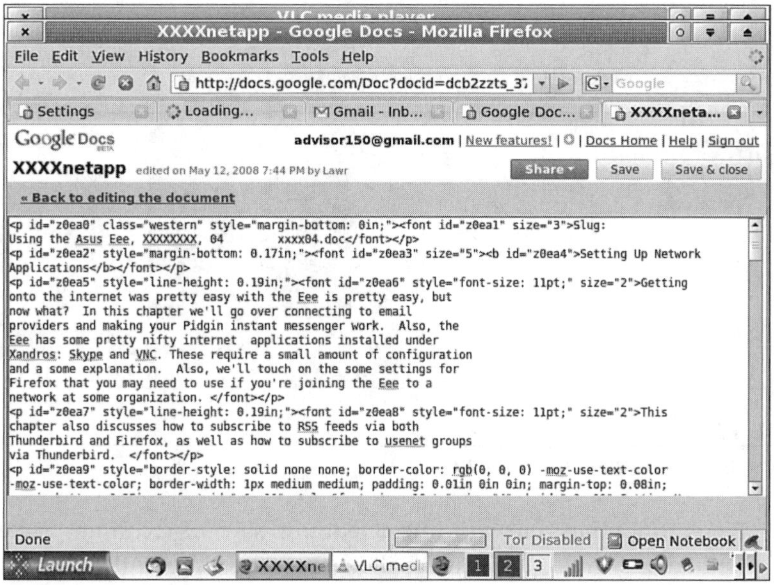

FIGURE 10.13
Editing a document's raw HTML in Google Docs.

Working with Presentations

You can create a Google Docs Presentation by selecting New, Presentation. Presentation has a fairly large set of slide templates and the basic formatting features you'd expect (see Figure 10.14). What it lacks is the ability to select from various formats that include lists, multiple columns, and various mixes for presenting text and graphics on the same slide. Instead, you can drop text boxes into the slide, which you can format with styles and formatting buttons. Amazingly, boxes dropped into a slide can be dragged around fairly smoothly, which is not easy in a web application.

You can also drop in some basic shapes, such as callout balloons and arrows, and you can change the color and size of these. Again, you can drag these shapes around with relative ease. You can also change text color and use a "highlighter."

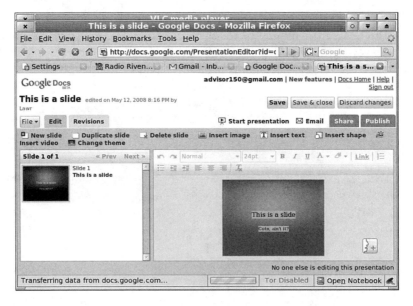

FIGURE 10.14

The presentation editing environment.

Presentation has a few advanced features, such as creating speaker's notes and adding multimedia to the slides. Because Presentation saves in PowerPoint format, you can send your presentations almost anywhere. Better yet, you can run a web presentation with this tool and invite viewers just as you would collaborators. Viewers can actually view the files at their own pace while the presenter is giving the presentation.

As with all Google Docs applications, you can publish the presentation to a website. This actually "embeds" a slide-viewing application in the web page, similar to a video player. Users can then "click" from slide to slide through the presentation.

Working with Spreadsheets

Like the other two applications, the spreadsheet is a basic but competent program with a wide variety of basic math and statistical functions. The Google-specific functions are rather mind-boggling. Figure 10.15 shows the Insert a Function list you can access by clicking the More link. For example, you can add Google-specific functions such as

```
=GoogleLookup("entity"; "attribute")
```

The "entity" might be any primary search string, such as "Pittsburgh Penguins" and the "attribute" would be the secondary search string, such as "NHL standings." Thus, when executed, the function will return some sort of information pertinent to the search.

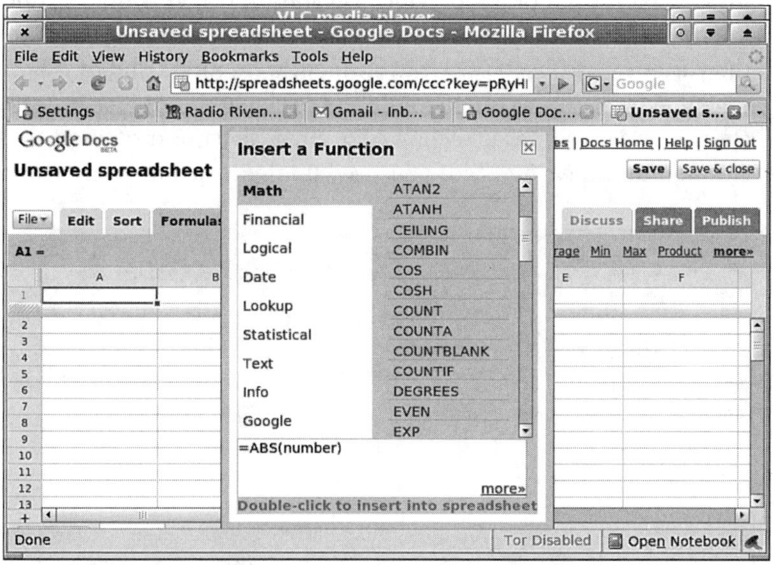

FIGURE 10.15

Functions in the spreadsheet application.

You can save files from any of the applications as Adobe Acrobat PDF files. This may not seem like a big deal if you're used to OpenOffice.org and its excellent PDF capabilities, but it's still very useful. Folks that you're collaborating with that have applications such as Microsoft Office will find this a great feature, because, without Adobe Acrobat or Distiller, they have no straightforward way to create PDF files.

Another feature that you'll only find in powerful content management systems is full-text search within all the documents stored in Google Docs. If you build up a considerable library of documents over time, finding things can become really challenging. For large document libraries, full-text search can be a life-saver. To search the library of stored documents, just use the Search Docs field as you would a general Google search.

Versioning in Google Docs

Like any good content management system, Google Docs stores versions of your documents (see Figure 10.16). This is true for all three document types: text, spreadsheets, and presentations. Within each application, there's a Version History (sometimes called Revisions) function. You can use either of these to view each of the previous versions and even what's changed between them. Google Docs saves each version of the file that you save. You can peruse the various versions to see what changes were made and by whom as the document evolved. This can prove to be extremely handy. For instance, if you change or delete a large section of a spreadsheet or a series of slides in a presentation and then find that you need it later, you can easily recovert.

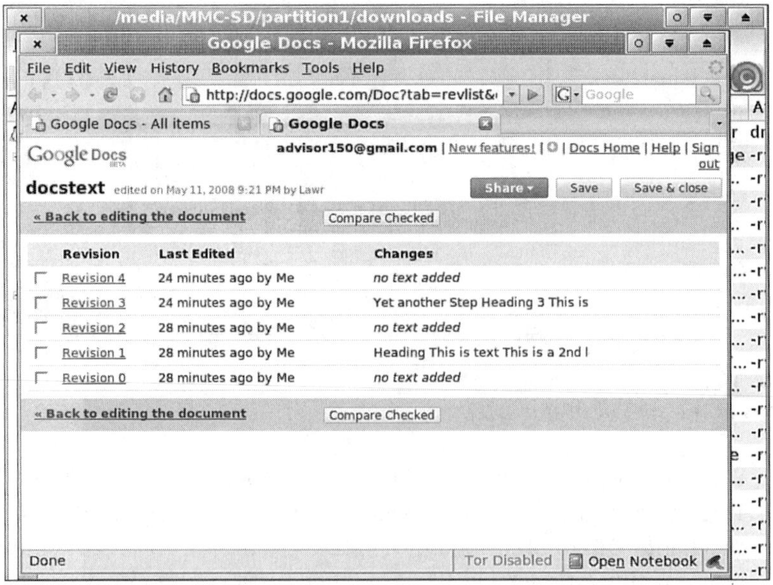

FIGURE 10.16
A list of versions from the Google Docs repository.

Collaborating in Google Docs

The real key to the power of Google Docs is collaboration. From within each of the applications, you can choose to share documents with others. You must first set up as Contacts in Gmail the email addresses of all your collaborators. Once they are in the Contacts list, you can simply choose collaborators and assign sharing permissions. Each file that you create (or upload, or email into the system using the email address provided to collaborators in their email invitations) is assigned to you as the owner. The owner can decide who can collaborate on each file (on a file-by-file basis) and what the collaborators can do. If you wish, you can change the owner so that one of the collaborators can control the file. This works well if you'll be on vacation or just got that big promotion.

On a basic level, collaborators can either simply view a document or edit and add comments to the document. Even viewers can save copies or print the document. You can also add some advanced permissions, which gets a little tricky. You can allow collaborators to invite other collaborators so that the entire world might be working with you on your document. You can also allow an invitation to be used by basically anyone, so that it can be forwarded on throughout the globe.

Each collaborator receives an email message with a URL link that leads directly to the document. Google Docs can actually allow multiple editors to work on the document at the same time. Updates between open documents occur very quickly, and the revision history logs not only changes but who made them. When a collaborator closes the document, they will find themselves in their own Google Docs page, but with the shared document added to their document list. This is an exceptional feature, because each Docs user can have their own document set, which isn't shared, plus the shared documents—all in the same file system.

Beyond all of this, you can publish your documents to a Google Blog or a web page. You can even make a document "public" and allow people to subscribe to changes to the document via an RSS feed.

Working Offline

The last bit of Google magic breaks the link to OpenOffice.org for offline use. By loading the Google Gears plug-in for Firefox, you can have the same functionality offline that you have online with Google Docs on your Eee PC's native file system. Google Gears synchronizes the files between the online repository and a local file store. On the Eee PC, these local files and all the goodies that allow you to edit offline are stored in /home/user/.mozilla. There isn't any way to move this, so the offline storage is kept in the file storage area, where space is the most precious. This is unfortunate, and Google could help us out a lot by providing a way to move the storage location.

To set up the offline functionality, you must first install the Google Gears plug-in. This is much like any other Firefox plug-in. To install it, navigate to http://gears.google.com/ and click Install Google Gears to install the plug-in (see Figure 10.17). It will correctly identify the combination of Linux and Firefox. As with most plug-ins, it will close your current Firefox session and restart it to load the plug-in.

FIGURE 10.17

Adding the Google Gears plug-in.

Google Gears is a flexible Google technology that provides a way to run web applications offline. It installs a local web server to run the web applications and installs a database to store the information contained in the websites. After Google Gears is installed, Google Docs will synchronize its documents with the database on your Eee PC.

After Google Gears is loaded and Firefox is restarted, navigate back to http://docs.google.com. The menu bar now contains a green synchronization icon (to the right of your login name).

Initially, Gears takes a bit of time to build the database and set things up. If you click the green sync icon and then select Preferences, you'll see the Offline Access Settings dialog box shown in Figure 10.18, which includes a tempting button to place an icon on the KDE desktop (this won't work for Easy Mode, of course). Give it a shot if you like, but it didn't work for me. If you tire of synchronizing to Google Gears, you can also deactivate syncing from the Offline Access Settings dialog box.

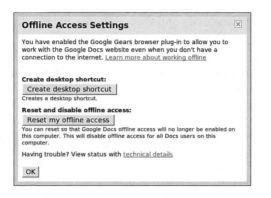

FIGURE 10.18

Google Gears preferences.

Aside from the desktop icon, Google Gears works perfectly in either Easy Mode or Full Desktop. To give it a try, first make sure it's synchronized. Click the green icon to determine the current state (the icon will also turn into a check mark if everything is synchronized). Now shut down Firefox and disconnect from your network. Open Firefox again. Even though you are currently disconnected from the network, navigate to http://docs.google.com. Your document repository appears. Click a document to open it, and the familiar Google Docs application appears. However, you'll find a message at the top of the file reminding you that you're working offline and that you'll have to connect to Google Docs via the Internet to upload this file (see Figure 10.19).

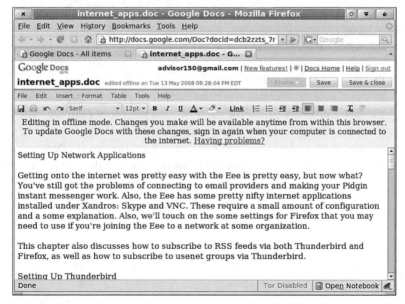

FIGURE 10.19

Offline Google Docs editing via the magic of Google Gears.

If you make some edits and then close the file via the Save & Close button, you'll see a message to the left of the filename saying that the file was "Edited Offline," as shown for internet_apps.doc in Figure 10.20. Also, if you add a check mark beside the file and look under the More actions menu, you'll see that everything other than Preview is disabled. Functions such as versioning and publishing require you to be online.

FIGURE 10.20

A document saved offline.

Reconnect to your network and then refresh the http://docs.google.com page in your browser. To force a synchronization, you can put a check mark beside the files that were edited offline and then use More Actions, Sync Now. The "Edited Offline" message disappears, and all the functionality of Google Docs is back. If you open the document, you'll see that your changes are intact and that the version history now contains a version with your offline edits.

Summary

Clearly one of the big limitations of the Eee PC is storage and one of its chief benefits is portability. So, remote file storage and applications that can be accessed from anywhere make a lot of sense with this platform. Gmail, by itself, provides both a webmail program and a mail server, which you can connect to Thunderbird (covered in Chapter 3). You can get Gmail simply by setting up an iGoogle account, which also gives you access to a lot more functionality. For example, you can plug RSS feeds into your iGoogle home page.

By adding the Gspace plug-in to Firefox, suddenly you have a flexible network file system. You can upload and download files from there as you please. The only drawback is that you can't mount it and open files directly there.

By adding Google Docs, you have a basic suite of office tools and a content management system to go with it. More importantly, you have the ability to collaborate and share content with anyone else that has a Google account. So, now the tiny Eee PC is an ultra-portable node in a global collaboration environment.

You can take this one final step via Google Gears. By installing the Google Gears plug-in via Firefox, you can edit any document in your Google Docs repository locally, without a network connection. By reconnecting, you can synchronize your documents. The penalty is that it requires space on your local file system to load the Gears components and the most current version of your files. Still, that's an awesome amount of capability that's basically free.

Introduction to the Linux Command Line

Regardless of how simple the graphical user interface (GUI) becomes, to efficiently use and control a Linux system, you should at least become familiar with the shell commands. "Shell" is just another term for the command-line prompt. The prompt provides an interface to the underlying Linux system, but through typed commands instead of a GUI. The original UNIX shell was called the Bourne shell, and the default Linux shell for the Eee PC, as well as most Linux systems, is Bash (Bourne-again shell). The Bash shell is a sophisticated and powerful environment from which you can perform just about any task on the computer.

This chapter provides a quick reference to the Bash shell commands and some basic Linux concepts, such as Linux file permissions. At the end of the chapter, you'll find a very quick reference to the most useful Bash commands.

IN THIS CHAPTER

- An introduction to Linux Shells
- How to launch a shell in both Easy Mode and the KDE (Full Desktop)
- A description of how to use a basic set of Linux commands
- A command reference

Launching the Shell in Easy Mode

In Easy Mode, you can launch what's called an xterm window. This is nothing more than a terminal-emulator window, harkening back to the days when one interacted with a computer via a terminal. To launch it, press Ctrl+Alt+T. The window that appears has a prompt that looks like this:

`/home/user>`

The prompt, by default, displays the current directory. Note that I said "directory" instead of "folder." "Folder" is used more in the context of a GUI that actually uses folder icons. When discussing the shell, however, the term "directory" is the preferred term. But when you get down to the file system itself, the two terms refer to exactly the same thing.

> **note** There is a convention in Linux command documentation to use the $ prompt to mean user commands and the # prompt to mean "superuser" or root commands. But for simplicity, throughout this chapter (and the book), you'll see the prompt shown as >. If the sudo command is required, it'll be specifically included in the examples. Thus, > sudo means the command is being used with root authority. sudo is required whenever your command affects the system as a whole. While modifying a file in your user directories doesn't require sudo, changing a system configuration file does.

In Full Desktop, you can launch an xterm window by choosing Launch, Run Command, and entering xterm &. However, you can launch a much nicer terminal emulator called Konsole by entering konsole &. Konsole is a powerful terminal emulator, with lots of features configurable via menus.

One more bit of background: In Linux, to protect your system, you are given somewhat restricted permissions and privileges in your user account. On the Eee PC, these are simply the permissions that any default user might have. To have administrative, or root, privileges, you must preface a command with sudo. However, do this with extreme care, as you can render your system unusable with a mistake (though this is unlikely). At least with the Eee PC, it's easy to reimage the solid-state drive.

Comparing the Linux File System to the Windows File System

The following are several of the major apparent differences between the Linux file system and the Windows file system:

- The character used to separate directories in Linux is a slash (/), not a backslash (\). This will drive you crazy if you must switch between Windows and Linux machines during the day.

- There is only one top to the Linux file system, the root, instead of a number of peer drives (such as C:, D:, and X:). Various "drives" on the Eee PC, such as flash drives and DVD drives, are accessible through the /mnt or /media directories.

- The Linux file system uses file links, of which there are two types. A symbolic link (also called a sym link or soft link) is a shortcut across the file system to another directory or file. It's actually a shortcut file that's easy to distinguish from the file or directory to which it points. It's very similar to file shortcuts on Microsoft Windows systems. But there is also a "hard" link, which is actually a pointer at the file-system level. Hard links are difficult to distinguish from the target to which they link, which makes them a lot trickier to use than symbolic links.

- Linux is case sensitive. In Windows, MYFILE.DOC, Myfile.Doc, and myfile.doc are considered the same filename and extension. Not so in Linux, where all three would be different files.

- Architecturally, Linux has no concept of a separate filename "extension" as there is in the Microsoft world. Although filenames *can* be in the form <name>.<ext>, and in fact usually are, in the Linux and UNIX world, this is nothing more than a naming convention; the dot (.) character is treated as any other character. The only special meaning is that if a file or directory name begins with a dot, that file or directory is hidden to a number of commands (ls in particular).

One way in which the file systems are the same is in the way they treat filenames that include spaces. Once upon a time, when UNIX boxes roamed the earth, you couldn't have spaces in filenames. But now that you can in Linux, you must enclose them with double quotes so that the commands can deal with them, like so:

```
"this is a very tediously long filename"
```

In Chapter 8, I said that most new applications that you install have instructions. If you wish to delve further into the intricacies of the various commands covered in this chapter, you can take a look at either the man page or manual. To see the man page for the ls command, for example, simply enter:

```
> man ls
```

You can scroll up and down, and when you're done, enter q (for "quit") to exit. Some commands also come with a manual file, which has more detailed information. For example, for a full manual on the bzip2 command, enter:

```
> info bzip2
```

Again, use q to escape. If the manual doesn't exist, you'll get the man page. Manuals can have links to jump to other sections. To use these, simply use the arrow key to navigate to a link (links are easy to recognize, as they are preceded with an asterisk) and press Enter. Figure 11.1 shows a number of links in an info file.

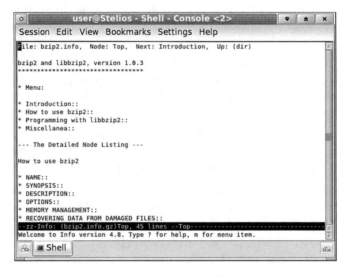

FIGURE 11.1

The Info file for bzip2, showing a number of links.

Working with Files and Directories

The following sections list the most commonly used commands for viewing information about files and directories, as well as manipulating them.

Listing Directory Contents

The command to list the contents of a directory is ls (short for "list"). For example:

```
> ls
Desktop/    MMC-SD      My Documents/    Trash/
media
```

You'll see a number of files listed, some of which are displayed in different colors. Although the colors can be changed in the settings for the console program, by default they mean:

black: file

dark blue: directory

light blue (cyan): symbolic link

If you want to see all the files, including hidden files and directories, use the
-a switch:

```
/home/user> ls -a
./                      .fbrc              .kdesession      .scim/
../                     .FBReader/         key.asc          .Skype/
.adobe/                 .firstrundone      .lesshst         .thumbnails/
.AsusLauncher/          .fontconfig/       .lgames/         .thunderbird/
.audacity               .fonts.conf        .local/          Trash/
.bash_history           .fullcircle/       .macromedia/     .tuxmath/
.
.
.
```

If you want to see all the information about files, such as their current permissions, use the -1 switch, as follows. This also shows the target of the symbolic
link:

```
> ls -l
total 52
drwx------   2 user user   4096 2008-05-27 18:21 Desktop/
-rw-rw-rw-   1 user user   1730 2008-02-22 08:12 key.asc
lrwxrwxrwx   1 user user      6 2008-05-18 13:44 media -> /media/
lrwxrwxrwx   1 root root     13 2008-05-27 18:21 MMC-SD -> /media/MMC-SD/
drwxrwxrwx  11 user user   4096 2008-05-11 22:08 My Documents/
-rw-rw-rw-   1 user user   1364 2008-04-01 00:25 RSS
drwxrwxrwx   3 user user  36864 2008-05-26 13:40 Trash/
```

Some translation is now required. The first 10 characters in each line lists the
entry's type and permission flags. For directories, the first character is a d (such
as with Desktop), and for symbolic links, it's l (such as with /media) For files,
the first flag is -. Although you probably will not encounter these in your daily
travels about the Eee PC file system, for completeness' sake, you should know
that p is a pipe, s is a socket, c is a character device, and b is a block device.
These have the following, if somewhat esoteric, meanings:

- Pipe is a special file used for communications between two processes. It
  connects the output of one process to the input of another.

- Socket is another special file that's used for communications between
  processes.

- Character is a device file type for a serial device. Serial devices take
  input and output as a stream of data. One of the really neat things

is that all hardware devices, except for network devices, are treated as files. These device files handle permissions information and configuraton for the various devices on the system.

- Block is a device for devices that have random access data.

The next nine characters are the permissions settings, and they are owner (first three characters), group (middle three characters), and world, or all (last three characters). Because the Eee PC is essentially a single-user Linux system, you're basically interested in owner, and that's either going to be you or root. This is where the sudo command comes into play, because if you're not the owner, and group and world don't have permissions on the file, you need to use sudo to manipulate the file.

The permissions break down as a triplet of r (read), w (write), and x (execute). You can change the permissions with the chmod command, which is covered a bit later in this section. You can change owner with chown, which is covered with chmod. To read a file, you must have the r permission. To change a file, you must have the w permission, and to run a script or program, you must have the x permission.

The next number is the link count, which simply indicates the number of hard links to the file or directory. Following that are the owner and group, both of which are called "user" or "root" in the preceding example. You can manipulate user files without sudo, but root files require you to preface the command with sudo.

After the user and group comes the size of the file, in bytes. Following the file size is the date and time stamp for when the file was either created or last "touched" (which normally means edited or updated). Finally, the last entry is the name of the file or directory, and if it's a symbolic link, it shows the destination after an arrow.

Creating, Removing, and Moving Around in Directories

Now that you can list and understand the contents of a directory, you need to know how to create and remove one. If you're going to create a directory, you use the mkdir command. So, if you're in your /home/user directory, try this:

```
> mkdir mydir
```

If you use ls -l, you'll find that you're both the owner and group, which is only fair because you created it.

Changing into the directory requires the cd command. Because this is a subdirectory of the current directory, you don't need the "fully qualified" path and can just use a relative path, which means just the path from your current directory. In this case, the cd command is:

```
> cd mydir
```

If you had wanted to use the fully qualified path, that would be:

```
> cd /home/user/mydir
```

Note that the prompt now changes to reflect the current directory.

To change back to the next directory "up" (/home/user), you can use the shortcut of . ., like this:

```
> cd ..
```

Also, because /home/user is your home, you can use the ~ shortcut to return to your home directory:

```
> cd ~
```

To jump all the way to the root, use:

```
> cd /
```

Copying Files

Suppose that you're back in the mydir directory and want to copy a file. For that, you need to use the cp command. The file you'll copy is a hidden config-uration file in your home directory, and you'll rename it in the process:

```
> cp ../.bash_profile mybash.txt
```

That copies .bash_profile and gives the copy the name mybash.txt. Now that you have a file in mydir, jump back to the home directory and try to delete the directory:

```
> cd ~
> rmdir mydir
```

Note that the Eee PC refuses and complains:

```
rmdir: mydir: Directory not empty
```

Clearly, you need to hunt down mybash.txt and remove it. To do that, you need to use the rm command (but don't type this yet):

```
> rm mydir/mybash.txt   (BUT DON'T TYPE IT YET!)
```

Now, because you just entered the rmdir command, you can use something called command memory. Just press the up-arrow key twice. The first press produces the last command and the next press produces the previously issued command. You can use the down-arrow key to navigate back down through the command stack. When you see the rmdir mydir command, press Enter and this time it will remove the directory.

Treat the rm command with some respect. Combined with wildcards, it can be devastating to your system. The * means match everything, so rm * will delete all the contents of the current directory. There are two switches for rm:

- ■ -f means to "force" the deletion. Occasionally, the system may ask if you really want to delete something, and using -f is a polite way of saying "don't ask, just do it."

- ■ -r means "recursive" deletion, which means to go down through the subdirectories and remove their contents.

So, for example, to force the deletion of the file "bob," you'd enter:

```
> rm —f bob
```

Sometimes, you'll want to move a file from one directory to another—that is, place it in another directory and remove it from its source directory. You could do that by issuing back-to-back cp and rm commands, but you can instead use mv. For example:

```
> mv /somewhere/myfile.txt /else/
```

You can also use mv to move or just rename a directory (and all of its subdirectories). For example, to rename the "zane" directory to "kira," you would enter:

```
> mv zane kira
```

To move kira and its subdiretories under the hope directory, you'd enter:

```
> mv kira hope/
```

Note that the trailing slash makes all the difference, as it identifies hope as a directory.

Checking Free Storage Space

Suppose you're interested not in listing the contents of directories, but in how much space is left on the Eee PC. Simple, use the df ("display freespace") command:

```
> df
rootfs                1454700   1203160    177644   88% /
/dev/sda1             1454700   1203160    177644   88% /
unionfs               1454700   1203160    177644   88% /
tmpfs                  453356        12    453344    1% /dev/shm
tmpfs                  131072      3420    127652    3% /tmp
/dev/sdb1             3971584   1423456   2548128   36% /media/
➥MMC-SD/partition1
```

The information you want is in any of the first three entries. In the case of my machine, 88% of the solid-state drive is full, with a mere 177,644 bytes left. My Eee PC is a 701 4G, so I have a little breathing room. Folks with a 900 series machine will have much more space.

You might be wondering if the file system has a single root, why are there six entries. Mounted devices and disk partitions are also shown. The top three are actually just different references to the same thing. Note that the MMC-SD drive is shown as a device in the /mnt directory (which is because it's mounted).

Creating Symbolic Links

Symbolic links are handy things, because they can provide a shortcut to any location in the file system. They're easy to create with the ln command. For example, to create a symbolic link docs directory that links to a directory on the MMC-SD drive, use the following:

```
> ln -s /media/MC-SD/partition1/Documents/ docs
```

Note the trailing slash after Documents, which makes it specific that this is a directory target.

Creating Tarballs

Now and then, you might want to make backups of your home directory and your MMC-SD drive. A common way to do this is to create a "tarball," which is a tar file compressed by bzip2. A tar file is a single file that contains a collection of files, so the tar part of the exercise gathers all the files from the target directory path into a single file. You can both tar and compress in one single command.

> **tip** The name "tar" comes from the fact that, way back in the mists of time, the format was originally used for (T)ape (AR)chives.

Given that space is at a premium on 700 series Eee PCs, make sure the target (such as a USB flash drive) has sufficient space for the tarball.

As a rule, tar does not follow symbolic links, but rather backs up the symbolic link file itself. However, if you throw in the h switch, it will follow symbolic links, which will back up all your /media directories (such as the MMC-SD drive). However, the problem with this is that it will also follow along to wherever you're creating the backup file, which would be bad. If you're going to use the h switch, have the target be on a network share.

To create a tar file of the user directory, issue:

```
> tar -cjf /whatever/your/target/directory/is/backupfilename.tar.bz2
/home/user
```

where `/whatever/your/target/directory/is/` is the directory path to the directory that will hold the tar file, and `backupfilename.tar.bz2` is some name that you choose for the tar file.

If you write another tarball with the same name to the same location, it will simply overwrite the first one.

The `-cjf` switches simply tell `tar` to create a file with the following argument as the name of the file and compress it with bzip2. To restore the file, issue the following command:

```
> tar -xjf backupfilename.tar.bz2
```

Issue the restore command from where you want the directory and its contents, including subdirectories, restored. It will re-create its parent directory structure as well.

Changing File Ownership and Permissions

You'll want to know how to change the ownership of a file and its permissions. Now, of course, you can easily do this through the graphical file manager, but you can also use `chown` and `chmod`.

The `chown` command can really have only two arguments on the Eee PC: `root` and `user`. To change the ownership of a file from root to user, you need to use `chown` with `sudo`:

```
> sudo chown user filename
```

where `user` is the new owner and `filename` is the name of the file whose ownership is to be changed.

Changing permissions is almost as easy. The `chmod` command has as switches a (all users), g (group), and u (user). Each of these switches has several arguments: + (add), - (remove), r (read permission), w (write permission), and x (execute permission). So, to make yourfile.ext have read, write, and execute permission for all users, which includes the group and the owner, you would issue this command:

```
> chmod a+rwx yourfile.ext
```

To remove write permissions from the group, you would issue this command:

```
> chmod g-w yourfile.ext
```

Finding Files

This section discusses how to find files or sets of files, and how to find information contained within files.

You can find files easily with the `find` command. All you need for `find` is to know, more or less, what you're looking for and where to start. By the way, this is a really great command to use if you're looking for a file that you installed via `apt-get` or the Synaptic Package Manger and you know the name of the file. To search for a fictitious file called key.asc in the /home/user directory (and any of its subdirectories), you'd issue this command:

```
> find /home/user/ -name "key.asc"
```

To find all JPG graphics files in the Eee PC's built-in file system, issue this command:

```
> find / -name "*.jpg"
```

To find the same set of files on the attached flash drives, issue this command:

```
> find /media/ -name "*.jpg"
```

The `find` command is pretty fast, even though it's doing a brute-force search. If you want to find the location of a program file that's currently installed, you can use the `which` command. For example, to use `which` to report the location of the GIMP executable, gimp, you'd use this command:

```
> which gimp
```

The `which` command depends on things being in the path. The path is actually a set of directories, stored in an environment variable (PATH) that tells Linux where to look for programs. If you want to see the current path, use this command:

```
> echo $PATH
```

The `echo` command "echoes" the current value of the variable, denoted by the dollar sign, to the screen. On the Eee PC, the path returned is actually pretty short:

```
/usr/local/bin:/usr/bin:/bin:/usr/games
```

Using environment variables is simply a way to set some information so that programs can access it. The great thing about environment variables is that they can be redefined and, by doing so, programs get the new definition. If you want to take a look at all the environment variables that are currently set, run this command:

```
> printenv
```

So, what if you want to find something inside of a file or files? That's where `grep` comes in. For `grep` to work, the files must be text files. So, if you want to find a file that contains the string "winning lottery" and there are a number of TXT files in the directory, you'd issue this `grep` command:

```
> grep 'winning lottery' *.txt
```

grep will report back any file in the specified directory with the .txt extension that contains the search string. The grep command also understands regular expressions, and using those makes it an incredibly powerful search tool. Regular expressions are the subjects of entire books and thus beyond the scope of this book. However, you can find more than you even want to know about regular expressions at http://www.regular-expressions.info/reference.html.

The grep command can also search for strings of information "piped" through it. We'll cover pipes and redirection in the "Command-Line Tricks" section.

Viewing Text Files

If you now want to view the text files you've found, you have two ways of doing that: cat and less.

The cat command is designed to join two text files together; however, if you give it a single file as an argument, it will simply spew the contents of the file to the console. Clearly, this is really only good for short files, unless you can read faster than the console can spew text. So, to do this with a file, you would issue:

```
> cat yourfile.txt
```

A better way is to use the less command, which fills a single screen full of text. Then, you can scroll up and down with the up- and down-arrow keys. If you want to scroll up and down faster you can use the Page Up and Page Down keys. Use q to exit from the file. To run less on a file, issue this command:

```
> less yourfile.txt
```

If you want to compare two text files, you can do that with the diff command. If fact, you'll likely hear UNIX and Linux folks using this as a verb as they discuss "diffing" two files. Usage is pretty simple:

```
> diff thisfile.txt thatfile.txt
```

The diff command will echo any lines that aren't identical to the console, and won't show any lines that are identical. You'll also see > and < signs at the beginning of the lines: < means that the line came from the first file in the command, and > means that the line came from the second file (see Figure 11.2).

```
○ ▐███████████  user@Stelios - Shell - Console <2>  ▐██  ▼  ▲  ✖
Session  Edit  View  Bookmarks  Settings  Help
/home/user> diff file1.txt file2.txt
1c1
< The diff command will echo any lines that aren't identical to the console, and
 won't show lines that are identical at all.  You'll also see greater-than and l
ess-than signs at the beginning of the lines.  A less-than sign means that the l
ine came from the first file in the command and a greater-than sign means that t
he line came from the second file.
\ No newline at end of file
---
> The diff command will echo any lines that aren't identical to the console, and
 won't show lines that are identical at all.  You'll also see greater-than and l
ess-than signs at the beginning of the lines.  Another less-than sign means that
 the line came from the first file in the command and a greater-than sign means
that the line came from the second file.
\ No newline at end of file
/home/user> █




⊠  ■ Shell                                                               ▓
```

FIGURE 11.2

Results from "diffing" two text files.

Command-Line Tricks

In this section, you'll learn about ways to work with the command line, including command completion and command editing. You'll also find a few other handy tips, such as how to stop a script or how to clear the screen. Finally, this section covers redirections and pipes, which are poweful ways of working with command inputs and outputs.

Command-Line Completion

Command-line completion is a tremendous time-saver (and hand-saver), because Linux will fill in parts of the command line for you. Suppose you're sitting with a command prompt in front of you, and you want to change directories to this rather long path: /media/MMC-SD/partition1/downloads. After you enter the cd command and the following space, simply enter /me and then press Tab. Because no directories that are children of the root other than /media begin with "/me," the system knows which directory you mean

and fills in the rest of the path. If there were more than one directories beginning with "/me," cd would list the possible choices for you so that you could
type enough letters to make the choice clear. You can keep pressing Tab
throughout the directories in the path and have the Bash shell fill in the
blanks for you as you go. This even works for individual filenames.

Editing Commands

If you make a mistake on a long command, you can use the left- and right-
arrow keys to move the cursor back and forth along the command line. Ctrl+A
will jump to the beginning of the line, and Ctrl+E will jump to the end. If you
want to delete everything before the cursor, press Ctrl+U. Pressing Ctrl+K
deletes everything from the cursor position to the right.

If you want to clear the current xterm or Konsole screen, simply enter the following command:

```
> clear
```

I've mentioned this before, but adding a space and then an ampersand (&)
after a command spawns it off from the current console, freeing your command prompt for the next command. Thus, launching gimp with the ampersand gives you back your prompt, but neglecting the ampersand means that
the prompt is frozen until the gimp session is complete.

Stopping Scripts

If a script is running, you can usually stop it with a simple Ctrl+C command.
If this does not work, look ahead to the next section on controlling processes.

Creating Aliases

If you tire of typing the same long command over and over again, you can make
up your own short command name that's actually the long command and its
arguments. This is done through the alias command. For example, the following
will back up the /home/user directory into a tarball on the MMC-SD drive:

```
> tar -cjf /media/MMC-SD/partition1/backup/homebak.tar.bz2 /home/user
```

You can simply create a command called backme that has all of that defined in it:

```
> alias backme='tar -cjf /media/MMC-SD/partition1/backup/homebak.tar.bz2 \
/home/user'
```

Now, when you issue the `backme` command, it will actually run the big, long `tar` command.

Redirection and Pipes

In Linux, you can combine commands by taking the output of one command and sending it to another command. This is called "piping." You can also take the output of a command and send it to a file or to the console, which is called "redirection." For example, suppose that you're looking for all the JPG graphics files on the Eee PC that have the string "wallpaper" somewhere in their name. You could use `*wallpaper.jpg` as the argument to the `find` command, but what if "wallpaper" is merely the first part of a long filename? That won't match `*wallpaper.jpg`. However, you could find all the JPG files with `*.jpg`, and then "pipe" the output of the `find` command into the `grep` command, which can search for the string "wallpaper." To do that, you use the pipe character (¦):

```
> find / -name *.jpg ¦ grep 'wallpaper'
```

That's great, except perhaps you'd like to save these results to review later. Now you need a way of saving the results to a file. This is where redirection comes in. You can use the redirection character (>) to redirect the output from the console to a file that you specify, like so:

```
> find / -name *.jpg ¦ grep 'wallpaper' > wallpaper.txt
```

If you want to add additional information to the end of an existing file, you can use a pair of angle brackets rather than just one. For example:

```
> ls -l \home\user  >> mydir.txt
```

Controlling Processes

Each time you run an application on the Eee PC, that application starts one or more processes. Xandros also has its own processes, such as those in the X Window System. Some of these processes start when the system starts.

Using the top Command

To see what processes are currently running, run the `top` command:

```
> top
```

Figure 11.3 shows the output from the top command. The top few lines provide system status, some of which information is of more use on a multiuser system (such as the number of users). Still, this is all useful stuff. You can tell at a glance how much memory is being consumed and how much is left. You can also see the total number of tasks.

```
┌─────────────────────────────────────────────────────────────────────────┐
│ ○     user@Stelios - Shell - Console <2>           ▼  ▲  ✕                │
├─────────────────────────────────────────────────────────────────────────┤
│ Session  Edit  View  Bookmarks  Settings  Help                            │
│ top - 18:36:55 up  8:58,  1 user,  load average: 0.60, 0.48, 0.56      ▲  │
│ Tasks:  96 total,   4 running,  88 sleeping,    0 stopped,   4 zombie     │
│ Cpu(s): 15.0%us,  1.3%sy,  0.0%ni, 83.4%id,  0.0%wa,  0.3%hi,  0.0%si,  0.0%st │
│ Mem:     906716k total,    637076k used,    269640k free,    45552k buffers │
│ Swap:         0k total,         0k used,         0k free,   333352k cached │
│                                                                           │
│   PID USER      PR  NI  VIRT  RES  SHR S %CPU %MEM    TIME+  COMMAND        │
│  1411 root      15   0  292m  30m 4948 S  7.0  3.4  11:39.24 Xorg          │
│  2152 debian-t  15   0 14880  12m 5824 S  4.7  1.4   1:33.04 tor           │
│ 16311 user      15   0  167m  39m  18m S  3.3  4.5   0:42.35 firefox-bin   │
│  1545 user      15   0 37748  20m  15m R  1.0  2.3   6:42.93 kicker        │
│ 18131 user      15   0  2236 1136  860 R  0.3  0.1   0:00.12 top           │
│     1 root      16   0  1564  440  372 S  0.0  0.0   0:00.40 fastinit      │
│     2 root      34  19     0    0    0 S  0.0  0.0   0:00.27 ksoftirqd/0   │
│     3 root      10  -5     0    0    0 S  0.0  0.0   0:01.20 events/0      │
│     4 root      12  -5     0    0    0 S  0.0  0.0   0:00.01 khelper       │
│     5 root      10  -5     0    0    0 S  0.0  0.0   0:00.00 kthread       │
│    25 root      17  -5     0    0    0 S  0.0  0.0   0:00.01 kblockd/0     │
│    26 root      10  -5     0    0    0 S  0.0  0.0   0:00.13 kacpid        │
│   128 root      13  -5     0    0    0 S  0.0  0.0   0:00.00 ata/0         │
│   129 root      20  -5     0    0    0 S  0.0  0.0   0:00.00 ata_aux       │
│   130 root      10  -5     0    0    0 S  0.0  0.0   0:00.13 kseriod       │
│   148 root      25   0     0    0    0 S  0.0  0.0   0:00.00 pdflush       │
│   149 root      15   0     0    0    0 S  0.0  0.0   0:00.00 pdflush    ▼  │
│ ┌──────────┐                                                              │
│ │ ▣ Shell  │                                                              │
│ └──────────┘                                                              │
└─────────────────────────────────────────────────────────────────────────┘
```

FIGURE 11.3

The output from the top command.

The processes themselves are listed by percentage of available CPU cycles in use (the %CPU column). The columns in the listing have the following meaning:

PID: The process ID, which is a unique number assigned to each process. If you want to stop (kill) a process, you need to know this.

USER: The owner of the process. On the Eee PC, it'll either be user or root. Most of the root processes are in fact system processes.

PR: The priority of the process. This number changes depending on the order of processes in the CPU queue.

NI: The "nice" value for the process, which can range from -20 (highest-priority processes) to 19 (lowest-priority processes). You can change the "niceness" of a process by using the renice command, covered at the end of this section. Keep in mind that some high-priority processes, especially system processes, are set that way for a good reason.

VIRT: The amount of virtual memory consumed by the process.

RES: The amount of physical memory consumed by the process.

SHR: The amount of shared memory consumed by the process.

S: The task status. Normally, this is R (running) or S (sleeping).

Occasionally you'll have a z, or zombie process. This is usually junk, and is normally a child process left behind after the parent process was killed.

%CPU: The percentage of available CPU cycles in use.

%MEM: The percentage of available physical memory in use.

TIME+: The amount of time that the process has been running.

COMMAND: The name of the process.

If you press the ? or H key, you'll get help on the top command. If you press the spacebar, top immediately updates its display. It automatically updates every few seconds. Pressing A toggles the display between a "multiwindow" display, which is really just a grouped display, and the normal display.

Entering q quits top and returns your xterm or Konsole window to your control.

Determining Parent and Child Processes with pstree

If you want to see which processes own other processes (parent and child processes), use the pstree command, which provides a tree structure showing the parent/child relationships (see Figure 11.4). If you're running something like Konsole, you can easily scroll back up through the tree. You can also use the pipe character and pipe the output through the less command:

```
> pstree ¦ less
```

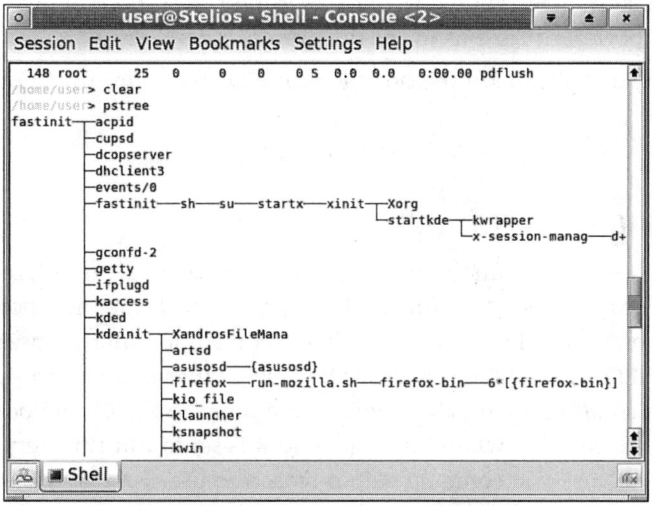

FIGURE 11.4

Output from pstree.

Given that you can now view processes and get their PIDs, you have all the information you need to manage them. You can either change the "niceness" (or priority) of a process that's hogging all of your CPU cycles or outright kill a process that's gone awry.

Changing Process Niceness

The renice command resets the priority of a running process. Priorities run from -20 (high) to 19 (low). You may need to add sudo to this if you get a permission denied. To set Firefox (PID 3918) on my system to a lower priority than its default of 0, I'd run this command:

```
> renice 10 3918
```

Killing a Process

To stop a process, you can use the kill command, which takes the PID as its only argument. To kill PID 3918, for example, you'd use this command:

```
> kill 3918
```

Sometimes, issuing the kill command won't stop a process. Actually, kill is really sending signals to shut down the process. Many processes have some cleanup to do in order to "gracefully" exit, which includes writing buffers, cleaning up temporary files, etc. Database applications, such as mysql, are especially prone to data corruption if suddenly stopped. So, give the process some time to exit.

If, after a reasonable amount of time, the process simply won't shut down, you can stop it cold with kill -9. This is a last resort option and it like shutting off the power (at least as far as the process is concerned).

For example, to kill the process with PID 3918 right now, enter:

```
> kill -9 3918
```

Scheduling with crontab

The crontab command gives you a way to schedule a task to be run at a particular time. Given that the Eee PC is pretty much the most portable and personal of computers, I was having a little trouble imagining a case in which crontab would be useful. The Eee PC will likely be turned on when you need it and turned off pretty much the rest of the time. So the likelihood that the Eee PC will be running when the crontab task is set to run isn't very high. However, just in case you come up with a reason to use crontab, this section presents it. For the example, you'll use the command to back up the /home/user directory onto the MMC-SD drive as a tarball:

```
> tar -cjf /media/MMC-SD/partition1/backup/homebak.tar.bz2 /home/user
```

What you're really doing with `crontab` is editing the crontab file for "user," which lives in the /var/spool/cron/crontabs directory. To do this, you issue the `crontab` command with the `-e` switch:

```
> crontab -e
```

This loads the user crontab file into the nano editor. To set up the `backup` command, you need to first give it a time to execute. You do this by setting the minutes, hours, date, month, and/or day. These take the following values:

minutes: `0` through `59`

hours: `0` through `23`

date: `1` through `31` (be careful because not all months have 31 days)

month: `0` though `11`

day: `0` (Sunday) through `6` (Saturday)

You can also use the * wildcard to mean "all" for these settings.

So, to back up the home directory every day at noon, enter a line with nano that looks like this:

```
0 12 * * * tar -cjf /media/MMC-SD/partition1/backup/homebak.tar.bz2
/home/user
```

If you want to schedule more tasks, just put each one on a separate line. When you're done, press Ctrl+X to exit. Nano will ask you if you want to save the file. Press Y to say yes, and then nano will ask if it's okay to save the file in a subdirectory of /tmp. Press Enter and it'll save the file. If you want to change the crontab entry, simply issue `contab -e` again. If you want to take a look at your current crontab settings, enter this command:

```
> crontab -l
```

You can remove the current crontab settings by using this command:

```
> crontab -r
```

Another way to schedule tasks, which probably makes more sense on the Eee PC, is to use Anacron. Anacron doesn't rely on specific times or days, but rather you can give it a period. For example, every seven days you could run the same `backup` command. The only catch is that Anacron isn't on the Eee PC by default. However, the Debian repositories listed in Chapter 8, "Getting More Linux Applications," do reference Anacron, so you can install it by using the Synaptic Package Manager.

The `anacron` command is run automatically at bootup. The configuration file is called anacrontab, and is in the /etc/ directory. You need to use the `sudo` command to edit it. The syntax for the anacrontab file is a little different from cron, and consists of the period (in days), the delay after its run at bootup before running the task, some arbitrary name you assign to the task, and the command itself. Instead of the period being the number of days, you can also set it to run monthly with @monthly. The delay is really important, and you should give it several minutes. Attempting to run a command while booting can have unpredictable, and potentially bad, effects. The name you assign can't have spaces, so use the old UNIX trick of substituting an underscore for a space (for example, my_backup_job).

When you edit the anacrontab file, you'll find some entries already in there. Simply make yours the next line after the others. These entries also provide examples.

Quick Reference

The following is a very abridged, noncomprehensive quick reference to the Linux commands discussed in this and other chapters. For detailed command information, use the man and info commands. This is just a "cheat sheet" to get you by until you're comfortable with these commands.

alias

To create a command:

```
> alias newcommand='oldcommand -arguments'
```

To display existing aliases:

```
> alias
```

 tip To delete an existing alias, see **unalias.**

apt-cache

To search through the existing APT database:

```
> aptcache search package_name
```

To display information about a package:

```
> aptcache show package_name
```

To display dependencies for a package:

```
> aptcache depends package_name
```

apt-get

To install new packages:

```
> sudo apt-get install package_name
```

To remove a package:

```
> sudo apt-get remove package_name
```

To (attempt to) upgrade all packages:

```
> sudo apt-get upgrade
```

To update the APT database:

```
> sudo apt-get update
```

To delete old package installation files:

```
> sudo apt-get clean
```

bzip2

To compress a file (the file is replaced by the compressed file unless you use the -k switch):

```
> bzip2 -k filename.ext
```

cat

To list a file:

```
> cat filename.ext
```

cd

To change directories:

```
> cd /directory/path
```

chmod

To change permissions for a file or directory (a = all, u = user, g = group, r = read, w = write, x = executable):

```
> chmod a+rwx filename.ext
```

chown

To change ownership of a file to "user":

```
> chown user filename.ext
```

clear

To clear the screen:

```
> clear
```

cp

To copy files:

```
> cp filename.ext /directory/path/
```

crontab

To edit the crontab file to schedule a task (command) to recur at a given time:

```
> crontab -e
```

df

To display the amount of free space in the file system:

```
> df
```

diff

To show the differences between two text files:

```
> diff file1.txt file2.txt
```

dpkg

To install an installation package (DEB file) on the local file system:

```
> dpkg -i packagename.deb
```

To remove an installed application (but not the configuration files):

```
> dpkg -r packagename
```

To remove an installed application, including the configuration files:

```
> dpkg -R packagename
```

exit

To exit from an xterm or Konsole window:

```
> exit
```

find

To find a file in the file system, starting from the specified directory:

```
> find /directory/path -name 'filename.ext'
```

free

To see current memory usage:

```
> free
```

grep

To search a file for a specific text string:

```
> grep "search string" filename.txt
```

gzip

To compress a file and replace it with the compressed version (this is an older compression tool):

```
> gzip filename.ext
```

help

To list Bash shell commands:

```
> help
```

info

To display the manual (or, if it doesn't exist, the man page) for a specific command:

```
> info command_name
```

kill

To stop (kill) a specific process:

```
> kill PID
```

less

To display the contents of a text file, allowing you to navigate through the file:

```
> less filename.txt
```

ln

To create a "hard" link to another directory:

```
> ln /target/directory/path/ link_name
```

To create a symbolic link to another directory:

```
> ln -s /target/directory/path/ link_name
```

ls

To list the contents of a directory (or the current directory if no directory path is given):

```
> ls [/directory/path]
```

To list all files, including hidden files:

```
> ls [/directory/path] -a
```

To list information about the files:

```
> ls -l
```

man

To display the man page for a specific command:

```
> man command_name
```

mkdir

To create a directory:

```
> mkdir directory_name
```

mv

To move a file from one directory to another:

```
> mv filename.ext /directory/path/
```

printenv

To list the current environment variables and their definitions:

```
> printenv
```

pstree

To view a tree of parent and child processes:

```
> pstree
```

renice

To change the priority, -19 (high) to 20 (low), of a running process:

```
> renice priority PID
```

rm

To remove a file:

```
> rm filename.ext
```

rmdir

To remove a directory:

```
> rmdir MyDir
```

sudo

To run a command with root privileges:

```
> sudo command
```

tar

To bundle a group of files into a compressed tarball:

```
> tar  cjf filename.tar.bz2 /path/directory/
```

top

To display the currently running processes:

```
> top
```

unalias

To remove an alias:

```
> unalias alias_name
```

which

To provide the location of an application in the path:

```
> which application
```

Summary

This chapter covered the basics of the Bash shell and a set of the most commonly used Linux commands. If you are new to Linux, mark this chapter as it will be a good reference. You'll come back to it time and again as you master the command line. If you decide to try one of the other versions of Linux covered in the next chapter, this command reference will still be useful.

12

Loading Other Linux Distributions

This chapter introduces three other flavors of Linux that you can run on the Eee PC. Two of them, Ubuntu Eee and Pupeee, are maintained by volunteers. The third, Mandriva Linux, is a commercial offering from Mandriva S.A. The Mandriva Linux One version (which is free) is a "Live CD" that can also be installed on the system. A live CD is a complete version of the operating system that can be booted and run entirely from the CD.

If you're seriously considering switching your Eee PC's operating system, take a look at this chapter and the next two (Chapter 13 covers switching to OpenSolaris, and Chapter 14 covers switching to Windows). You'll probably want to add a DVD R/W unit with a USB interface as well, as discussed in Chaper 3. Most of the OS distributions come as an ISO file, which is intended for a CD or DVD. This chapter also covers how to load an ISO file onto a flash drive.

This chapter begins by explaining how to restore Xandros on your Eee PC, in case you change your mind about using any of the operating systems covered in this or the following few chapters or you encounter problems while switching to a different Linux distribution.

Restoring Xandros

The Eee PC ships with either a support DVD or CD, which is an amazing resource for this little machine. I've used everything on it, and it's one of the reasons that the Eee PC is so versatile. It contains all the Windows drivers, the documentation, and the Eee PC's default Xandros image. I've lost track of the number of times I've reinstalled the default image in the course of writing this book.

Reinstalling does require that you have access to other hardware: either a DVD drive or a Windows-based computer. You can restore directly from the DVD itself or you can put the image on a flash. Either way works fine, but if you anticipate doing this more than once, you should consider the flash drive method. It's much faster and more convenient. The only catch is that you need access to a Microsoft Windows machine to put the Xandros operating system image on the flash drive.

Restoring from a Flash Drive

You should invest in a 2GB flash drive if you want to use one for re-imaging. The Asus documentation has ominous notes about the Eee PC sometimes not recognizing flash drives with more than 2GB of storage.

Creating a Bootable Flash Drive

To place the Xandros image on a flash drive plugged into a Windows machine, pop the Asus Support DVD into the drive of a Windows machine and wait for the DVD to autorun. If you have turned off autorun, using Windows Explorer, access the DVD and double-click Setup. After the support application appears, click the Utilities tab and then click the Asus Linux USB Flash Utility button. On the next screen, select to Copy Eee PC Image Files to USB flash and Make it Bootable. Click the Run button. If prompted to insert the Recovery DVD, do so.

The next screen warns you that this process will delete everything from the flash drive and asks whether you want to proceed. Click the Yes button and you're on your way. When the Confirm dialog box appears, follow the instructions and remove and reinsert the flash drive. Click Retry to complete the copy process. When the Success dialog box appears, click OK.

Now for the fun part:

1. Plug the flash drive into your Eee PC and boot the computer.

2. Press the F2 key at the prompt to enter the BIOS configuration screens.

3. Use the arrow key to navigate to the Advanced tab and make sure all of the hardware is enabled.

4. Also under the Advanced tab, set the OS installation option to Start.

5. Use the arrow key to navigate to the Boot tab and, under Hard Disk Drives, make the USB drive the 1st Drive in the list. Under Boot Device Priority, select the USB drive as the 1st Boot Device.

6. Press F10 to save the changes and continue to boot.

7. You'll be prompted to indicate whether you want to reinstall the images. Type **yes** and press Enter. When you've completed the process, unplug the flash drive and, on next bootup, make sure that the BIOS settings are returned to boot 1st from the internal drive and that the internal drive is 1st in the boot order. Also, under the Advanced tab, set the OS Installation to Finished.

Restoring from the DVD

To restore from a DVD:

1. Attach a DVD drive with a USB connector to your Eee PC, insert the recovery DVD (or support DVD, if your Eee PC shipped with a single DVD), and reboot the machine.

2. Press F2 when you see the prompt to launch the the BIOS configuration screens.

3. Use the arrow key to navigate to the Advanced tab and set OS Installation to Start.

4. Use the arrow key to navigate to the Boot tab and, under Boot Device Priority, select the DVD drive as the 1st Boot Device.

5. Press F10 to save the changes and continue to boot.

6. You'll be prompted to indicate whether you want to reinstall the images. Type **yes** and press Enter.

When the operation is complete, make sure you change the boot order in the BIOS so that the internal drive is 1st on next reboot. Also, on the Advanced tab, set OS Installation to Finished.

Comparing the Various Distributions

The following table provides a quick look at the three Linux distributions discussed in this chapter.

Distribution	Supports 2 GB?	Best Features	Worst Features
Mandriva Linux One	No	Has excellent support for Eee PC hardware.	Free version lacks some important features, such as printing support, and lacks a large number of package repositories.
Pupeee	Yes	Will run from a flash drive or CD as a plug-in operating system. Runs extremely well on 512 MB systems.	Spartan GUI and configuration files, if saved, take up significant space.
Ubuntu Eee	Yes	Supports Eee PC wireless and video. Has huge base of respositories for installing software.	Implementation has a few bugs; for example, the battery life indication is useless and the wireless light is always on. However, the web site provides workarounds for problems.

Mandriva Linux One

Mandriva Linux is an absolute gem and, if you don't mind plunking down the $89 USD (69 EUR), Mandriva Linux Power Pack is probably the best operating system for the Eee PC. The Mandriva Linux One installation, which is a free "live" version of the software, provides pretty much everything you need, with all the drivers the Eee PC requires. However, it lacks a lot of other things that you might want, such as printer configuration. I'll cover only how to install it from a Live CD; however, you'll find all the information you need to install networks, flash drives, and so forth at http://wiki.mandriva.com/en/Docs/Installing_Mandriva_Linux#Installation_from_Mandriva_Linux_One.

There is also a Mandriva Linux Free version, but it lacks the drivers that come with Mandriva Linux One to support the Eee PC.

One of the best features of Mandriva Linux One or Power Pack is the Metisse window manager. With Metisse, you can scale individual windows, including their fonts, so that larger windows can fit within the small Eee PC screen. This is an elegant solution to limited display resolution.

Frankly, Mandriva Linux Power Pack is my candidate for best Linux OS for the Eee PC. It's well stocked with applications, knows all about the Eee PC's hardware, and can do some amazing things. However, if you want to use Mandrive Linux One as your operating system, you'll need to consider if you can live without printer support or extensive software repositories.

Installing Mandriva Linux One

You can download Mandriva Linux One from http://www.mandriva.com. Simply burn the ISO file to a CD and you're ready to begin. The installation is extremely straightforward. Drop the CD into an attached USB CD drive and reboot the Eee PC. Press F2 at the prompt and set the following in the BIOS setup screens:

- On the Advanced tab, enable all hardward and set OS Installation to Finish.
- On the Boot tab, under Hard Disk Drives, make the USB drive the 1st Drive in the list. Under Boot Device Priority, select the USB drive as the 1st Boot Device.

Press F10 to save the changes and continue to boot. Mandriva Linux will boot itself from the CD. After the desktop is active, click the Live Install icon on the desktop (see Figure 12.1). I selected to use the entire disk. Check the latest on partitioning and file systems in the various wikis and forums for the partitions and file systems that are currently recommended.

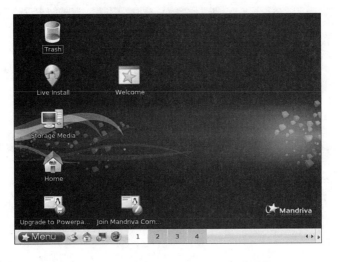

FIGURE 12.1

Starting the Mandriva Linux installation.

Once Live Install begins, you can pick the various language and regional options to run on your Eee PC. Pay close attention to your login account name, password, and administrative password settings. You'll need those after the installation is complete (this isn't like Xandros, for which you don't have to log in). After installation is complete, remove the CD, reboot, and reset your BIOS boot settings.

After you've logged in, you need to set up your network (you may be prompted before login). Choose Menu, Tools, System Tools, Configure Your Computer. You'll be prompted for the administrative password. In the Mandriva Linux Control Center window, click Network & Internet. Select Set Up a New Network Interface and click Next. In the next window, shown in Figure 12.2, select either Ethernet or Wireless and click Next. For wireless,the utility will scan for networks and allow you to select any of those that are detected. You can enter you security settings (if any) and set Mandriva Linux One to automatically connect to a designated wireless network on bootup.

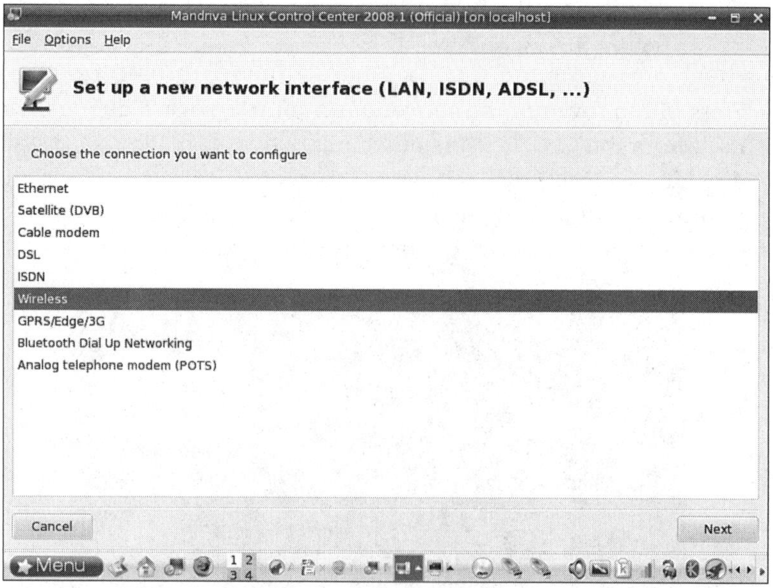

FIGURE 12.2

Mandriva Linux wireless configuration.

Metisse

The Metisse 3D window manager, shipped with Mandriva Linux, lets you shrink any given window and its fonts to fit the screen. The more you shrink the window, the fuzzier the text will become. However, you can shrink things quite a bit and still have readable text.

Aside from shrinking windows, Metisse does some amazingly cool and useful things

> **note** Actually, Mandriva Linux comes with two 3D window managers: Metisse and Compiz Fusion. Compiz Fusion is quite similar to Beryl, which, as discussed in Chapter 6, is a 3D window manager that you can run under Xandros.

that can make working on the 701 or 900 series screen a lot easier. Like the KDE, Metisse has virtual desktops. However, it has nine of them instead of the default two with the KDE. Also, you can rotate screens, navigate through a table of screens, and even clone windows. The cost of all this is processing power, so the Eee PC will respond a little, though not painfully, sluggishly. Figure 12.3 shows some of the windows effects available in Metisse.

You can activate Metisse by choosing Menu, Tools, System Tools, Configure Your Computer. Once again, you'll need your administrator password. Click Hardware, and then click Configure 3D Desktop Effects. From there, you can select Metisse. You need to log out and then log in again to reset the X Window System server.

Right-click the corner of any window, and you'll get a number of arrows with labels such as Scale, Z-Rotate, and Resize. Drag the mouse pointer in any of the directions shown and the magic happens. You'll be able to rotate windows and scale them, which is the trick you need with smaller screens.

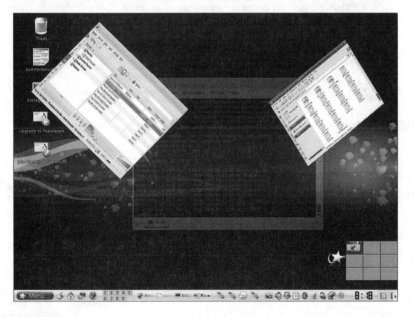

FIGURE 12.3

Metisse windows effects.

Right-click the title bar of any window and you'll get a menu of options, including the ability to set the transparency of the window. You can also use this menu to rotate in the third dimension, making 3D windows.

The widget at the lower right, aside from being your access to the nine virtual desktops, can expand to full screen so that you can easily arrange things between windows. If you have a mouse attached to the Eee PC, simply put your mouse pointer over it and rapidly spin the mouse wheel. If you're using an Eee PC 900 or higher, you can use two-finger scrolling. Figure 12.4 shows the nine virtual desktops in the "table view."

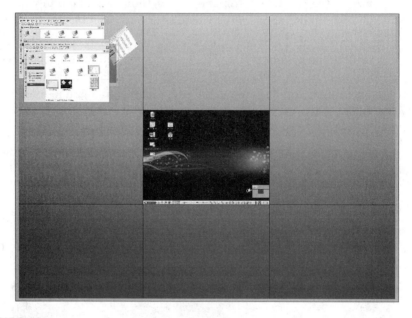

FIGURE 12.4

Metisse table view of virtual desktops.

If you want to know more about what Metisse can do, check out its documentation at http://insitu.lri.fr/metisse/docs/using.html. I think it's the most innovative windows manager I've ever seen.

tip No screen-capture program works in Metisse. However, screen-capture capability is built in through the Super(Windows)+F key combination. The full screen is saved to a JPG image in your home directory. The utility can't overwrite an existing snapshot, so you need to rename it before you take another.

Pupeee

Pupeee, which is a derivative of Puppy Linux, is so lightweight that you can carry it around on a fairly compact flash drive.

Suppose that you're using Windows but you'd like a Linux distribution that you can boot when you want to use a Linux application. Or suppose that you want another version of Linux to play with, or that you have a 2GB version of the Eee PC and want a smaller, "lighter" operating system. Pupeee is the ideal operating system for any of these situations.

Pupeee loads into a mere 256MB of memory, and it loads the entire OS into memory on bootup. Moreover, it includes a whole lot of stuff, including:

- AbiWord (word processor)
- SeaMonkey (a scaled-down Firefox browser)
- CD- and DVD-ripping software
- Simple graphics applications
- xine media player
- Audacity audio editor

Figure 12.5 shows some of the other applications included in the Eee PC version of Puppy Linux.

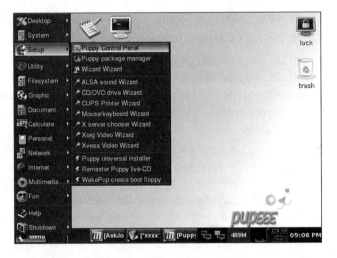

FIGURE 12.5

Some of the applications in little Pupeee.

But wait, there's more! Pupeee also has driver support for the Eee PC's hardware, so wireless configuration is trivial. It also easily fits on even the 701's diminutive screen.

Pupeee is kind of self perpetuating: launch it and you can then install it easily on something else, such as a flash drive.

You can get the ISO disk image file from http://puppylinux.ca/members/ Pupeee/. This is based on Puppy 3.01, which probably won't be anything close to current by the time you read this. Your best approach is to do a Google search for Pupeee and pick the one that has all the drivers.

When you have the ISO file, you can burn it to a CD or write it to to a flash drive and make the flash drive bootable. Boot up the system and press F2 to enter the BIOS when prompted. On the Advanced tab, make sure that all hardware is enabled and that the the OS installation option is set to Start. Also, make sure that boot device (CD or flash drive) is first in the boot priority. Press F10 to save and exit, and you're on your way. Pupeee boots up very quickly, and loads into the Eee PC's memory. You'll be asked to pick a keyboard language and graphics resolution, and that's it.

Configuring wireless is just about as easy, as Pupeee knows about the Eee PC's Atheros wireless hardware:

1. Launch the Puppy Control Panel by choosing Menu, Setup, Puppy Control Panel, as shown in Figure 12.5 (the window manager panel autohides on the bottom of the screen, so just place the mouse cursor there).

2. From the Control Panel, click the Connect button.

3. Click the Network Wizard.

4. On the Puppy Network Wizard page, click the ath0 button.

5. On the next wizard page, click the Wireless button. Clicking the Scan button will find any wireless networks in range, and then you can select the network you want and create a profile to link to the network (as shown in Figure 12.6). You can also enter any security configuration information.

6. When you save the profile, click Back and then test it and set it to AutoDHCP (if that's the type of network).

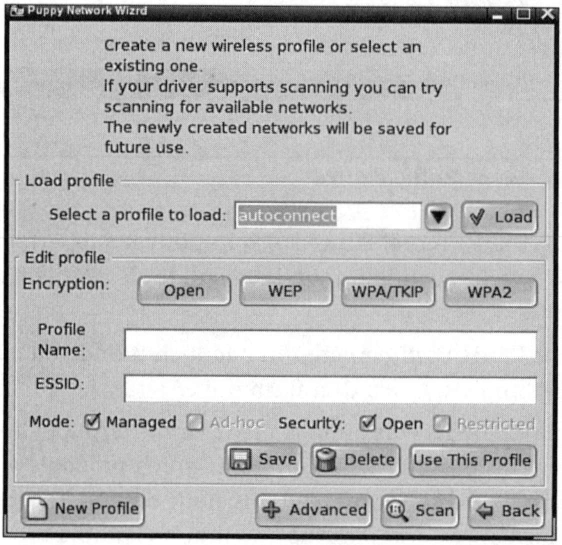

FIGURE 12.6

Configuring wireless in Pupeee.

When you plug in a storage device in Pupeee, it does not automount. You can mount it by choosing Menu, File System, Pmount Mount/Unmount Drives. Simply plug in your flash drive, MMC-SD card, or other device, and click Refresh. The Pmount Puppy Drive Mounter, shown in Figure 12.7, scans the hardware and provides a list of available devices. Click the button to the right of each entry to mount it (it will turn green when successfully mounted). Click again to unmount the device.

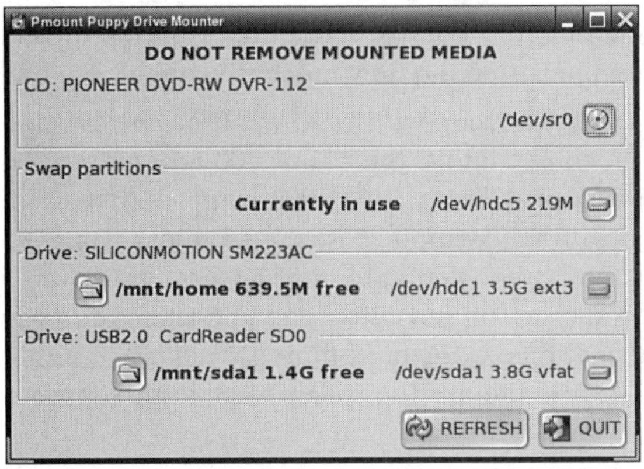

FIGURE 12.7
Mounting devices in Pupeee.

Finally, you might want to build another installation of Pupeee on a CD, flash drive, etc. You can do that through the Puppy Universal Installer. Choose Menu, Setup, Puppy Universal Installer. You can choose the device to which you wish to install Pupeee.

Looking over the vast array of utilities that comes with Pupeee, Pupeee appears to be best suited (aside from fitting even the most modest Eee PC quite nicely) for troubleshooting networks, broken computers, and so forth. It also has a lot of productivity applications.

When you shut down Pupeee, it'll offer to write its files and so forth to your Eee PC. Consider this offer carefully, as it'll take up about 600MB or more.

Installing Ubuntu

I've run the KDE version (Kubuntu) of Ubuntu for a while, so I was looking forward to seeing Ubuntu on the Eee PC. I wasn't disappointed. I chose to run Ubuntu Eee, but EeeXbuntu is available as well. Ubuntu Eee is located at http://www.ubuntu-eee.com, and is a CD-sized, live version of the operating system packaged as an ISO file. Since it is a live CD, you can choose to either run it directly from the CD or install from the CD.

Boot up the system and press F2 to enter the BIOS when prompted. On the Advanced tab, make sure that all hardware is enabled and that the the OS installation option is set to Start. Also, ensure that the CD/DVD is first in the boot priority. Press F10 to save and exit and, when prompted, choose to install.

Installation is extremely simple. You will select the language and keyboard, as well as the usual username, password, and so forth. The only slightly tricky spot is when you select the installation disk. Make sure that you select /dev/sda1 if you are installing on the internal SSD. When I installed it, I was left with about 1.2GB of free space on the SSD at the end. That's fairly impressive by itself, considering how much is installed.

Ubuntu Eee is a version with GNOME. It has a very clean interface, with short, compact menus, that fits the 701 or 900 series nicely. Figure 12.8 shows the GNOME desktop. Ubuntu Eee comes completely stocked with basic applications and with the Synaptic Package Manager pointed to repositories. For example, after I had configure my wireless connection, when I pulled up an Internet radio station in Firefox and told Firefox to open the M3U file with /usr/bin/rhythmbox (the built-in music player), it immediately launched Synaptic to find the missing codecs to play the streaming media.

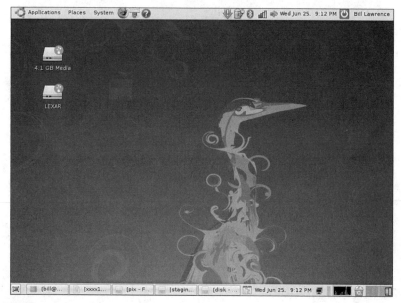

FIGURE 12.8

Ubuntu Eee, sporting one of the brown themes.

Some of the other applications onboard are the ubiquitous OpenOffice.com (without which I couldn't have written this book), Firefox, Mozilla, Thunderbird, and Pidgin—pretty much the basics of Internet and productivity software. Conspicuously missing are GIMP and K3b, although there is a CD/DVD writer.

If you're concerned about your Eee PC being stolen and someone getting access to proprietary or valuable data, you'll be happy to know that you can install the TrueCrypt encryption package via Synaptic. Unlike under Xandros, TrueCrypt works under Ubuntu Eee.

Getting onto wireless is trivial, as the hardware is supported. Simply choose System, Network to open the Network Settings window, shown in Figure 12.9. You can't make any changes until you click the Unlock button and enter your password. Click Wireless Connection and then click the Properties button. Make sure roaming mode is enabled. I had to reboot at this point to get Ubuntu to find my wireless network, and I then I got the network icon in the top panel. Right-click this icon and choose Edit Wireless Networks. You can then configure your network by selecting it and adding the necessary security information.

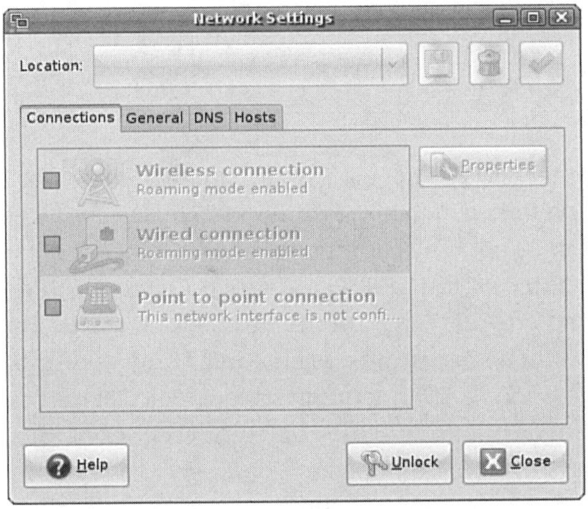

FIGURE 12.9

You need to unlock the network settings with your password.

That's about all that you need to do. Almost everything else just seems to work, including Bluetooth. The following are a few of the issues that I encountered:

- The battery indicator is reporting meaningless values.
- It doesn't play DVD movies, but that seems to be a codec problem.
- I'm still struggling with GPS and the GPS daemon, gpsd.
- Shutdown doesn't work properly, and you must press the off button to get power to go off. There is a workaround for this posted on the Ubuntu Eee site.
- The wireless light remains lit even when wireless isn't enabled. Again, there is a workaround on the Ubuntu Eee site.

In fact, Ubuntu Eee is almost as functional as Xandros. Actually, some things that don't work in Xandros work quite well in Ubuntu, such as the Scribus desktop publishing system. This would not run under Xandros, but downloaded directly from the Ubuntu repositories and ran perfectly.

Ubuntu Eee comes with a limited, though very nice, set of themes and wallpaper. You can add your own if desired, but first try the brown and tan themes that come by default.

While I think the commercial version of Mandriva is a wonderful option for an operating system for the Eee PC, Ubuntu Eee is almost as good (albiet a little buggy at this point). Because of the vast amount of software available, Ubuntu Eee is my choice for an operating system for my Eee PC. The default Xandros Linux is certainly useful and well tuned to the machine, but Ubuntu Eee is elegant and provides more software choices. Over time, the small glitches will be ironed out and it will be as completely functional as Xandros.

Summary

This chapter covered how to restore Xandros onto your Eee PC, which is a good thing to know about regardless of whether you ever try another operating system or not. The chapter also covered installing three alternative versions of Linux for the Eee PC: Mandriva Linux One, Pupeee, and Ubuntu Eee. Depending on your Eee PC configuration and tastes, you may find that you like one of these better than the default Xandros distribution. The next chapter covers a true UNIX operating system (Solaris) and the following chapter covers the installation of three different versions of Microsoft Windows. So, if you want something other than Linux, you have a lot of choices.

Loading OpenSolaris

OpenSolaris is the Sun Microsystems version of the UNIX. While Linux is very similar to UNIX, they aren't the same. If you ever wanted to learn about UNIX or you just happen to be a UNIX user, OpenSolaris is a great choice for the Eee PC operating system. It comes with OpenOffice and has enough applications to be useful for general computing.

When I first thought about this chapter, I imagined that I would write about loading Mac OS on the Eee PC, and thus began researching what would be required to run Leopard on the Eee PC. However, as luck would have it, OpenSolaris became available at just the right time. Unlike OS X Leopard, there are no licensing infringement issues involved in running OpenSolaris on the Eee PC. Also, Sun Microsystems and the OpenSolaris community have taken an interest in the Eee PC, so you'll find blogs and web sites devoted to this. Moreover, drivers and workarounds are freely available. OpenSolaris has a pretty big community to support this sort of stuff, with more than 60,000 registered members.

IN THIS CHAPTER

- Install OpenSolaris on the Eee PC
- Fix the internal keyboard.
- Install the wireless driver
- Install OpenOffice

For those unfamiliar with Solaris in general, it's Sun Microsystems' version of UNIX (derived from UNIX V). Solaris is a very powerful, mature operating system. OpenSolaris is an open source version of Solaris that's packed with lots of built-in goodies, such as a graphical package manager. In fact, I'm writing this chapter using OpenOffice while running my Eee PC under OpenSolaris, and I used the OpenSolaris screenshot tool to take the screenshots of the desktop for this chapter.

Challenges to Running OpenSolaris on the Eee PC

Running OpenSolaris on the Eee PC does pose some challenges that you should be aware of before you decide whether to embark on installing it:

- OpenSolaris does not have the driver for the Atheros wireless built into the Eee PC. However, you can easily download and install it, as described in the "Fixing the Wireless Issue" section later in the chapter. This does mean that you'll either have to download it first or have access to another computer.

- The internal keyboard does not work on some Eee PC models (such as my 701 4G) unless you unload and reload the keyboard driver module. You can't do this until you've installed OpenSolaris, which makes trying to install OpenSolaris rather daunting. The workaround is to plug in a USB keyboard for the installation, after which you can then modify some startup files to unload and reload the keyboard driver module, as described in the "Fixing the Keyboard Issue" section later in this chapter.

- The Eee PC sound hardware isn't supported by OpenSolaris. However, you can get it to work by using the latest Open Sound System driver. I don't recommend doing that just yet as it isn't stable, so I don't cover it in this chapter. By the time you read this, things may be a bit more stable. It works, but folks are reporting high CPU load from Open Sound System (and on the Eee PC, that's a bad thing). Check http://www.4front-tech.com/download.cgi for OpenSolaris versions.

- Suspend/resume doesn't work (yet). So, you won't be able to save your battery during slack times by suspending operation.

Downloading and Installing OpenSolaris

Note that after OpenSolaris 2008.05 is loaded on a 4GB Eee PC, you have about 630MB of free space on the solid-state drive. That's not a lot of space compared to the Linux operating systems, so you'll need to by very choosy about what applications you'll install. Also, you'll really want an MMC-SD flash memory card for additional storage. Like some of the Linux operating systems, OpenSolaris is available as a Live CD. This means that after you write the ISO file for OpenSolaris to a CD, you load and run the operating system from the CD before actually installing it. This gives you a chance to give OpenSolaris a try before committing to installation and, if you don't like OpenSolaris, your Xandros installation remains intact.

You'll need the following to install OpenSolaris on the Eee PC:

- A USB CD drive
- A USB keyboard (for some Eee PC models)
- A USB flash drive (for the drivers)

You can download OpenSolaris from http://www.opensolaris.org/index.html. This is a sizable download, over 685MB, so it'll take a while. It's an ISO file, so you need to burn this to a CD before installing. This is also a Live CD, so it will actually boot into OpenSolaris before the installation. (This is where the USB keyboard comes into play for some models, because, until you've loaded OpenSolaris and fixed the problem, the Eee PC's keyboard won't work.)

If you are downloading the ISO file using Xandros, you'll want something like K3b (which is covered in Chapter 9, "Must-Have Utilities"). On Windows machines, you can use applications such as Nero to "burn" the CD.

Before you begin, back up any information that you have on your Eee PC. The installation will overwrite everything on the solid-state drive.

When you're ready to install, make sure the USB keyboard is plugged in and then load the CD into the drive. By the way, the installation will go much faster if you make sure that you don't have an MMC-SD card in the slot. Some folks have reported that the installation takes many hours if there is an MMC-SD card in the slot; however, OpenSolaris installed in less than an hour when I did it with an MMC-SD card in the slot.

note If you want to restore Xandros at any point, see the section, "Restoring Xandros" in Chapter 12.

Start the Eee PC and press F2 when prompted. You'll want to set the following under Advanced: all devices enabled under Onboard Devices Configuration, and OS Installation set to Start. Tab over to Boot Order and set the CD drive to the top of the list. Press F10, save the changes, and exit. OpenSolaris will load from the CD. After configuring the "Live CD" desktop, you'll see an Install OpenSolaris icon on the desktop (see Figure 13.1). Double-click the icon to start installing OpenSolaris on the Eee PC.

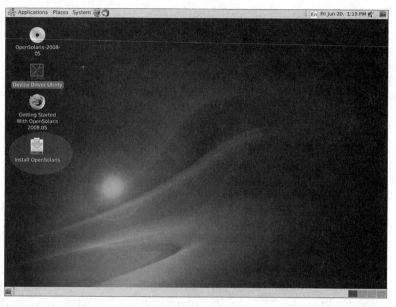

FIGURE 13.1
The Install OpenSolaris icon.

As you go through the installation process, click Next on each OpenSolaris Installer screen until you reach the Where Should OpenSolaris Be Installed? screen, shown in Figure 13.2. Choose to use the whole disk and then click Next.

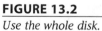

FIGURE 13.2
Use the whole disk.

Select the Region, Location, Time Zone, and so forth, and click Next. Select your locale (and language) and then click Next to move on to the Users page. The Users page is a big deal for OpenSolaris. You need to set your username and password. This is one of the two accounts (along with the password for root privileges) you'll have on the Eee PC. You'll need that administrative password to do any of the tasks you'd normally do under sudo in the OpenSolaris environment. In this environment, you'll need to use the su (substitute user) command, and you'll become the administrative account after you enter the password. When you've set this, click Next.

The Installation screen tells you that OpenSolaris will take up 3GB of space; however, it really takes up 3.4GB. Look over everything to make sure it's correct (if it's not, click Back to return to the previous screens to fix things). If it's all okay, click the Install button and go make coffee.

The CD whirs and chugs for about 40 minutes (longer if you didn't take out your MMC-SD chip) and eventually opens the Installation Is Complete screen, as shown in Figure 13.3. Click Reboot and be patient.

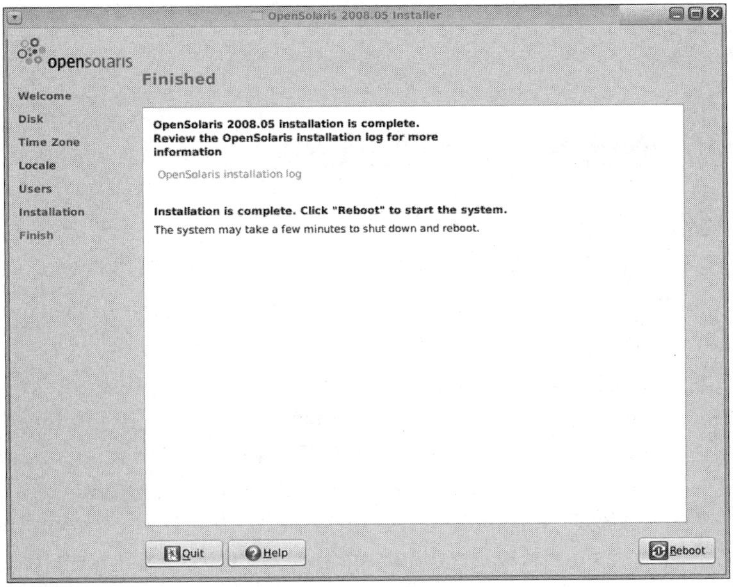

FIGURE 13.3

Time to reboot.

There's a lot more to load and it'll take a lot longer than Xandros or Windows does to load. Eventually, you'll find yourself staring at the lovely, deep blue OpenSolaris wallpaper. Note that this is a GNOME desktop, with the Applications menu in the upper-left corner and four squares in the lower-right corner representing your four virtual desktops (see Figure 13.4).

FIGURE 13.4
Welcome to OpenSolaris.

Fixing the Keyboard and Wireless

Fixing the Keyboard Issue

Fixing the keyboard problem is a fairly trivial matter, though it took me quite a while to track down the problem and the fix on the Internet. You need to unload and then reload the keyboard driver, as follows:

1. Launch a terminal window by choosing Applications, System Tools, Terminal. This opens the Bash shell that you're familiar with from Xandros. Note the $ prompt. This indicates that you're logged in as your account, which doesn't have privileges to change anything outside of your home directories. I'll use the $ and # (root) prompt conventions in the following examples so that you can keep this straight.

2. Enter the following:

   ```
   $ su
   ```

3. When prompted, enter the administrative password you entered during installation. The prompt should now contain the pound sign (#), which denotes that you're running as the administrative account.

4. Enter this command:

   ```
   # modinfo
   ```

5. Scroll up until 99 (in the leftmost column) is visible, as shown in Figure 13.5. That should be the number for the following entry:

```
99 f7fa0000    2a34 101    1   kb8042 (PS/2 Keyboard 1.68, 07/10/18)
```

```
                              Terminal
 File  Edit  View  Terminal  Tabs  Help
 83 f7f4e2c0    e4c  12   1  sad (STREAMS Administrative Driver ')
 85 f7f57000   3694   0   1  consconfig_dacf (Consconfig DACF 1.40)
 86 f7f5b000    3f2c   -  1  usbser (USB generic serial module 1.21)
 87 f7f5f000   2340c   -  1  usba (USBA: USB Architecture 2.0 1.66)
 88 f7f82000   4408  96   1  i915 (I915 DRM driver 1.2)
 89 f7f87000   7c54   -   1  drm (DRM common interfaces 1.3)
 90 f7e16000   118c   -   1  agpmaster (AGP master interfaces v1.7)
 91 f7f8f000   402c   -   1  gfx_private (gfx private interfaces 1.1)
 92 f7f92000  238c 103   1  conskbd (conskbd multiplexer driver 5.69)
 93 f7f95000    3b2c   -  1  kbtrans (kbtrans (key translation) 1.32)
 94 f7f98000  1524 143   1  consms (Mouse Driver for Sun 'consms' 5)
 95 f7e18000   113c  15   1  wc (Workstation multiplexer driver )
 96 f7f9a000.   7cec   -  1  tem (ANSI Terminal Emulator)
 97 f7e1557c    9fc  14   1  iwscn (Workstation Redirection driver )
 98 f7f9e000  133c 100   1  i8042 (i8042 nexus driver 1.41)
 99 f7fa0000  2a34 101   1  kb8042 (PS/2 Keyboard 1.68, 07/10/18)
100 f7f9d8bc    7e4 116   1  mouse8042 (PS/2 Mouse 1.48, 05/10/25)
101 f7fa2000   1b7c   -   1  vuid3ps2 (mouse events to vuid events)
103 f7fb5000   c010  55   1  uhci (USB UHCI Controller Driver 1.59)
107 f7fe3000   dcbc   -   1  ibtl (IB Transport Layer v1.15)
110 f803e000  15b44   -   1  pcmcia (PCMCIA Nexus Support 1.149)
111 f7fd0000   3a9c   0   1  elfexec (exec module for elf 1.128)
117 f7f5edac    2ac  39   1  hubd (USB Hub Driver 1.8)
118 f8080000   74dc   -   1  fctl (SunFC Transport v20080304-1.67)
```

FIGURE 13.5

Look for kb8042.

If not, find the entry for kb8042 (PS/2 Keyboard...) and note that number.

6. Press Enter to jump back to your prompt. Enter the following set of commands:

```
# modunload -i 99
# devfsadm -i kb8042
# modload /kernel/drv/kb8042
```

Your Eee PC's internal keyboard should now work. That's great, but you really want to make this permanent. The basic procedure for this is explained at http://unixsysadmin.net/2008/04/02/solaris-express-on-the-asus-eeepc/, which is the method shown here (with a few modifications):

1. Choose Applications, Accessories, Text Editor and launch a text editor.

2. Use the following for your script (and not what's on the blog page, which has a typo):

```
#!/bin/sh
modunload -i `modinfo¦awk '/kb8042/ {print$1}'`
devfsadm -i kb804
modload /kernel/drv/kb8042
```

3. Save the file as **keyfix** (it'll pop into your home directory).

4. Make keyfix a file belonging to the root account and set it to read/write/execute permissions for that user. Enter the following at the administrative prompt:

```
# chown root keyfix
# chmod u+rwx keyfix
# ls -l
```

You should see something like the following, showing that the ownership and permissions were successfully changed and that it can now execute:

```
-rwxr--r-- 1 root staff      105 2008-06-21 18:46 keyfix
```

5. Copy keyfix to the /etc/init.d/ directory and then link it from the /etc/rc2.d/S99keyfix so that it automatically runs:

```
# cp keyfix /etc/init.d/
# ln /etc/init.d/keyfix /etc/rc2.d/S99keyfix
```

Now, when you reboot, you'll have keyboard support and you'll be able to use your keyboard.

Fixing the Wireless Issue

Fixing the wireless issue is simple procedure:

1. Download the Atheros driver. Go to http://opensolaris.org/os/community/laptop/wireless/ath/. Scroll down and click the binary package link. The file should be ath-0.7.1-pkg.tar.gz.

2. Plug in the flash drive and wait for the desktop to show the icon for the flash drive.

3. Double-click the icon and navigate to the driver file.

4. Open a second file browser and navigate to your home directory.

5. Double-click the compressed driver file and drag the SUNWatheros file to your the other file browser to place the file in your home directory.

6. From an administrative command prompt, issue this command:

```
# pkgadd -d ./SUNWatheros SUNWatheros
```

7. Reboot. When the machine comes up, Solaris will detect your wireless network and prompt you for a security key (if you need one).

Getting OpenOffice.org

You'll probably want to get OpenOffice.org next. This is a roughly 400MB download, which will eat up a lot of your remaining space. However, there are no other office applications onboard with OpenSolaris, so if you want to have a word processor, illustration package, and so forth, you'll need to download OpenOffice.org.

> **note** See Chapter 7 for more details on the OpenOffice.org suite.

Here's where things get just a little dicey. OpenSolaris has a dandy utility called Package Manager, which is very similar to Synaptic, but running it on the Eee PC kills your keyboard (including your USB keyboard). Also, the package manager is very slow. If you launch it, the "starter" icon comes up…and then it goes away, with nothing to tell you that it's loading. Wait several minutes and the package manager will appear. Click Reload to update the repository database, and that update is even slower. When it's done, you'll find OpenOffice.org under the Office category. Right-click it to select it for downloading and then click Install/Update. After exiting from the package manager, the keyboard will work again.

Summary

OpenSolaris is a powerful, but rather large, operating system to run on the Eee PC. It also taxes the processor a bit. However, most things work pretty well. Under System, Preferences, you'll find that the display settings work nicely. Also, you'll find that a lot of the applications you're looking for, such as GIMP, Firefox, and Thunderbird, are already installed. Sun seems at least somewhat engaged in solving problems for this platform (from the forum and bug entries that already exist). Given that, over time, OpenSolaris on the Eee PC will become even more stable. With the addition of OpenOffice.org, you have pretty much everything you need.

Is it practical? Well, it's more practical than trying to run Mac OS Leopard. Also, if you're really a fan of UNIX, it's great to be able to run it on the Eee PC. Besides, it has a very high "geek coolness" factor. It's certainly functional, especially if you download OpenOffice.org as well.

Loading Windows

Switching from Xandros to Windows

Up to this point, most Eee PCs come preloaded with Xandros Linux. Asus estimates that for 2008, the numbers of Eee PCs shipped with Windows XP will grow to be about 60%. Clearly then, XP is a viable option for your Eee PC. Getting an XP equipped Eee PC comes at a price, however. These machines are traditionally a little more costly or have a smaller SSD than a similar model with Xandros Linux. So, if you have a copy of Windows XP that you can load on the Eee PC, buying the comparable Xandros-equipped model and loading XP yourself might be a better option.

Before we begin, it's important to note that your Eee PC will need at least a 4GB SSD for this installation. Also, loading Windows will eat up most of your built-in storage space and leave you with precious little unless you follow the instructions in this chapter to free up some room. On the plus side, you can install many Windows applications on an attached MMC-SD flash card.

Currently, there are a lot of Xandros Linux utilities written specifically for the Eee PC. There are a few Eee PC specific Windows utilities, and the best of these are mentioned in this chapter.

While loading Windows to your built-in SSD will remove Xandros, if you want to run both, it is possible. You can load Windows to a large (4GB or greater) installed MMC-SD flash card and leave Xandros intact. This chapter assumes that you'll be replacing Xandros with Windows. Also, should you wish to return your Eee PC to the Xandros Linux operating system, Chapter 12 covers this process in detail.

Installing Windows XP Home Edition

Installing Windows XP Home Edition on the Eee PC is pretty straightforward and is much like installing XP on a desktop or laptop PC. However, there are a few potentially confusing spots. First off, you need to have the following available:

- A copy of Windows XP Home Edition that has not already been activated
- A USB DVD drive

By default, the Eee PC has its SSD divided into four partitions. As part of this exercise, you'll delete all four partitions so that you have only a single partition for Windows. Here's how to load Windows XP on your Eee PC:

1. Power down your Eee PC.
2. Plug your USB DVD drive into a USB port on your Eee PC.
3. Place the Windows XP DVD into the USB DVD drive, and then start the Eee PC.
4. As the system boots, press the F2 key to enter the setup screen.
5. Choose Advanced, Onboard Devices Configuration, and make sure that all options shown there are enabled.
6. Choose Advanced, OS Installation, and select Start.
7. Change the boot options so that the first drive is the USB DVD drive.
8. Press F10 to save your changes and continue booting your Eee PC.
9. As the system boots, press the Esc key until the Please Select Boot Device screen appears.
10. Select your DVD drive and press Enter.
11. The system will show you the four drive partitions, and you'll need to delete each one. When there are no drive partitions left, proceed.
11. Windows XP will begin the tedious steps of preparing the drive and copying its components over to the Eee PC. Time to make lunch.
12. After you complete the Windows installation and find yourself staring at the green hillside of the default Windows wallpaper, reboot the system.

13. As your Eee PC boots, press F2.

14. When the setup screen appears, go to Advanced, OS Installation, and select Finished. Also, reset the boot order so that the SSD is first.

15. Press F10 to save your changes and reboot.

16. Now the fun begins. You must load all the Eee PC drivers from the Eee PC support DVD or CD. This is an autoloading DVD or CD, so just insert it and wait a bit.

17. Install the ACPI drivers. After this is installed, the support DVD/CD will be able to detect hardware and install the drivers.

18. When the Eee PC Software Support application launches, click the Drivers tab and then click the InstAll Drivers Installation Wizard (see Figure 14.1).

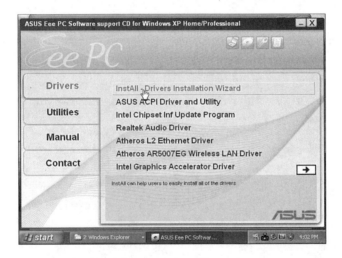

FIGURE 14.1

Selecting the InstAll Drivers Installation Wizard.

19. Choose the Install Drivers Automatically from InstAll (Recommended) radio button and click OK (see Figure 14.2).

20. For each driver that has a "Yes" in the Reboot column (see Figure 14.3), the system must reboot after the installation of that driver. The DVD/CD must remain in the drive during the reboot, and what complicates things is that the DVD/CD has a bootable copy of Linux on it. During each reboot, you will be asked if you want to boot the Linux operating system on the DVD/CD (and you don't) or continue booting from the operating system on the Eee PC (this is the option you want). Choose to skip booting the DVD/CD; that is, type something other the "yes" and press enter. Actually, any key other than "y" will do.

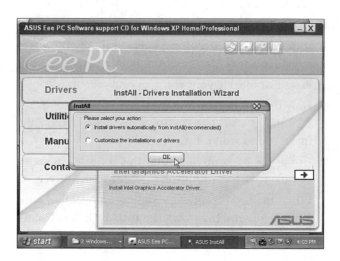

FIGURE 14.2

Selecting to install all drivers automatically.

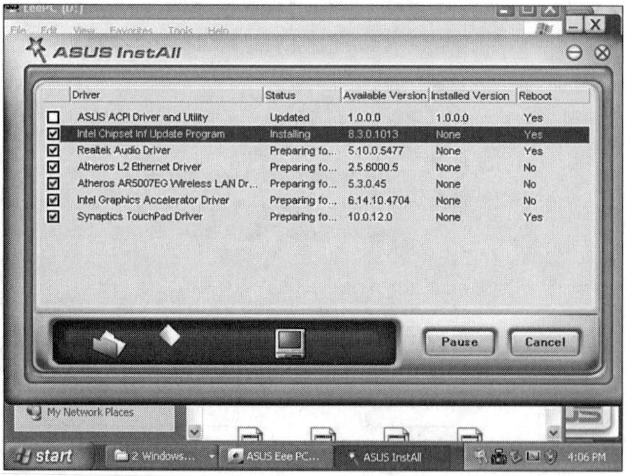

FIGURE 14.3

The driver installation screen.

21. After each driver is installed and Windows has booted, the DVD drive will open. A dialog box will appear, asking you to insert the support CD/DVD.

22. Close the DVD/CD drawer and then click OK (see Figure 14.4). The whole process will start all over again until the last driver is installed (which starts the reboot process again).

FIGURE 14.4

Close the DVD/CD drawer before you click this button!

23. After all the drivers have been loaded and you exit the support application, you're ready to start setting up and optimizing Windows (covered in Chapter 15, "Windows Configuration").

Loading Windows XP Professional

This process is almost identical to the XP process in the previous section, with a couple of additional things:

- You will get an opportunity to set an administrative password during the actual Windows setup.

- When you're done, you'll have a little less free disk space before you begin the optimization process covered in the next chapter. You're starting with only around 670MB of free space on the hard drive.

Loading Windows Vista Home Basic

I approached this installation with anxiety, because I wasn't really sure how well Vista would run on the Eee PC. As is well advertised, Vista is a resource hog and can drag even a fairly powerful machine to its knees. The trick to getting Vista to run well on the Eee PC is to pare down the Vista installation using the vLite utility before you install it. What you'll delete depends a bit on the options you wish to use in Vista. Generally, you can remove any other languages than perhaps English and your native language. Also, you can remove drivers you won't use, such as drivers for printers other than those that you actually have. Speed-wise, a pared-down version runs surprisingly well on the Eee PC's little mobile processor.

A little background before we begin: I loaded Vista on an Eee PC that has a 4GB drive and 2GB of memory. I wouldn't try installing Vista on an Eee PC with less than 1GB of memory, and preferably you should upgrade to 2GB (see Chapter 17 for instructions on adding memory to your Eee PC).

Also, you'll need an additional Windows machine with lots of drive space and a DVD reader/writer attached. You're going to write your "pared down" version of Windows to a DVD when you're done so that you can use that DVD to install Vista on the Eee PC. To write the DVD, you'll need software that can burn a DVD from an ISO file. You can do it with a DVD-ROM and a flash drive, and installing from the flash drive is a little faster, but the DVD installation isn't that slow and it's an easier route.

Follow these steps to install Vista on your Eee PC:

note I used the 1.1.6 version of vLite, which was the stable, production version at the time I wrote this. I ran this on an XP Home Edition machine, so your experience may vary depending on the version of the software and your operating system. If you have questions, refer to the vLite website, which has some brief, but very useful, documentation.

1. Using your desktop or laptop PC, download vLite from http://www.vlite.net/.

2. Create a directory that will hold your pared-down version of Vista. Also, you'll need a temporary directory (vLite will pick one, or you can create one and redirect vLite there) that has a minimum of 8GB of free space. vLite will write a full copy of Vista, which it takes from your genuine Microsoft installation DVD, to the temp directory. It will then use that full copy of Vista in the temp directory to build the pared-down version.

3. Install vLite on your desktop or laptop PC and launch it.

4. On the Start page, vLite asks for the location in which you want to install Vista. Choose to install Vista on your DVD drive.

5. vLite then prompts you to choose the version of Vista you want to install (see Figure 14.5). Given the diminutive size of the Eee PC's built-in storage, I recommend that you choose HOMEBASIC (which is the Basic Home Edition).

6. After you've made your selection, click OK and vLite will copy those files to the temp directory you set up on your desktop's or laptop's hard drive. Be patient, as this process will take a while.

7. After vLite copies the files to the temp directory, it displays the Tasks page, shown in Figure 14.6, which enables you to choose the pages of options that you want to edit to pare down Vista. It also enables you to choose to create an ISO file. Make sure to select the following pages by checking their corresponding check boxes:

   ■ Components

   ■ Tweaks

   ■ Unattended Setup

   ■ Bootable ISO

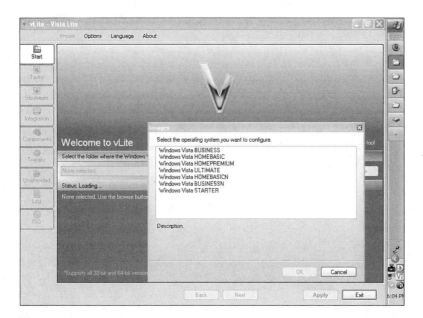

FIGURE 14.5

Choosing the Vista edition. Choose wisely.

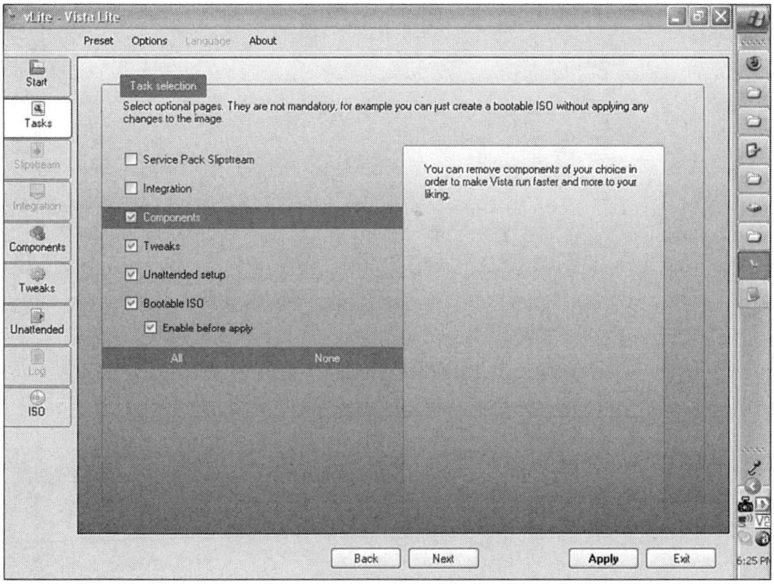

FIGURE 14.6

vLite options you'll need to check.

8. In the Compatibility pop-up window, make sure recommended is selected, then press OK.

9. Once you've selected those options, their icons on the left side of the screen become active, giving you access to their corresponding pages. As you fill in options and click the Next button, each of the icons will highlight in turn The Components icon, and its options, which automatically loaded when you closed the pop-up window.

10. On the Components page, choose the Vista components that you want to remove (see Figure 14.7). Remember, the more you remove, the smaller the installed OS becomes. Easy targets for removal are languages and printer drivers that you won't use. When you've picked what to remove, click Next.

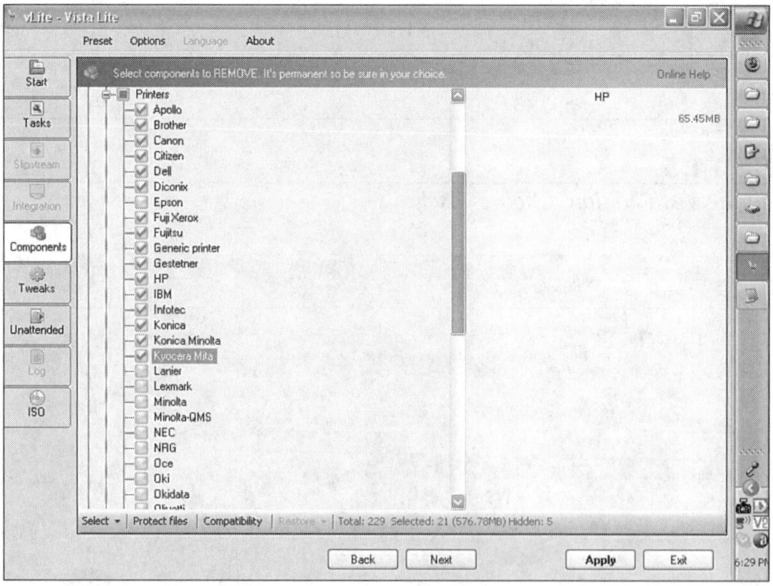

FIGURE 14.7

Some of the options you can choose to keep or cut.

11. The Tweaks page contains options for setting default behaviors for Vista security, system, file explorer, and Internet Explorer. These settings are personal preferences, and won't help reduce the size of Vista. However, they are worth looking though and setting. Press Next when you're done.

> **caution** Use extreme care when removing any option marked "Caution." Don't delete those unless you are absolutely sure you know what you're doing.

12. The Unattended page (see Figure 14.8) has options for presetting your license key, turning off automatic registration, automatically accepting the license, and selecting the temporary trial key (Skip Product Key). You can also enter any personal and organizational information here, such as your name, the machine name, workgroup, etc. If you are sure that you want to keep Vista and use your license key, don't worry about the license setting. If you just want to try Vista for a while, select the temporary trial key. This will give you a few weeks to try it out before you must register. Click Next when you're done.

> **tip** If you don't need the accessibility features or even the IIS web server, take them out. If you want to tear out Internet Explorer (and really, who doesn't?), it's a good idea to have a portable apps system on a flash drive that has Portable Firefox installed. Portable apps are Windows applications (with a menu-driven launcher) that can be installed entirely on a flash drive. Using portable apps gives you the ability to plug-in one of more flash drives with whatever Windows applications you want without using up room to install them on the Eee PC's SSD. This is covered in Chapter 15.

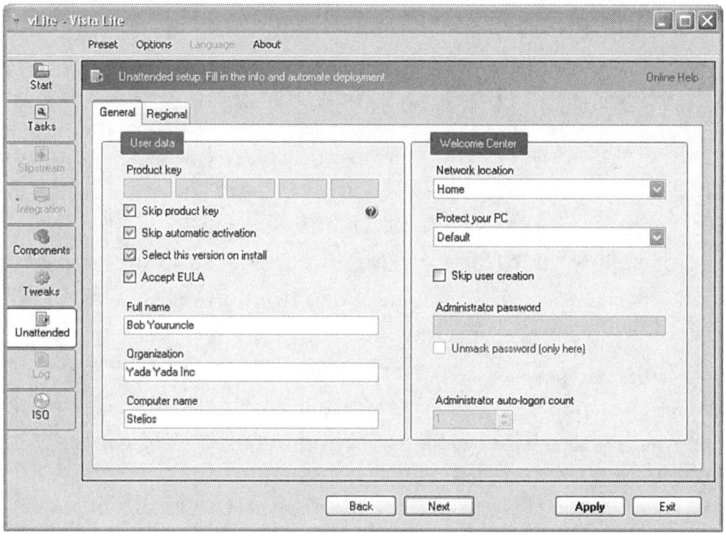

FIGURE 14.8
The Unattended options.

13. The Make Bootable ISO for Testing or Burning page lets you create a bootable ISO file from your pared and tweaked Vista settings. You can then use the ISO file to burn to a DVD or CD (if you get it small enough). Click Make ISO to build the file. Click Apply when this is done. The Apply process will rebuild the temp image to the smaller settings you created.

> **caution** Make sure during the "apply" process that you select to Rebuild One (the Vista version you selected) instead of Rebuild All.

14. At this point, you now have a DVD that you can use to install Vista on the Eee PC (see Figure 14.9). The BIOS setup is the same as for XP Home Edition listed at the beginning of this chapter, meaning that you

> **note** I was able to get Vista down to under 1GB on my first try, and could have done better on subsequent attempts had I been more economical with the options I chose. When installed on the Eee PC, it left a bit less than 1GB of free space on the built-in SSD.

must have the DVD drive first in the boot sequence. You may also need to delete the various Xandros partitions and create a single partition. This is, as you may imagine, a rather lengthy installation.

PREFAB vLITE CONFIGURATIONS

If you don't feel like playing with settings and experimenting, you can hop on over to http://www.eeeuser.com and search for vLite. A number of members have posted their own configurations in a form that you can cut and paste into an INI file for vLite. This preloads the settings, which these kind folks have tried out for you. Read through the whole thread for the posts for the various offerings. You paste the settings listing from the web page into Notepad (or some other text editor) and save it as a file named last session.ini. This file is automatically created after each run. You just copy your last session.ini file to /program files/vlite/presets and overwrite the preset file that vLite made from your first run.

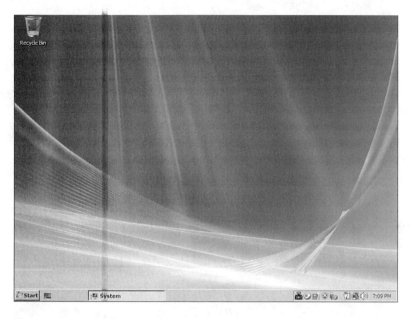

FIGURE 14.9
Vista, Eee PC style.

Installing Wireless Drivers for Vista

After the Vista installation is complete, you'll have a functional Vista system on the Eee PC except that you won't have wireless connectivity—not at first, anyway. This is a bit of a problem, as the driver installation software on the Asus Support disc simply won't run under Vista. However, you can skip the Driver Installation Wizard and manually install the driver from the disc. You should also check the Asus Eee support web site as there may be newer Atheros wireless drivers there. To install from the support DVD/CD:

1. Open the support CD/DVD Windows Explorer.

2. Navigate to the Drivers\Wireless\Install_CD directory.

3. Double-click setup.exe to install the Atheros client utility. You'll need to click the ever-present I Accept the Terms of the License Agreement radio button and click Next. The utility will install.

4. To install the driver, pull up the Windows Control Panel menu (it's on the right) and select the Device Manager.

5. Expand the network adapters and right-click one of the undefined entries.

6. Select to update the driver, and then browse to the Asus Support DVD.

7. Browse to the Drivers\Wireless\ Install_CD directory and click OK.

8. After the driver is installed, you can select the Atheros utility from the Windows Start menu and configure your wireless connection.

> **caution** After your installation is complete, don't forget to reset the boot sequence in the BIOS so that it boots first from the Eee PC's drive and not from the DVD drive.

9. Once connected, launch a browser and verify your connection.

And there you have it: Vista running on the miniscule Eee PC (see Figure 14.10). What's really amazing is how well it actually runs. Now, if you have a 4GB 701, you won't be installing Office 2007. But if you have an 8 GB 701, 900 or 901, which have larger SSDs, you certainly could.

FIGURE 14.10

Vista with wireless running.

Summary

In this chapter, you learned how to install Windows XP Home Edition and XP Professional. Both make excellent choices for the Eee PC, although the smaller footprint of XP Home Edition makes it a better choice for Model 701s with 4GB of storage. You also learned how to trim what you don't want or need from Windows Vista and install it on the Eee PC.

Windows Configuration

Basic Windows XP Setup

After you have installed Windows XP on your Eee PC (see Chapter 14), you need to optimize the video for the Eee PC and wireless connectivity.

Eee–PC Specific Notes for Setting Up Graphics Properties

The following are some things to keep in mind when configuring the graphics options on the Eee PC. The tip about making a larger virtual desktop is specific to the Eee PC's internal display. The tip concerning the screen settings automatically reverting is simply a handy thing to know, whether you're setting up the internal display or an external monitor.

Setting up the graphics properties requires you to use the Intel Graphics Media Accelerator Driver for Mobile applications, which may be found in the system tray (or what Microsoft now calls the notification area). Right-click the icon and select Graphics Properties. (You can get to the same menu by right-clicking on an open part of the desktop.) Let's go over a few things about the default Intel control itself:

- You can set the built-in Eee PC display to a greater resolution than the the display supports. This seems like a silly idea, but doing so sets a virtual desktop larger than your actual display space. Having a larger virtual desktop means that you can "push" the mouse pointer at the top or bottom of the screen, which scrolls the display up or down in this larger space. This is a great ploy for working with the limited space on the internal monitor. You can set this under the Display Settings option. For example, on the 701, you can set this to 800×600 instead of 800×480.

- Whenever you make changes, the Apply button gives you a chance to try out the changes. If something goes wrong and you don't accept the changes in 15 seconds, the display reverts to its old settings. While automatically reverting to previous settings is handy when playing with settings for the internal display, it becomes invaluable if you hook up an external monitor.

- If you plug an external monitor into the Eee PC, you'll see additional devices appear if you click Display Devices. Essentially, you can opt to have two monitors with separate displays (Extended Desktop), have two monitors that show the same thing (Display Clone), or shift the display entirely to the external monitor (Single Display).

Keep the above in mind when configuring both the internal display or an external monitor. You have a few more display configuration options in Windows than in most version of Linux (except Mandriva). If you want to set up a virtual desktop even larger than the 800 × 600 option allowed by default in the Intel driver, this is covered in detail in the next section.

Expanding the Display Scrolling Space

If you work with the internal display on the 701 (or even the 900 series), you'll soon discover that many Windows applications take up more space than can be shown. If you create a virtual desktop larger than the real desktop, you can move into the "virtual space" by placing the mouse pointer at the top or bottom of the screen (it will scroll). This is a great advantage for dealing with those oversized dialog boxes that are larger than the screen.

However, suppose you need a scrolling space much bigger than 800×600. No problem. Follow these steps:

1. Choose Start, Control Panel, Display.

2. In the Display Properties dialog box, click the Settings tab.

3. Make sure that Digital Flat Panel is selected for the display type, and then click the Advanced button.

4. Click the Monitor tab.

5. Clear the check mark from the Hide Modes That This Monitor Cannot Display check box (see Figure 15.1).

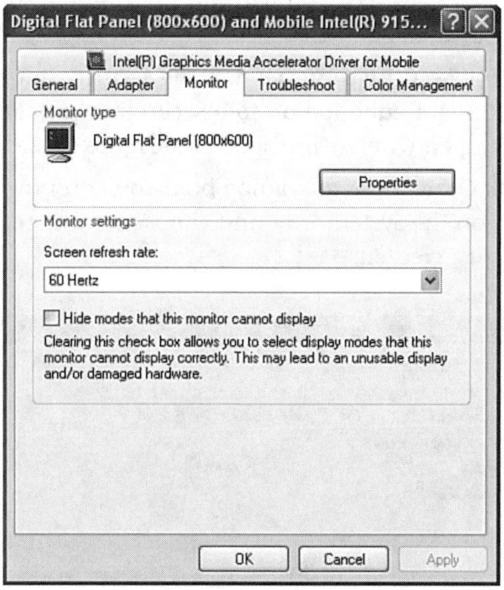

FIGURE 15.1

Clear the Hide Modes That This Monitor Cannot Display check box.

6. Click Apply and then click OK to return to the Display Properties dialog box.

7. Using the Screen Resolution slider, set the virtual resolution to whatever you like.

8. Click Apply and then click OK.

The screen now scrolls when the mouse touches any edge.

> **note** Later in this chapter, "Increasing the Screen Resolution" discusses downloading an updated Intel driver and increasing the resolution without scrolling. You can't do that with the default driver, but you can with the combination of a utility and the updated driver.

Setting Up Wireless Connectivity

To set up wireless connectivity, you should use the Atheros Client Utility, not the native Windows Wireless wizard. The Atheros Client Utility is located in the system tray/notification area. Right-click the icon and choose Open Atheros Client Utility. The Atheros system allows you to set up "profiles" for each wireless network to which you connect. To set up wireless connectivity, follow these steps:

1. From the Atheros Client Utility, choose the Profile Management tab.

2. On the General subtab, set the name for the profile, which is any arbitrary name you'd like to choose, though if you connect to multiple wireless networks, you will want to name it something that won't be confusing later.

3. On the Security subtab, enter the security information (WPA, 8021.x, or WEP) required to log on to a secure network (or no information if it's a wide-open wireless hot spot). See Figure 15.2.

4. Click OK to close the dialog box. You can now right-click the network icon on the system tray and choose to connect to the wireless profile you just created.

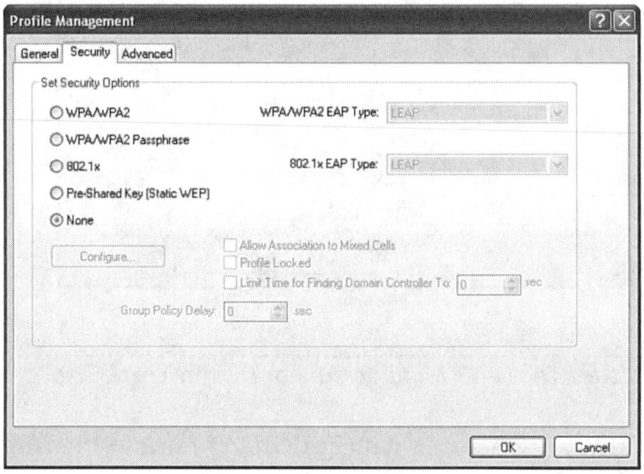

FIGURE 15.2

The Security tab in the Atheros Client Utility.

Optimizing Windows Settings for the Eee PC

The following sections provide tips for both maximizing the amount of free space left on your SSD, which potentially increases its life. Some of these suggestions include moving Windows directories to an attached MMC-SD card, so if you don't have one, you should consider purchasing one. The prices of MMC-SD cards has fallen quite a bit. I recently purchased a 4GB SD card at an office-supply chain for a mere $20.

Configuring the Swap File

By default on the Eee PC 701, 200 MB of space is taken up by the Windows swap file. The swap file is simply a part of the storage space (in this case, the SSD) set aside so that as your Eee PC runs out of memory, it can swap things between memory and the file. You can think of it as virtual memory on your SSD.

Under Xandros, swap space is disabled. Under Windows, by default, it isn't disabled.

If you're running with 512MB of memory, the recommendation is currently to set the Swap File Initial Size and Maximum Size to 256MB.

caution If you want to protect your Eee PC and its data by encrypting the hard drive and using on-the-fly encryption, ignore this section. If you encrypt the C: drive, you'll want to keep everything on it.

My recommendation is that if you're running Windows, you really should upgrade your memory so that you can eliminate the Swap File entirely. This will not only improve performance, but it will likely lengthen the life of your Eee PC.

The Swap File can get a lot of "reads" and "writes," and flash memory will eventually start to fail after a very large number of reads and writes. Using it as a substitute for real memory is a great way to reach that failure point in a much shorter time frame. Not good.

There is an alternative to eliminating the Swap File, by the way, but it means that your MMC-SD card must stay installed in the computer. Yes, this will contribute to a shorter life for the MMC-SD drive, but you can replace that easily. Replacing the SSD itself is, to date, not a simple affair.

The down side to having an MMC-SD card that you can't remove is that you can't have multiple MMC-SD cards—say, some with music, others with photos—and pop these in and out as needed. You'll need to make do with USB drives instead.

Assigning a Drive Letter to the MMC-SD Card

By default, the Eee PC sets your MMC-SD card as drive E:. As long as you leave it plugged in, the Eee PC won't reassign its drive letter. However, if you want to ensure that the drive letter stays the same, you can simply assign it a new drive letter (it doesn't really matter which one). Before you make the change, close any applications that are accessing files on that card.

To change the drive designation:

1. Click Start, right-click My Computer, and select Manage.

2. Click Disk Management under Storage.

3. Right-click the MMC-SD card in the upper-right pane (it'll likely be designated as the E: drive, but take a look at the size and make sure it matches the size of the card), and then click Change Drive Letters and Paths.

4. Click the Change button, and then assign it a new letter from the drop-down list.

5. Click OK; because you already closed any applications accessing or running from the card (you did, didn't you?), you can be sure that it won't cause any problems (see Figure 15.3).

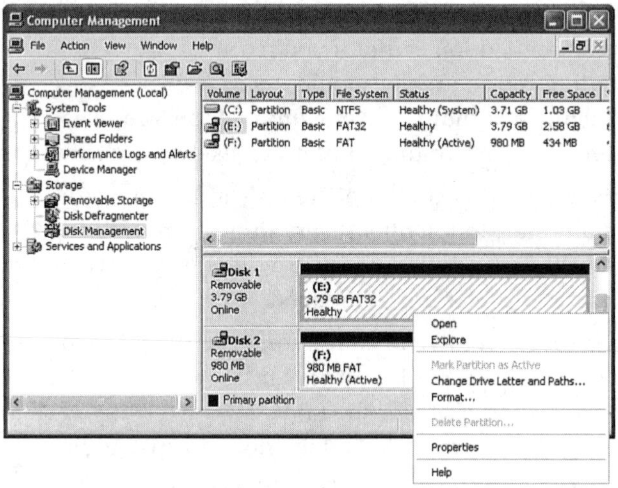

FIGURE 15.3

Assigning a different drive letter to the MMC-SD drive.

To change your virtual memory settings:

1. Press the Windows key+Break to launch the System Properties dialog box.

2. In the System Properties dialog box, click the Advanced tab.

3. Click the Settings button in the Performance area.

4. In the Performance Options dialog box, click the Advanced tab.

5. Under Virtual Memory, click Change.

6. If you want to eliminate the swap space altogether or move it, select the No Paging File option. If you want to maintain 200MB (in case you only have 512MB of memory installed), select Custom Size and set both the Initial Size and Maximum Size values to 200MB. When moving the swap drive, select the drive on which it will reside and then set the values.

7. Click OK three times to exit the System Properties dialog box.

If you chose to eliminate the swap file, the Eee PC may have already created it, so turning it off by itself won't free up any space. You need to erase the swap file. Doing so is perhaps easiest from a command prompt. Choose Start, Accessories, Command Prompt. Enter the following:

```
> cd \
> dir /AS
```

If you see a file called pagefile.sys, delete it with this command:

```
> del /AS pagefile.sys
```

Moving My Documents and Other Windows Directories to the MMC-SD Card

If you wish to move your My Documents folder to the MMC-SD card, choose Start, right-click My Documents, and select Properties. In the My Documents Properties dialog box, click the Move button on the Target tab. Navigate to the MMC-SD card, which is E: by default, and either select an existing folder or click the Make New Folder button. Click OK and, when prompted, indicate that you do indeed want to move the files. Your My Documents folder will now be safely tucked away on the MMC-SD card.

You can play this same trick with anything that keeps temporary data, such as an Internet browser. In Internet Explorer, choose Tools, Internet Options. On the General tab, click the Settings button under Temporary Internet Files. Click the Move Folder button, navigate to a directory on the MMC-SD drive, and then click OK. See Figure 15.4.

FIGURE 15.4

Moving the Internet Explorer Temporary Internet Files folder.

The good thing about having things on the MMC-SD card is that you can back it up easily. Just take it to a machine with a card reader, plug it in, and drag everything off it into a backup directory. You can also burn a DVD with the contents directly from the Eee PC. Should the MMC-SC card suddenly fail, you can simply restore your last (and hopefully recent) backup to a new card and you'll be "back in business."

Compressing the SSD

The manual suggests that you should compress the SSD to get more space, so I gave it a try. It takes about 20 minutes and I did get considerably more space. It also doesn't slow operation down appreciably, so I'd recommend compressing the SDD. You might want to turn off the indexing service while you're there, as this will both slow operations down a little and use up space.

To do both, choose Start, My Computer. Right-click the C: drive and choose Properties. On the General tab, check the Compress Drive to Save Disk Space check box and uncheck the Allow Indexing Service to Index This Disk for Fast File Searching check box. Click Apply. Fairly soon in the process, you'll need to tell Windows to ignore all errors.

After completing all of the suggestions under Optimizing Windows Settings for the Eee PC, I have almost 3GB of free space on my C: drive. Not bad considering I only had 4GB to start.

Reducing the Size of the Recycle Bin in XP

You can also save space by reducing the size of the Recycle Bin. By default, the Recycle Bin is set to take about 10% of the available space, but you can reduce this to whatever percentage you wish. To reduce the size of the Recycle Bin:

1. Right-click the Recycle Bin icon on the Windows desktop.
2. Select Properties.
3. On the Global tab, slide the bar to the desired percentage.
4. Click Apply.
5. Click OK.

If you wish to eliminate the Recycle Bin entirely, select Do Not Move Files to the Recycle Bin. If you eliminate the Recycle Bin, files will be removed when you delete them, instead of being stored in the Recycle Bin for possible later recovery.

Reducing the Size Allocated for System Restore

By default, 12% of your storage space is set aside for the System Restore function. System Restore automatically creates "Restore Points" that you can use to return to a previous, good configuration. If you reduce the space, the number of Restore Points that can be saved is decreased; however, the amount of free disk space is increased.

To reduce the allocation for System Restore:

1. Right-click the My Computer icon on the desktop.
2. Select Properties.
3. Click the System Restore tab.
4. Move the slider to the desired percentage of disk space allocated.
5. Click Apply.
6. Click OK.

Loading Microsoft Office on an MMC-SD Card

Let's face it, having Microsoft Works is better than nothing and will help you complete simple tasks, but it isn't designed for full-blown, day-to-day business, academic, or even home tasks. What you really want is an office suite such as Microsoft Office. You especially want Microsoft Office if your business, organization, or educational institution has settled on Office as a standard. (If you don't need Microsoft Office, skip this section and read about the much lighter, and free, OpenOffice.org suite.) This section explains how to load Microsoft Office on an external drive, first a legacy version of Office (XP) and then the current version (2007).

The only real trick to loading Office is determining where to put it. To save space, you could move the My Documents folder to your MMC-SD card (it's the E: drive on my Eee PC). This is covered in the previous section. You could also try to keep the installation folders for applications there as well (Office will prompt you during installation for the location in which you want to place the installation files).

Because a number of people have reported problems in loading Microsoft Office, I must admit I installed Office with some trepidation. I decided to start with a smaller, legacy version of Office. I dug out a copy of Office XP, plopped it into the DVD drive, and started the installation. Compared to Office 2007, Office XP is miniscule. It weighs in at a mere few hundred megabytes when fully installed.

Loading Microsoft Office XP

Moving Office XP to the MMC-SD card is pretty simple. In preparation, create a folder called Office on the MMC-SD card (which is probably mounted as the E: drive):

1. Put the Office XP CD into a CD/DVD drive and allow it to autorun.

2. Enter your license key and then click Next.

3. For the Install To field, browse to the Office folder of the MMC-SD drive.

4. In the same screen, select Install Now and then click Next.

5. Click Install.

The total installation will take up about 200MB of space on the MMC-SD drive. If you have a legacy copy of Office, rest assured it will run just fine in this environment.

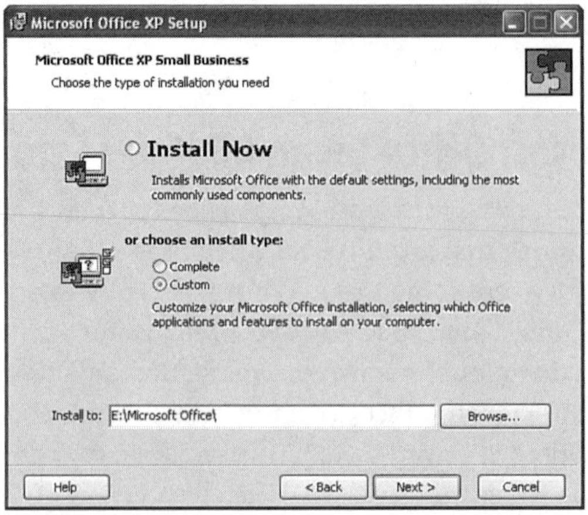

FIGURE 15.5

Redirecting the installation to the E: drive.

Loading Microsoft Office 2007

After testing the applications, rebooting, and writing in Office XP for a while (just to make sure all was indeed working), I uninstalled it and pulled out the Office Professional Plus 2007 DVD. This is a massive application, taking up about 800MB when fully installed. Once again, I had set up a Microsoft Office folder on the SD drive as the installation directory. This is a little trickier on Office 2007 because Microsoft has taken the option to install it into an alternate directory from main dialog boxes and tucked it away. When you reach the Choose the Installation You Want dialog box, click the Customize button. Customize launches the typical tree-control-laden dialog box that allows you to pick which parts of the application you want to load. However, it also has a File Location tab, which, when clicked, reveals the field for an alternate folder (see Figure 15.6). You can click the Browse button and navigate to whatever installation directory you've set up on the SD drive (or create the folder from within the file browser dialog box).

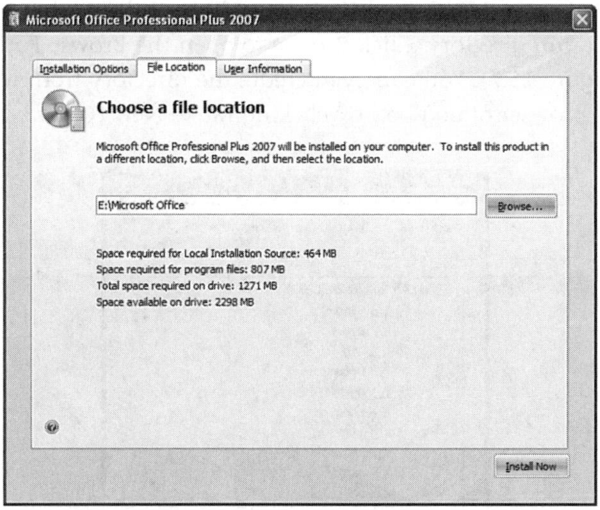

FIGURE 15.6

Redirecting the installation for Office 2007 to the E: drive.

This is a very, very long installation. However, once done, Office 2007 worked perfectly on my Eee PC. I rebooted, pulled up several Office applications, and used it as my main writing tool for a while with no problems. It did suck up a lot of storage space, however. The E: drive installation directory contained almost 600MB of files, with about 200MB taken up in the various common directories on the C: drive.

Installing OpenOffice.org

OpenOffice.org is a much "lighter," full-featured office suite that is available for just about every imaginable platform. It is shipped with the Xandros Linux versions of the Eee PC, as well as most KDE-equipped versions of Linux. You can read more about OpenOffice.org in Chapter 7. Suffice it to say that I think so highly of it that I used OpenOffice.org to write this book.

What makes OpenOffice.org especially interesting for Eee PCs with Windows is that it has much less overhead than Microsoft Office and installs nearly completely on the E: drive. Compared to the 800MB that Microsoft Office consumes, OpenOffice.org uses up only a dainty 132MB. Unless you have a requirement to run Microsoft Office, I strongly suggest you choose OpenOffice.org instead. If you only need a word processor, then AbiWord is an even lighter-weight choice. The setup file for AbiWord is 6MB and the actual installation takes up only 24MB.

The only trick in the installation of OpenOffice.org, if you want to put it entirely on the MMC-SD drive, is to redirect it there when it asks about the installation directory. Click Browse to open the Browse For Folder dialog box (see Figure 15.7). You can even create the directory from within the Browse For Folder browser dialog box by clicking Make New Folder.

FIGURE 15.7

Redirecting the OpenOffice.org installation to the E: drive.

Once installed, OpenOffice.org runs perfectly under Windows. (This can't be said for OpenOffice.org under Xandros, because the database application simply doesn't work in the default OpenOffice.org installation.)

Overclocking in Windows

The Eee PC, as shipped, has its processor underclocked to conserve battery power. For example, the 701 4G has a 900MHz Celeron processor that's underclocked to 630MHz.

The machine still seems zippy enough, but it could do much better. In Windows, controlling the Eee PC's processor and fan, as well as the backlight, is a simple matter of downloading and running a free utility called eeectl (http://www.cpp.in/dev/eeectl/). Eeectl places an icon in your system tray/notification area that tells you the current temperature of the CPU and at what percentage of full speed it's running.

note eeectl is another example of an Eee PC–specific utility developed by the Eee PC community. It was crated by "Anthony," a 22-year-old programmer from Russia. By the way, while you're at the website, you can click a button to donate some cash to Anthony to support his efforts.

Anthony did an outstanding job with eeectl. It works perfectly. As part of my journalistic duty, I felt compelled to make sure that it was really resetting the clock, so I downloaded a small CPU benchmarking program called CPUFreeBenchMark2. I can't attest to the quality of this tool, but the results of running it were interesting. Before eeectl, at its default speed, it took my Eee PC 126.31 seconds to complete the benchmarking test. After installation, I selected the Medium processor speed, and the Eee PC completed the drill in 103.29 seconds. Encouraged, I kicked it up to Full speed, and this time the Eee PC ran through the benchmarks in 87.74 seconds. That's a pretty impressive speed boost.

Eeectl is a simple executable file, packaged in a ZIP file with an INI file and a very terse readme file. Just double-click it to run it. When it runs, eeectl puts a square icon in the notification area, which alternates between displaying your current speed settings and the CPU temperature. Right-click the icon and you'll get a menu that you can use to select between Stock (normal), Medium, or Full processor speed (see Figure 15.8). You can also select the percentage of time the fan runs and display the backlighting intensity. What more could you want?

Well, you might want it to automatically launch. If so, go to whatever directory you've installed eeectl in and make a shortcut file from the eeectl executable file. (Right-click eeectl.exe and select Create Shortcut.) Once you've created the shortcut file, select it and press Ctrl+X to "cut" it. Choose Start, All Programs, right-click Startup, and select Open. In the Startup directory, press Ctrl+V to paste the shortcut file. Now eeectl will launch whenever you start your Eee PC.

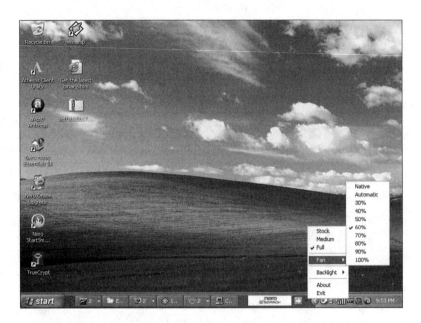

FIGURE 15.8

The eeectl menu.

Getting Free Antivirus Software

Linux isn't entirely immune to viruses, Trojan horses, rootkits, and other malware, but the Windows community is the "target of opportunity." Windows represents over 90% of the desktop OSs, so that's what the crooks go after. So, how do you defend yourself? You can, of course, purchase either McAfee or Symantec and have top-notch protection. Most companies, government agencies, and other large organizations use one or the other. However, if you don't want to spend the money, you can get excellent protection with the free version of either AVG (http://free.avg.com) or avast (http://www.avast.com/). At various times, I've run I've run one or the other of these products, and for the price of nothing, they are great. See Figure 15.9.

One problem is that these applications won't install onto a removable device. So, installing them on the MMC-SD drive is not an option. Folks on the forums report using one or the other, and the usual "mine is better" discussion wars break out. Both seem to slow the system down slightly, but not overly much. Also, either work just fine even if you've chosen to encrypt the drive (covered next).

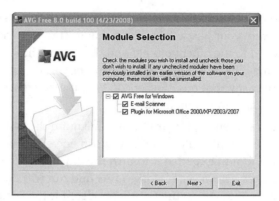

FIGURE 15.9

Installing AVG, and selecting email and Office support.

Both applications have these features:

- Configure to dynamically watch your browser and your email
- Support Outlook
- Can be set to autoscan your various logical drives
- Automatically update themselves when you are connected to the Internet
- Provide a significant level of protection

So which should you choose? Really, either does a great job.

Encrypting Your Data

The Eee PC is so portable, so handy, and so cool that it is a tempting target for thieves. Although the Eee PC itself is relatively inexpensive compared to other laptops, loosing the data you have stored on it might be a much more serious problem. It might be merely important, highly proprietary, or downright sensitive information that you don't want to either lose or share with others. Fortunately, a Windows version of TrueCrypt is available. You can download it from http://www.truecrypt.org/. TrueCrypt provides military-grade encryption and is a very tough nut to crack.

TrueCrypt has two basic ways of protecting your data:

- You can create an encrypted volume file, which can reside on either the SSD or any removable device (either a USB flash drive or the MMC-SD card). Once you enter the password, this file (really something like an encrypted TAR file) becomes a logical drive on the system. Moreover, you can create a volume within a volume. This hidden-volume scheme is an extra precaution in case you fear that someone may coerce you to reveal your password to the volume. Thus, you can give them the password to the outer volume, and they'll not know about the hidden volume. The TrueCrypt creators describe this as "plausible deniability." They say that an attacker can't tell the difference between the hidden volume and random data.

■ You can encrypt your C: drive, meaning the system will not boot unless you provide the password. You can encrypt a compressed drive. I tried it and half expected it to turn the machine into a plastic brick in the process. However, it worked fine and ran without a hitch for several days. Encrypting the C: drive is ideal for the Eee PC, because if someone steals it, they'll need the password to get any use out of it. (Well, unless they download the Asus Support DVD/CD contents and one of the myriad operating systems that'll run on it.)

Encrypting your C: volume requires that you rethink where you locate things. Up to this point, I've made a point of telling you how to move things off of the C: drive and onto the MMC-SD drive (E:). However, you don't want to do this if you're encrypting the C: volume, for a few reasons:

■ Your data won't be encrypted unless it's stored on the C: drive.

■ You can't encrypt the E: drive if components and directories that Windows needs are there. That could prevent Windows from working at all. The reason is part of a chicken-and-egg problem. You won't be able to run TrueCrypt to unencrypt the E: drive until Windows boots, as the TrueCrypt bootloader will only unencrypt the C: drive. However, Windows won't run until the E: drive is unencrypted.

If you want to go this route, store all of your Windows directories and vital applications on C:, and use E: and USB flash drives for data storage. These can then also be encrypted as file volumes. Any of these can contain a volume within a volume if you're feeling especially paranoid.

You also need a CD or DVD burner hooked up to the Eee PC to be able to encrypt the C: drive. This is because TrueCrypt creates a rescue disk that will enable you to get your drive back if things go badly during the encryption process. It insists on this step, and won't proceed until it has made a rescue disk and verified it.

To either encrypt the C: drive or simply create an encrypted volume (file) on any drive, launch TrueCrypt and click the Create Volume button. It will walk you step by step through either process, and you select which process you want to use in the first screen (see Figure 15.10). The setup includes selecting the encryption algorithm, wiggling your mouse over an arcane screen to "increase the strength of the hash code," and other fun spy stuff.

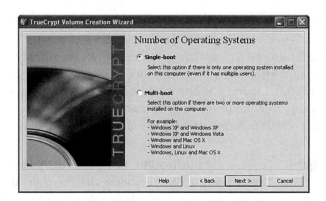

FIGURE 15.10

Selecting the encryption type in TrueCrypt.

If you choose to encrypt the C: drive, it will automatically burn your rescue disk and verify it. It will also run a bootloader test just to make certain that the bootloader will work.

After encryption, when you start the Eee PC, aside from being challenged for the password you created, you'll notice that the system runs just a trifle slower. This is because it's doing on-the-fly encryption. However, if your Eee PC becomes the target of a smash-and-grab theft from your car, the thief (unless it's a tech-savvy thief) will have no way of using it or getting to your data.

note The actual time to encrypt the C: drive depends on how much is stored in it. I had about 1GB of free space on my 4GB SSD when I tried it, and it took a little less than 20 minutes. You can pause this process if you need to use the Eee PC for something, and then pick up the encryption later.

Increasing the Screen Resolution

Clearly, you can't fit too much on a 701's screen. However, the video display panel and the Intel graphics accelerator are capable of more resolution than the native Eee PC allows. If you want to increase your screen resolution, you can do so simply by upgrading the graphics driver with the latest genuine Intel driver and installing an additional system tray graphics switcher. I suggest you keep the original Asus switcher as well, as the new one doesn't handle external monitors very well. This combination gets you to 1024×768 on the Eee PC screen *without scrolling*. Frankly, I find the letters at that resolution a bit teeny-tiny and rough-edged, but it's great for some things such as running Photoshop or GIMP.

A number of folks have created experimental display drivers for the Eee PC, many of which can be found on the EeeUser forum (http://forum.eeeuser.com). Most of these push the display to really high resolutions and are not terribly useful for everyday computing. However, on the EeeUser wiki, I found a utility called AsTray Plus that is useful for everyday computing (though at the highest resolutions, it causes so much interpolation that the screen becomes difficult to read). Thus, I will cover AsTray Plus in this section.

At http://wiki.eeeuser.com/astrayplus, you'll find the page that describes AsTray Plus. This was written by EeeUser senior member "BASSAM." BASSAM has done a truly wonderful job with AsTray Plus. Coupled with the eeectl utility, these two applications truly improve the Eee PC user experience. My jaw dropped when I saw what could be done with the updated Intel driver. Frankly, I don't see why Asus didn't include this capability. The following explains the steps to get AsTray_plus running on your Eee_PC:

1. To change the screen resolutions, first you need the Intel driver, which you can download from http://downloadcenter.intel.com/ Product_Filter.aspx?ProductID=1764.

2. Select your flavor of Windows and then download the EXE version, which is the easiest to install.

3. Once the driver is downloaded, simply double-click it and you'll be guided through the installation.

4. If you set the graphics options to display video modes beyond what the driver could do so that you can scroll the video (as described earlier in this chapter), you'll want to undo that.

5. Get AsTray Plus from BASSAM's latest download link, which is currently http://forum.eeeuser.com/ viewtopic.php?id=18260. If this link doesn't work, search for "AsTray Plus" at http://wiki.eeeuser.com.

6. Unzip the files for AsTray Plus to a directory and double-click astray.exe.

> **note** While you're there, you can make a donation to BASSAM for his excellent work via PayPal. At the time of this writing, the ZIP file was a download from MediaFire. I had a bit of trouble downloading from MediaFire via Internet Explorer; however, Firefox worked perfectly.

7. You'll see the graphics properties icon in your system tray (see Figure 15.11). You can switch graphics modes via Quick Switch. The Native setting returns the Eee PC display to its default resolution.

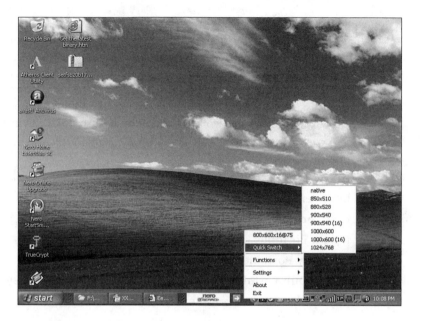

FIGURE 15.11
The AsTray Plus menu, showing onboard screen resolutions.

If you have an Eee PC 701, I suggest keeping the original Intel graphics properties switcher because I had some odd, and sometimes comical, effects when running dual-monitor mode. Switching graphics resolutions via AsTray Plus tends to affect the external monitor, and sometimes it also rotates it 90 degrees. So, use the original Intel control when you're using the dual-monitor mode and use AsTray Plus when you're using only the built-in display. The Eee PC 900 seems immune from this weird behavior.

To autorun AsTray Plus at startup, make a shortcut file from the astray.exe file. (Right-click astray.exe and select Create Shortcut.) Once you've created the shortcut file, select it and press Ctrl+X to "cut" it. Click Start, All Programs, right-click Startup, and select Open. In the Startup directory, press Ctrl+V to paste the shortcut file.

Installing PortableApps.Com

Portable apps are the ultimate space savers because you can install them directly on a USB flash drive. This is ideal for applications that you rarely use and don't want to install directly on the Eee PC. The great thing about PortableApps.com is that they come with their own launcher, so you'll have a system tray icon that will pop up the launcher for all of the portable apps installed on the flash drive.

You can download PortableApps.com from http://portableapps.com (see Figure 15.12). PortableApps.com includes a basic launcher, a basic suite that comes with Firefox, Thunderbird, and various other utilities, and the AbiWord word processor. There's also a full-fledged version that has OpenOffice.org instead of AbiWord. Click Download Now on the website's main page to fetch these. However, keep in mind that this is simply a starter set. There are lots of additional applications on the PortableApps.com site that you can install on a flash drive. For instance:

- **XAMPP:** A full Apache web server plus mySQL, PHP, and phpMyAdmin.
- **GIMP Portable:** An open source Photoshop alternative that's a must-have item for the Eee PC under Linux.
- **Nvu Portable:** A complete, open source web-development environment.
- **Pidgin Portable:** A multisystem chat client.
- **Audacity Portable:** A complete sound-editing system.
- **VirtualDub Portable:** A reasonably capable video-editing system.
- **VLC Media Player Portable:** My favorite music player.

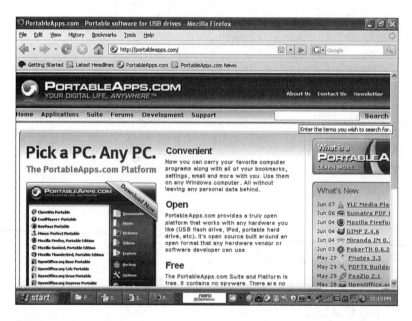

FIGURE 15.12

PortableApps.com.

All you need to do to add these files to the launcher is:

1. Download each of the portable apps.
2. Either double-click them or click Options, Install a New App in the PortableApps.com Launcher.

If you want even more portable apps, check out http://en.wikipedia.org/ wiki/List_of_portable_software, a massive list of portable apps on Wikipedia. Literally hundreds of applications are listed there, ranging from full-blown wikis to BitTorrent clients.

Surfing Anonymously

Chapter 9 described Tor and Privoxy as important applications for anonymous web surfing. These programs might be especially important to people who live under regimes that censor the Web or do not allow freedom of speech. In the Windows world, there's a portable application that does pretty much the same thing as the combination of Tor and Privoxy: OperaTor. OperaTor bundles up the Tor and Polipo applications with the Opera browser, making for a complete and convenient package. Moreover, it's a portable application that can be stored either on your Eee PC or on a USB flash drive.

OperaTor can be downloaded from http://archetwist.com/en/opera/operator. It's a small download, only 6.3MB, and comes as a ZIP package. You simply unpack it to whatever folder you like. If you have installed the PortableApps.com launcher, simply unpack it to the PortableApps directory (if the launcher is running, you'll need to refresh the menu for it to appear).

OperaTor only anonymizes HTTP and HTTPS protocols, so stay away from FTP, BitTorrent, and so forth. If you want to check whether it's working, navigate to http://check.torproject.org/. You should see the web page shown in Figure 15.13 if it's working.

FIGURE 15.13

OperaTor, with verification that it's working.

Cleaning Up Your Storage Space

You can download an excellent disk clean-up utility called CCleaner, which will remove temporary files from Internet Explorer, Firefox, and Opera, as well as unnecessary temporary files left around by Windows. It will even empty the Recycle Bin, clean the Windows Registry, and remove temporary files form a variety of third-party applications. You can download CCleaner from http://www.ccleaner.com/.

To install CCleaner, double-click the executable file that you downloaded. During the short installation, you'll be given an opportunity to select the installation directory. So, if you wish, you can install it on the MMC-SD drive to minimize the amount of storage on the SSD CCleaner uses.

To run CCleaner, select Start, CCleaner, CCleaner. CCleaner presents you with two tabs and check boxes for removing temporary files, one tab for Windows clean-up and the other for Third Party cleanup. Set the check boxes for the types of files you like to clean up, and then click the Analyze button at the bottom of the screen.

Analysis will take a little while, as it will scan all of your storage for temporary and extraneous files. When it's done, it will fill the blank space above the buttons with a list of files to be deleted. Scroll the list to ensure that nothing you need will be deleted. If all is well, click Run Cleaner. When it's done cleaning, click the Close box to close the application.

Summary

This chapter is packed full of ways to optimize Windows for the Eee PC. If you follow the suggestions outline in this chapter, you'll have an Eee PC that runs faster, has greater screen resolution, and has more free storage space than you may have thought possible. You can trim the fat out of Windows and make it a really great choice for the Eee PC operating system.

Using Windows Live

Windows Live and the Eee PC

indows Live is Microsoft's entry into the world of "cloud computing." Simply put, cloud computing moves the installation of application and storage of files away from your personal computer and onto some third-party servers that you access via the Internet. This has tremendous advantage for computers such as the Eee PC. You can leverage the easy connectivity to the Internet to access your applications and files, instead of having to use the limited storage options on the Eee PC for all application and file storage.

There are other applications that do roughly the same thing, most notably Google Apps and the new offering by Adobe: Acrobat.com. These cloud computing alternatives can provide productivity applications, webmail, and online file storage. However, they go beyond that to allow others to easily and securely collaborate with you. Also, they provide "versioning" of your files, so that instead of merely storing the latest updated version of your file, each set of changes is saved and accessible. This allows you to retrieve previous sets of changes as well as track who made changes and when. These collaborative features coupled with file versioning are typically functions one finds in a content management system, such as Microsoft Sharepoint or Alfresco.

There are three major drawbacks to cloud computing in general:

- Everything is done through a browser. This means that your word processing applications, file managers, etc., are limited by what a browser can do. Google Apps attempts to be as universally accessible as possible, therefore it's user interface has limitations that are imposed by a set of actions that any common browser can accomodate. Adobe's Acrobat.com leverages its own technologies, such as Flash, Flex, and Air, to expand what the browser can do and make its applications more functional. The downside is that you must install the necessary Adobe plug-ins for the technologies. This limits which browsers can be used with the site; for example, Opera will not work with Acrobat.com.

- If you don't have access to the Internet, you can't access your applications. Cloud computing makers are addressing this in a variety of ways. For example, you can run many Google Apps applications while disconnected from the Internet through Google Gears. Essentially, Google Gears provides a small web server that you run locally on your computer that provides the applications to your browser.

- Your files are residing on someone else's servers. While this means that they'll get regularly backed-up, it also means that you must trust the third party to not peruse or make use of your information.

Cloud computing applications typically support the file formats of installed applications. For example, Google Apps supports both OpenOffice and Microsoft Office formats. This makes it possible to work disconnected from the Internet without having something like Google Gears running on your computer. However, there is often quite a bit of formatting lost in translating the files from Word or OpenOffice Writer to the HTML format used by most cloud computing applications.

Microsoft took a different approach to cloud computing in that they view Windows Live as an extension of the Microsoft Office suite. They go beyond using a browser as the interface to the cloud computing applications, and also add Microsoft Live commands to Microsoft Office Applications.

note To learn more about cloud computing, see *Cloud Computing: Web-Based Applications that Change the Way You Work and Collaborate Online*, by Michael Miller, published by Que.

In some ways, Windows Live is really "Microsoft SharePoint Lite," with document-management features found in the Microsoft Sharepoint Content Management System. It does Google Apps "one better" through its direct integration into the Office applications running on the Eee PC. It also has much more sophisticated collaboration functions, a la SharePoint, with various types of workspaces.

I thought that the combination of Microsoft Office installed on the Eee PC and Windows Live would be the best combination of technologies for the Eee PC. If it all worked together, it would make Windows with the addition of Microsoft Office the best combination of operating system and productivity software for the Eee PC. Moreover, Microsoft claimed to support both Internet Explorer 6 and 7, as well as Microsoft Office 2007, 2003, and XP. What could be better?

Unfortunately, what could be better is if Windows Live actually lived up to its promises. The big drawbacks with Windows Live, at least from my testing, are performance and reliability:

- It is much slower than Google Apps.
- Internet Explorer 6 crashed several times while I was working with Windows Live, and Word completely locked up at one point. Don't get me wrong—Windows Live isn't consistently unstable under IE 6, but it isn't as robust and dependable as Google Apps either.

Given the performance and instability problems, I was convinced that my Eee PC had been infected with a virus, so I scanned the system with avast. It was clean.

My next step in the quest for stability was to upgrade IE 6 to IE 7. That helped to a degree, but didn't completely clear up the problem. IE 7 also installed special Active X controls for Windows Live which seemed to improve stability (though not performance). However, despite the improvement in stability, performance was still noticeably slower than when running other online productivity suites. Also, Office XP eventually crashed when saving a file back to the online document space.

Finally, I uninstalled the Windows Live components, uninstalled Office XP, installed Office 2007, and reinstalled the Windows Live components. After this, I had only one or two crashes on the Eee PC in the following couple of days. Still, I'm left with that nagging doubt that it could crash at any minute. Worse, most of the instability seemed to occur when saving files to Windows Live from within Office, which is when you really don't want it to fail you.

The potential here is enormous if Microsoft could improve the performance and stability of Windows Live. By extending the onboard Microsoft productivity applications to the Internet and by providing content-management and collaborative capabilities that are, quite frankly, more powerful than the other online tools, the combination of Windows Live and Microsoft Office would make for an environment ideally suited to a device with limited storage, such as the Eee PC. Coupled with a GPS and Microsoft Streets & Trips, the Windows environment would be hands-down superior to Linux for many Eee PC users that spend much of their time on the road.

However, as Windows Live currently stands, it just isn't very useful for the Eee PC, even if you have Office 2007. It's clearly tailored for larger screens than any Eee PC currently sports, and its performance and stability make it a frustrating experience even with a larger monitor. Moreover, it's completely Microsoft-centric in its technologies, and requires you to download more and more ActiveX controls to add functionality. Your experience may vary, but just to write this chapter using the Windows Live capabilities, I had to use eeectl to crank up the processor to 900MHz (as described in Chapter 15) and use an external monitor to access all of the controls.

You can get around the screen resolution problems to some extent without an external monitor if you have attached a mouse with a scroll wheel to the Eee PC. Otherwise, if you wish to use the internal display, you'll need to either set your virtual screen larger than the actual screen or get the AsTray Plus utility plus an upgrade to the Intel graphics drivers in order to see and use the controls. How to do both of these is covered in Chapter 15.

To be totally fair, Windows Live is still "beta" software, so a certain amount of instability is to be expected, and one of its components, Writer (a blog editor, described later in the chapter), is considered a "tech preview" and is therefore still in an early testing phase. A tech preview is expected to be unstable. Therefore, Windows Live may improve dramatically by the time it has reached a fully "released" state, especially if Microsoft applies Silverlight technology to the interface. Silverlight is Microsoft's answer to the Adobe Flash, Flex, and Air technologies, and it should begin to replace ActiveX controls as it gains acceptance. Also, the Eee PC is not a particularly powerful machine. However, it is a platform that is served better than most with access to systems such as Windows Live.

Introducing the Windows Live Components

With a Windows Live account, you have access to the following Windows Live components:

- **Hotmail:** Set up a free Hotmail account, which allows you to send and receive email with your web browser.
- **Calendar:** Share calendars with other users and set up meetings.
- **Spaces:** Share file areas, called spaces, with special capabilities for sharing photos with family and friends. For example, there's a really nice event planner that enables you to set up the event and share photos taken at the event.
- **Skydrive:** Use collaborative workspaces and document "libraries" (similar to those in SharePoint).

- **Messenger:** Chat with friends and family online.
- **OneCare:** Get virus protection, online ID protection, and so forth.
- **Writer:** Create and publish your own blog.

Beyond the web-based functions, you can download components to integrate these functions into Microsoft Office (XP, 2003, and 2007). Because Office XP requires far less disk space than 2003 or 2007, and disk space is at a premium on the Eee PC, I decided to use Office XP.

If you don't have Microsoft Word 2007, based on my experience, you should carefully consider if you want to go through the process of setting up Windows Live. It was too unstable to be useful under any version of Word other than Word 2007.

In order to use Windows Live, you first must set up a Windows Live account.

> **tip** If you intend to use both Office 2007 and Streets & Trips, you need to have an 8GB or greater system. Each application occupies nearly 1GB, which, even with the inclusion of an MMD-SD drive, leaves you without much free space for other applications or file storage.

Setting Up a Windows Live Account

If you already have a Microsoft Passport, Hotmail, Windows Messenger, or MSN account, the name and password for that account will serve as your Windows Live ID. If you do not have any of these accounts, then you need to set up your Windows Live ID.

The following procedure is accurate at the time of writing; however, it may have changed significantly by the time that you read this:

1. Go to http://home.live.com and click the Sign Up link.

2. On the Sign Up for Windows Live page, shown in Figure 16.1, create an account name. After you enter the login name you want to use and select the domain (such as live.com) from the drop-down list, click the Check Availability button to see if that name is in use. If it's unavailable, keep trying until you find a name that works.

> **note** If you have an existing Microsoft account, simply click Sign In in the upper-right corner and sign in to Windows Live.

3. Choose a password. The password you select will be rated for its "strength," which is a measure of how difficult it might be to "crack" using software for that purpose. Strong passwords are usually a combination of upper and lower case letters, numbers, and special characters (such as $). You'll need to retype it as a confirmation.

Enter the information that you can use to reset your password. This consists of a question (which you'll pick from the drop-down list) and Secret Answer (which you'll type). If you lose your password, providing your Secret Answer to the question will provide access to your account.

4. Enter all the required personal information and type the characters that you see in the picture.

5. Review and accept the agreements (if you agree to Microsoft's terms). After a few seconds, you'll be redirected to your default home page. From there, you can install the Windows Live Update application, which provides the direct connection between Office applications and Windows Live. In fact, links to download the Windows Live Update application appear throughout the various Windows Live pages. You can also download it directly from http://www.microsoft.com/downloads/details. aspx?FamilyId=98DF1962-F351-4BD2-9ED2-EAAFED67996D&display-lang=en (you can select various language versions from there).

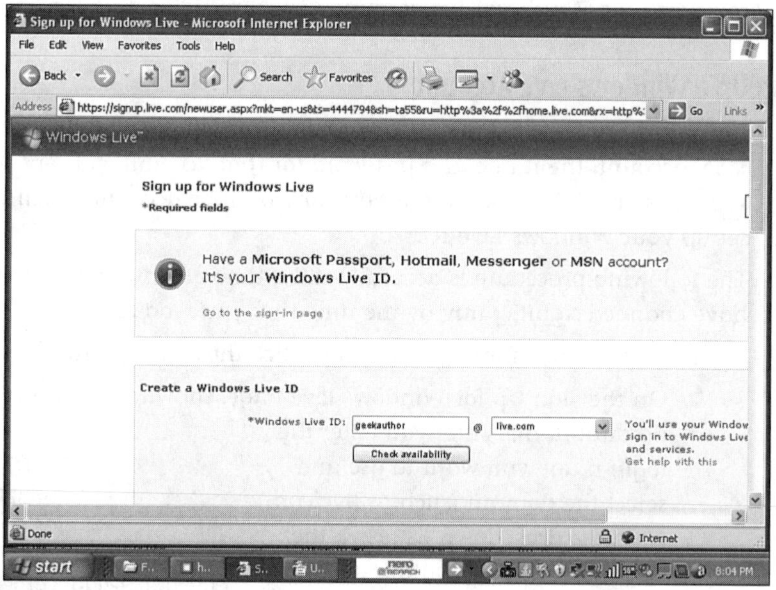

FIGURE 16.1

Signup page for Windows Live.

Live Update adds to Office XP and 2003 a menu bar with three buttons (see Figure 16.2):

- **Go to Office Live:** This button launches the default browser (which must be IE 7) and goes to the Windows Live home page. If you aren't terribly concerned about security on this account, you can set the home page to both remember the computer and automatically log you in.

■ **Open:** This button opens Windows Live and, if you're not logged in, signs you in. Once signed in, this button functions as a launch pad for opening files stored in your workspace on Windows Live.

■ **Save:** This button, obviously, allows you to save documents you create on Windows Live. You'll find that the first time you save a file, it will take quite a long time, even over high speed connection for the first save, but subsequent saves are tolerably fast.

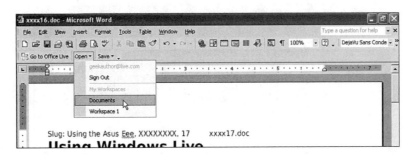

FIGURE 16.2

Windows Live buttons in Word XP/Word 2003.

Office 2007 incorporates two new items in the Microsoft Office button menu: Open From Office Live and Save to Office Live. These function just the same as the Open and Save buttons in legacy versions of Office.

Integrating Windows Live and Microsoft Office

For me, at least, Office integration with Windows Live is the single differentiating factor between this online suite and the cloud computing alternatives. Office integration is especially important because Windows Live lacks the option to use an online writing tool. Integration is tolerable under Office 2007, and frankly too unstable to be usable with legacy versions of Word. Opening files takes a little time, and the performance is limited (as you might imagine) by network connectivity.

Once files have been uploaded to the Windows Live site, they can be viewed online. Unlike Google Apps, which adds live collaboration to the various tools, Windows Live collaboration is done strictly from the online side. That is, you can't access collaborate directly from Word. You must do the writing locally and upload and download versions of the files, which is also the only way that reviewers can make changes to or comment on a file.

Sharing is done through the document workspace, which you access by clicking the Share button. You can send emails to both "editors" and "viewers" by using the corresponding address lines (see Figure 16.3).

Note that only people with Windows Live accounts can actually collaborate on files (as Editors), but anyone can view them (as Viewers). I discovered this when I attempted to share a file with someone who doesn't have a Windows Live Account. I entered the target recipient's email address on the Editors line. He didn't receive it. I then tried again, entering his email address on the Viewers line. That time he received it. The problem is easily remedied by having the other person sign up for a Windows Live account.

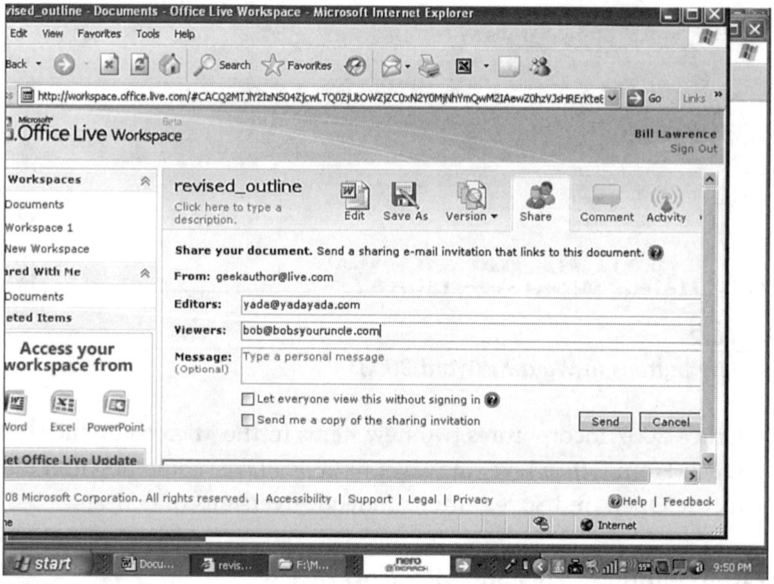

FIGURE 16.3
Sign-up page for Windows Live

Calendar

Windows Live Calendar, accessible via the web interface, is somewhat reminiscent of Outlook's calendar. In fact, Calendar will integrate with Outlook and Outlook users can accept or decline meeting invitations just as they would for those sent from Outlook itself. People who don't have Calendar must reply via email.

Calendar also has similar functions to set up appointments and events. For example, to create a meeting, just click a time slot in the day calendar (see Figure 16.4). From there, you can invite attendees via email, set a place for the meeting, specify a meeting type from a drop-down menu, and so forth. One nice feature is the ability to make an appointment private so that if the calendar is shared the appointment isn't visible. This is accessed through the Add More Details link.

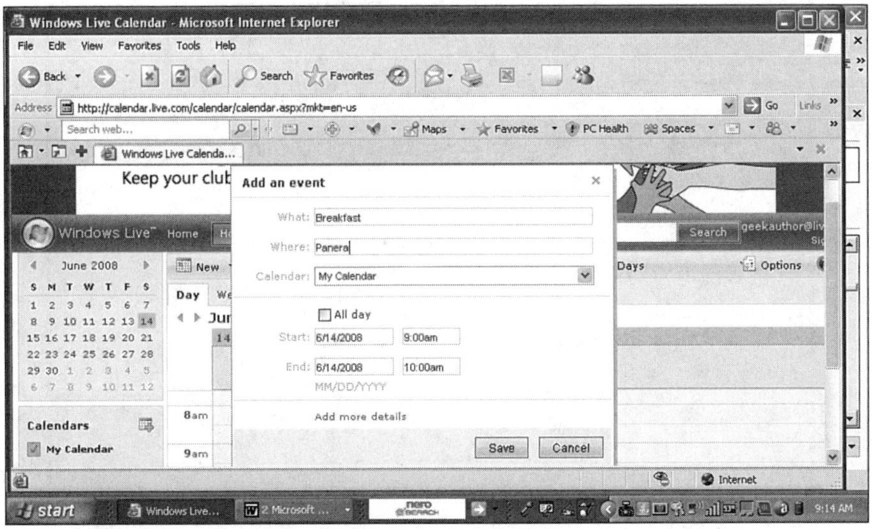

FIGURE 16.4

Creating an appointment in Windows Live Calendar.

Calendar supports the iCalendar format for calendar data exchange. This is also supported by most calendar applications, including Outlook 2007 and Apple iCal, as well as many websites. iCal files can be brought in through the Import button above the calendar. From there, you can browse to the iCal file.

You can share a calendar by clicking the Share button to open the Sharing tab, shown in Figure 16.5. You can choose to share a calendar with a group of fellow Windows Live account holder, email a view-only link (private URL) to your calendar (viewers do not need a Windows Live account), or make your calendar accessible to the public through a public link. Only users with a Windows Live account can add to or modify a calendar.

Spaces

Windows Live Spaces defines the real power of Windows Live. Spaces is a collection of applications that allows you to share files with other Windows Live account users that you specify. The following sections describe the features available on the various tabs of the Spaces main page (see Figure 16.6).

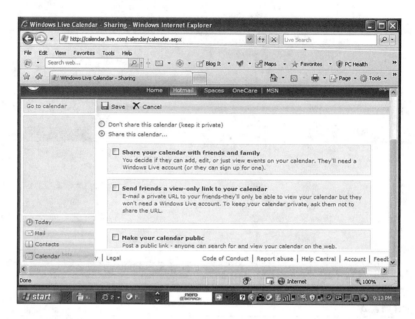

FIGURE 16.5

Sharing a calendar.

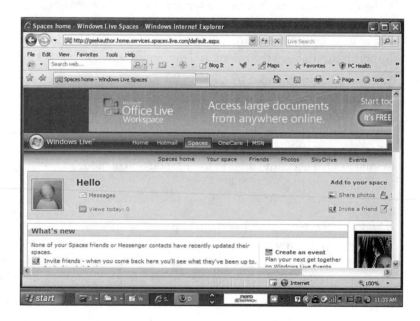

FIGURE 16.6

Spaces home page.

Your Space Tab

From the Your Space tab, you can control the various setup parameters (see Figure 16.7). Click Choose Web Address (you'll need to scroll to the left side of the screen to see this button) to set a generally accessible web address, which always takes the form http://*thenameyoupick*.spaces.live.com/default.aspx. This web page provides an access point for others to access blog entries, photos, and files that you set to public availability.

You can also click Edit Profile (on the left side of the screen) to set up your own "profile," which includes such personal information as the name (or alias) that you choose, as well as information about yourself that you want to share with the rest of the Internet. In addition, you can create lists of your favorite things, such as blogs, books, movies, and music, which you can share with the world.

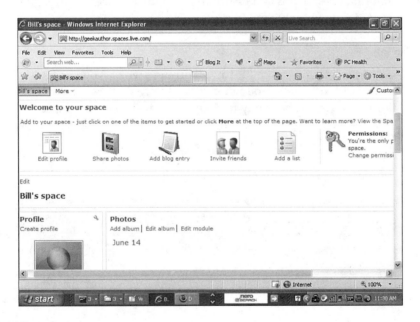

FIGURE 16.7
Your Space page.

The Your Space tab is also where you restrict permissions to your space by clicking the the Change Permissions link to the right of the screen. By default, it is publicly available on the Internet. However, you can restrict it to be accessible only to a set of users (with Windows Live accounts) that you choose. You can also restrict visibility of the web address to yourself.

Finally, you can also add blog entries to your Windows Live blog from this tab.

Friends Tab

The Friends tab is where you maintain your friends list and invite others to join and share files. The Invite Friends tool lets you invite people directly via email or add them through your contacts list. Once you've set up a list of friends, you and they can access each other's spaces to share photos, documents, videos, and other files.

Photos Tab

The Photos tab leads to a fairly typical photo-sharing facility, through which you can create various albums. One very nice feature is that it allows you to install drag-and-drop functionality through an additional IE ActiveX control. This provides a drag-and-drop space on a page, through which you can add multiple files. If you don't want to install this ActiveX control, you can browse to and upload individual files.

SkyDrive Tab

SkyDrive lets you create file folders through which you can share files, again either with a limited group or as a read-only set viewable by the world at large. This is a very handy tool with a limited-space device, such as the Eee PC. The ActiveX control that allows you to drag and drop multiple files to the photo albums also works here, so you can upload and share files easily (see Figure 16.8). This is one of the cases where an add-in ActiveX control provides significantly better capabilities.

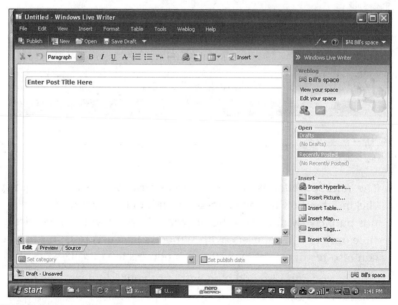

FIGURE 16.8

The bulk uploader, provided by the ActiveX control.

Events Tab

The Events tab leads to a very nice event planner (see Figure 16.9), with templates for various types of events such as birthday parties, anniversary parties, and family reunions. You can also change the layout of the events page that's generated. There is even a facility for adding a map. The whole thing can then be made visible to a select few or the Internet at large.

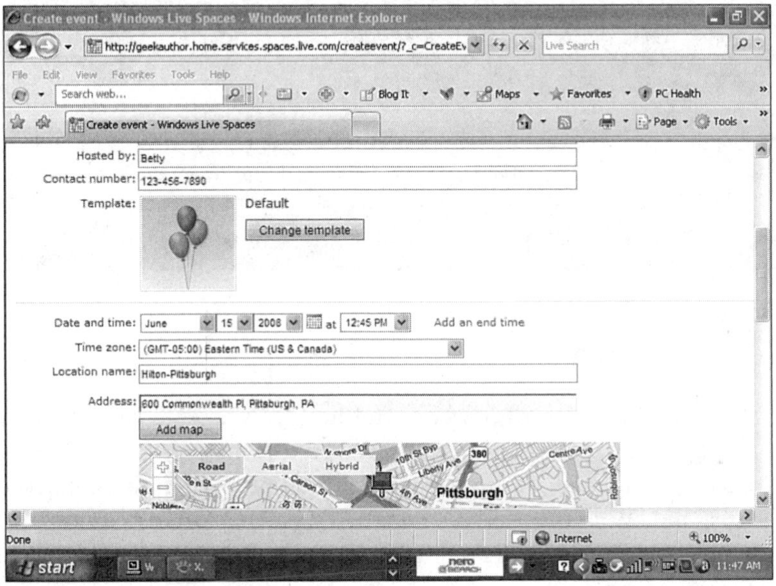

FIGURE 16.9
Events planner.

Hotmail

Hotmail is one of the long-time web standards for powerful, usable webmail applications (see Figure 16.10). From Hotmail, you can also easily access your calendar and contacts list. You'll find all the functions that you'd expect from a top-notch webmail application, including multiple folders, tools for managing your mail, and lots of customization features. There's also a more advanced view of Hotmail, but it doesn't work with screens even as large as 800×600 pixels. If you have an attached monitor, you can try this by clicking the Try The Full Version link at the bottom of the page.

FIGURE 16.10

Hotmail via Windows Live.

To appreciate the real power of Hotmail, you have to click the Options link (in the upper-right part of the window). That's where you can access all the tools, such as language settings, incoming mail processing rules, blocked sender lists, and even your "today" page settings. You can also automatically forward emails to another address or even, through Windows Live Mobile, send alerts to a mobile phone.

For example, if you click Automatically Sort Email Into Folders, you get a very Outlook-like rules editor that allows you to match emails coming in to filters that you create, and then presort them into folders (or delete them). For instance, you could sort all emails from your spouse into a folder with your spouse's name. By the same token, if you receive annoying forwards from a friendof a friend, you can send them right to the trash. You can also set the level of spam filtering from the Filters and Reporting function.

A serious shortcoming of Hotmail is that you can't activate POP3 without having a paid, premium Hotmail account. Given that practically every other free webmail system provides this (and usually IMAP support as well), this is one of the few real drawbacks to using Hotmail. Not having POP3 or IMAP means that you can't connect a third-party mail application, such as Thunderbird, to your Hotmail account.

Through the Contacts link on the main Hotmail page, you can access an Import Contacts link. This leads to a wizard that will walk you through the process of importing contacts lists form other mail or webmail systems. As you might expect, Hotmail can pull in a contacts list from either Outlook or Outlook Express. However, it can also read contacts lists from the likes of Yahoo Mail or any mail application that can export its contacts to a comma-separated values (CSV) file. Almost anything can write a CSV file, so you can even load contacts created through Google's Gmail if you like. Once again, there's an ActiveX control to assist with this, called the Contacts Importer, which you can download if you wish.

The Today page in Hotmail is the Windows Live version of the iGoogle page, but with a lot more Microsoft-centric content. It includes advertising for MSN content and news (again, only from MSN). You can't really change the content, and the only customization you can do is opt not to view it at all.

Messenger

Windows Live Messenger is Microsoft's chat application. As such applications go, it's loaded with features. There's an installer, which is an executable file that installs the chat application and configures Internet Explorer to use Messenger. You'll be prompted to load the installer as soon as you click any of the Messenger links from within Windows Live. Unlike the Google Chat function, there's no web interface to Messenger and no way to access it from another browser.

OneCare

Windows Live OneCare is an integrated, fee-based service that provides virus protection, online ID protection, printer sharing, and even content filtering. Unlike free applications, such as AVG or avast (see Chapter 15), or even commercial applications, such as Symantec or McAfee, OneCare includes multi-computer management and backup capabilities. It even provides online photo backup. If you are looking for a one-stop solution for all of these capabilities, you might consider OneCare.

Writer

Windows Live Writer is a downloadable blog editor. You can access it by clicking the Writer link (currently on the left side of the main Windows Live page).

To launch Writer, choose Start, All Programs, Windows Live, Windows Live Writer. Writer is a very competent blogging tool, with lots of advanced formatting features. It's actually superior to most of the online blogging tools and much more reminiscent of Google Docs than a mere blogging editor.

Live Writer includes formatting tools, on a Word-like toolbar, that correspond to HTML tags. For example, you can select block quotes, bulleted lists, and numbered lists directly from the toolbar. Heading tags are available from a drop-down list. There's even a very nice HTML table editor, again similar to what you might find in Word.

Writer excels at importing content, and has excellent map connectivity to Microsoft Virtual Earth. For example, the Insert>Map command launches Microsoft Virtual Earth, and once you've located the view that you want, you can just drop it in place into the blog entry.

You can save your draft until later, so you can work on blog entries in stages. When you're finished, it will publish directly to your Windows Live blog. You can even add Technorati blog categorization tags or set up tags for other blog search systems (see Figure 16.11).

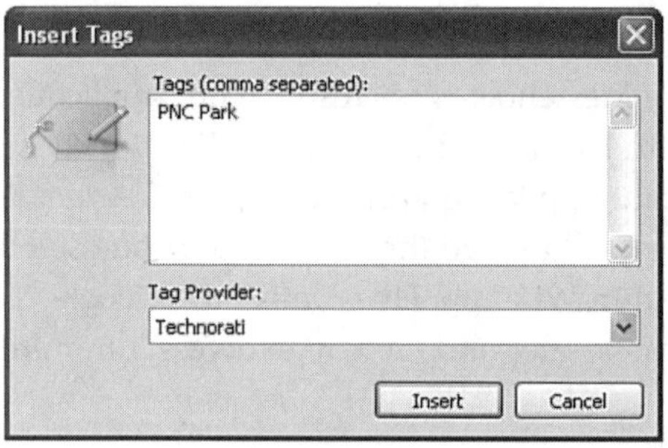

FIGURE 16.11

Windows Live Writer.

For those technically inclined, you can switch to a panel that shows the content in HTML (typically referred to as source code), and you can edit that code directly. There's also a preview function so that you can see exactly how the entry will appear in the Windows Live blog.

Summary

This chapter covered Windows Live, including the promise that it holds and the unfortunate reality of trying to use the current implementation on the Eee PC. You learned how to install it, some workarounds for using Windows Live on a small display, and what combinations of Microsoft Office and Internet Explorer work best.

I really wanted Windows Live to be much better than it is with the Eee PC. This could really be a great tool for Eee PC users, providing lots of online storage and useful online tools. Having a "SharePoint Lite" available on the Internet would be almost ideal, especially if you're an on-the-road worker that must collaborate with others who use Microsoft tools. Perhaps a later version of Windows Live will fulfill its promise.

Upgrading the Hardware

In this chapter, you'll learn how to speed up your Eee PC under Xandros with a utility that not only changes the clock speed, but also allows you to monitor the CPU temperature and control the CPU cooling fan. You'll also learn how to extend the capabilities of the Eee PC with a USB Bluetooth dongle and a USB GPS receiver. Finally, you'll learn how to expand the number of available USB connections by attaching a USB hub directly to the motherboard and mounting that hub within the Eee PC case. As an example of how this can allow for internal hardware expansion, you'll learn how to attach a USB device (in this case, a Bluetooth dongle) to the internal hub board.

Upgrading Memory

The memory hatch on the bottom of the Eee PC leads to the single memory socket. The Eee-PC uses DDR2 PC2-5300, 200-pin SODIMM memory. You can upgrade to 1GB or 2GB. Unless you're running Xandros, I suggest getting 2GB. Xandros can only use 1GB, so there's no sense wasting money on more than it can address.

Before you install memory, make sure that the Eee PC is off and the battery has been removed.

Overclocking the Eee PC 701 in Xandros

I continue to wait for a BIOS update that will allow you to adjust the speed of the 701 Eee PC's CPU. While in theory I agree with the idea that underclocking the CPU will extend battery life, there are times when I just want to crank the processor up to its full rating of 900 MHz. Fortunately, there finally is a utility for Xandros that gives you control over the processor clock rate and fan speed and lets you monitor the processor temperature: eeecontrol. Once again, this utility is the work of an EeeUser.com forum member, eee_and_me. You can find the thread about this utility and the download link at http://forum. eeeuser.com/viewtopic.php?id=19493&p=1.

After you download the program, simply right-click it in the File Manager (Launch, File Manager) and unpack it to any directory. You can install the .deb file either by double-clicking it or by entering the following from the command line:

```
> sudo dpkg -i /path/to/eeecontrol.0.2.1.deb
```

After installing eeecontrol, you can run it via Launch, Applications, Utilities, Eeecontrol 0.2. After you launch it, an eeecontrol icon (a black fan) appears on your panel. Click this icon and the eeecontrol panel pops up (see Figure 17.1). To control the processor speed with eeecontrol, click the Manual Control button. You are actually setting the Front Side Bus (FSB) value and not the actual megahertz. The default FSB value of 70 provides a CPU speed of 630MHz, which is the default. You can adjust the FSB value higher to increase the clocking speed of the processor. Be careful! Don't crank it up too much at first or you'll crash your Eee PC. If you want to clock it at 900MHz (or even 800MHz), make sure that you check the Activate Vmod check box.

I have my suspicions about the accuracy of the CPU temperature value. No matter what it has risen to, I can reset it to its starting value of around 54 degrees Celsius by just rebooting the computer. Admittedly, the CPU will begin to cool off as soon as the clock rate drops, but 10 degrees in a few seconds is a pretty hefty drop.

However, I am confident that the CPU speed increases when I increase the FSB value. I loaded a simple benchmarking program, xengine, that tests the efficiency of the X Window System. Although this is not a true CPU test, it should indicate higher efficiency if the CPU speed increases. It did, and its values increased with each CPU speed increase.

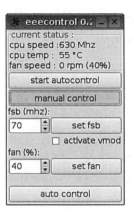

FIGURE 17.1

Eeecontrol's manual controls.

If you like eeecontrol, the Auto Control menu (see Figure 17.2) provides check boxes to automatically start it at PC startup and to run whatever autocontrol settings you make.

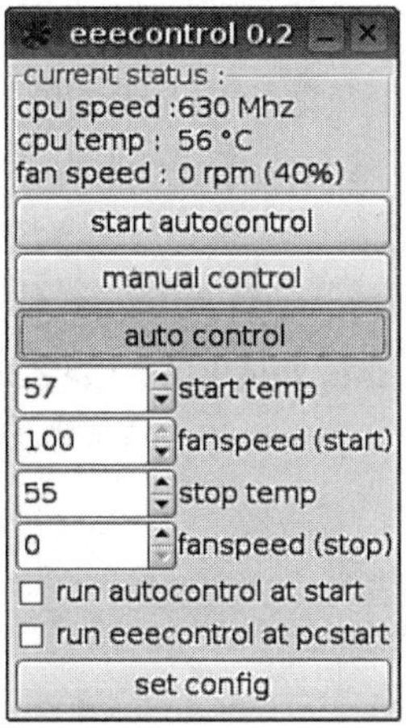

FIGURE 17.2

Eeecontrol's Auto Control menu.

Enabling Bluetooth

Enabling Bluetooth on the Eee PC is a trivial matter. Because the Bluetooth stack is built in to Xandros, all you need is a USB Bluetooth dongle. If you are going to use a mouse or keyboard, you need to enable support for that in the /etc/default/bluetooth file. Use your favorite editor (remember to preface the command with sudo) and open the file. For example:

```
> sudo nano /etc/default/bluetooth
```

Look for the line that says:

```
HIDD_ENABLED=0
```

and change it to:

```
HIDD_ENABLED=1
```

Save the file and then exit.

Issue this command to restart the stack:

```
> sudo /etc/init.d/bluetooth restart
```

Next, plug in your Bluetooth USB dongle and enter:

```
> sudo hciconfig
```

You should see something similar to the following output if the device has been detected:

```
hci0:   Type: USB
        BD Address: 00:00:00:00:00:00 ACL MTU: 0:0 SCO MTU: 0:0
        DOWN
        RX bytes:0 acl:0 sco:0 events:0 errors:0
        TX bytes:0 acl:0 sco:0 commands:0 errors:0
```

Note that the status was reported as being down. To bring it UP, enter:

```
> sudo hciconfig hci0: up
```

If your dongle has the almost-ubiquitous flashing blue light, that should commence flashing. Now that you have the dongle interface up, you need to find your device. Turn it on and then enter the following:

```
> sudo hidd --search
```

You should see something like the following output, indicating the devices in range and their addresses:

```
Searching ...
        Connecting to device 00:12:A1:63:07:DB
```

You should now be connected. If not, issue:

```
> sudo hidd —connect <addr>
```

where <addr> is the device address shown in the search.

If you want to shut down your USB dongle, enter:

```
> sudo hciconfig hci0: down
```

Using GPS in Xandros Linux

Unfortunately, at this point in development, the GPS navigation programs that are available for Xandros Linux are really not much beyond the toy and hobbyist category. Getting maps is tedious and the programs are not suitable for real-time car navigation. They are useful to a point in that they will track your position on maps.

To get most GPS applications working in Xandros, aside from a GPS receiver, you'll need to get GPSD and the GPSD client, as well as one of several available GPS applications—this section takes a look at both GpsDrive and Roadnav. While some GPS applications can actually connect to the GPS directly, having GPSD is a good approach because practically anything can work through GPSD.

First, you need to determine whether your GPS device is supported by GPSD. The best list is at the GPSd website, on its Compatible Hardware page: http://gpsd.berlios.de/hardware.html. I have two GPS receivers, the GlobalSat BU-353 and the Microsoft-labeled Pharos. Both work equally well, although the Pharos is smaller and can be attached directly to the side of the Eee PC, because it can be detached from the USB cable.

Getting gpsd and GpsDrive

To install gpsd and GpsDrive using the Synaptic Package Manager, follow these steps:

1. From Full Desktop, choose Launch, Applications, System, Synaptic Package Manager.
2. Click the Reload button, and then click in the packages list and type **gpsd**.
3. Mark both gpsd and gpsd-clients for installation.
4. Use the same method to find GpsDrive, and mark that for installation.
5. Find the festival and flite speech packages and mark those for installation.
6. Click Apply and wait a bit as Synaptic downloads and installs these packages.

Running gpsd

Next, you have to get gpsd running. Open a shell or terminal window (choose Launch, Run and enter **Konsole**). If you're using a USB-connected GPS receiver, enter the following command:

```
> gpsd /dev/ttyUSB0
```

If you have a Bluetooth unit (see "Enabling Bluetooth" earlier in this chapter), refer to http://gpsd.berlios.de/bt.html for instructions.

To see if the whole thing works, enter the following command:

```
> xgps &
```

xgps should launch and start reporting the present position of the satellites that your GPS device is using to pinpoint your position. If it's not working, check the GPSd website for troubleshooting information. If you stick with a GPS that's known to work (from the list on the GPSd site), this should be pretty fool-proof.

GpsDrive

Given it's inability to provide driving instructions, GpsDrive is a passive sort of GPS navigation program. It would be fine for a passenger in the car to check from time to time, but that's about it. It is interesting in that it does work with maps rather well and will track your position.

GpsDrive is the product of Jörg Ostertag and Fritz Ganter of Germany. It can plot out your position on a street or on a topographic (topo) map, although getting the topo maps has become something of a challenge. GpsDrive comes with a low-resolution world map, but that's it. However, downloading street maps is a cinch. At one point in its history, you could download topo maps as well from TopoZone and the option is still there. However, this option no longer works as TopoZone is now part of Trails.com and downloading the maps now requires a subscription fee.

The opening GpsDrive window shows your location on a world map, which at least tells you that your GPS device is running.

To download maps, simply click the Download Map button in the menu on the left side of the main GpsDrive window. You can select which Expedia you want to use (GpsDrive will download maps from either Expedia or Expedia Germany). Figure 17.3 shows the various maps scales you can select to download. These maps scales correspond to "zoom" levels. If you want to zoom in or out, you'll need to download a map to that scale. If you want to find other map sources, do a Google search for "maps" and "GpsDrive" and you'll find discussions on various forums that will help you find the currently best locations from which to download maps.

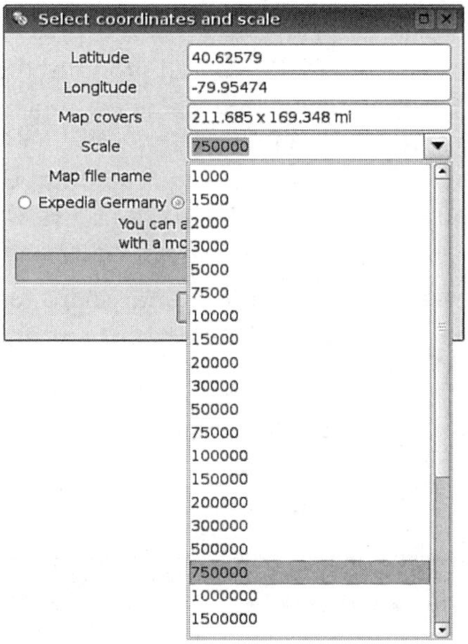

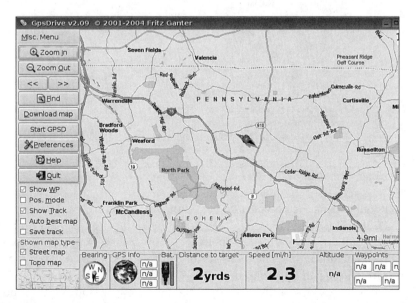

FIGURE 17.3

Downloading maps in GpsDrive.

Figure 17.4 shows GpsDrive in action, It accurately pinpoints your current location on a map and tracks your position, speed, and direction.

FIGURE 17.4

A typical map display on GpsDrive.

Roadnav

Roadnav is a much more full-featured program than GpsDrive, but it's very buggy on the Eee PC under Xandros. For example, it will go into an endless "recalculating path" loop if you ask it for driving instructions. Also, it has a tendency to crash while downloading map data. Unfortunately, it's also currently only really useful in the United States. However, it does function at a basic level and will, like GpsDrive, track your position against a map.

To get Roadnav, browse to http://roadnav.sourceforge.net/ and download the i586 Debian version. You can install it, once downloaded, by entering:

```
> dpkg -i /path/to/roadnav_0.19-1_i386.deb
```

Once installed, you can run it from the command line with:

```
> roadnav
```

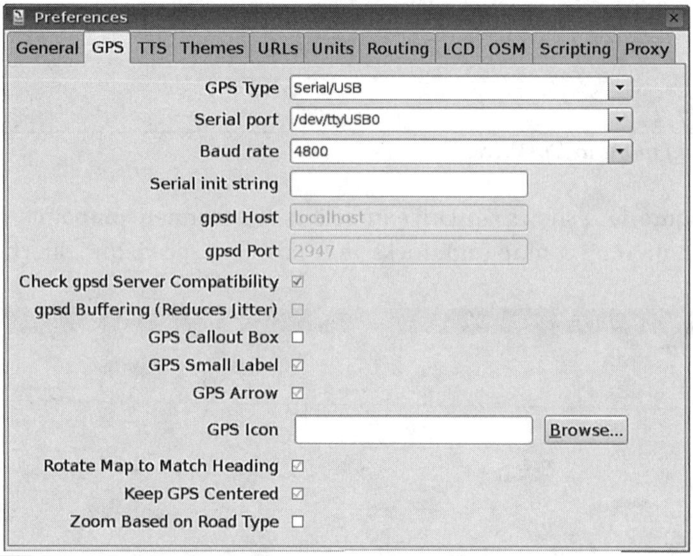

FIGURE 17.5

A typical display in Roadnav.

Roadnav has the potential to be a dandy navigation application on the Eee PC, but it isn't really "there" yet. You'll need to get maps first, and I suggest you pull down the TIGER (Topologically Integrated Geographic Encoding and Referencing) maps. These are vector-drawn street maps and are really quite nice. These can be accessed via Tools, Download TIGER/Line Maps(US). You'll get a county-by-county list, organized by state (see Figure 17.6), and you can click the county map you want. To select multiple maps, you can select a range with Shift+click or pick multiple maps with Ctrl+click. Note that using the scrollbars is very slow.

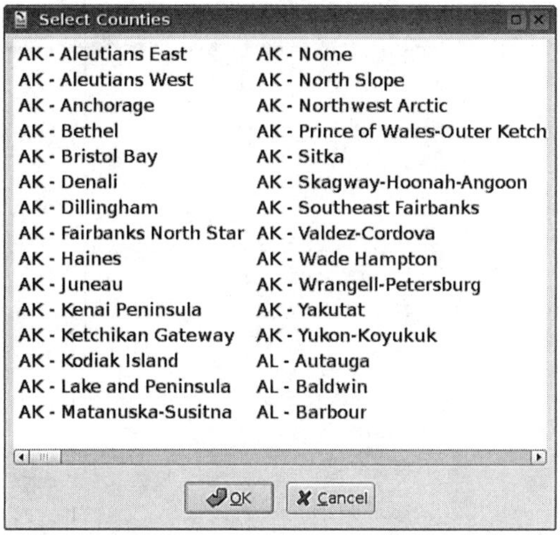

FIGURE 17.6

Roadnav's map-loading interface.

When I downloaded maps, Roadnav crashed after downloading a few and I had to restart. This was okay, because Roadnav highlighted the maps that I'd downloaded in the county list, but the process was tedious.

The View menu has some nice options, but also has some option that you should avoid. The GPS window gives you a display of your speed, position, heading, position, and current set of satellites. You can select to use the aerial photos, but beware: they will take a long time to download and will prevent you from doing anything else until they are all downloaded. They also eat up several megabytes of storage for each map.

Don't select the What's Nearby option. While the list is nice, Roadnav goes into an endless loop reloading the window. The 3D view option is, however, interesting and doesn't cause any harm.

Voice commands for driving directions can be provided via the flite speech synthesizer. If you want to use this, enter the following on the command line:

```
> flite &
```

From within Roadnav, select Tools, Preferences, Test TTS. Select Flite for the TTS type and then click Test Phrase to check the speech output (make sure your speakers are on).

Roadnav works quite well with GPSD, but if you wish you can set it to talk directly with the GPS. This is also set through the Preferences dialog box. If your GPS is USB, select Serial/USB in the GPS Type drop-down list, /dev/ttyUSB0 in the Serial Port drop-down list, and 4800 in the Baud Rate drop-down list (see Figure 17.7).

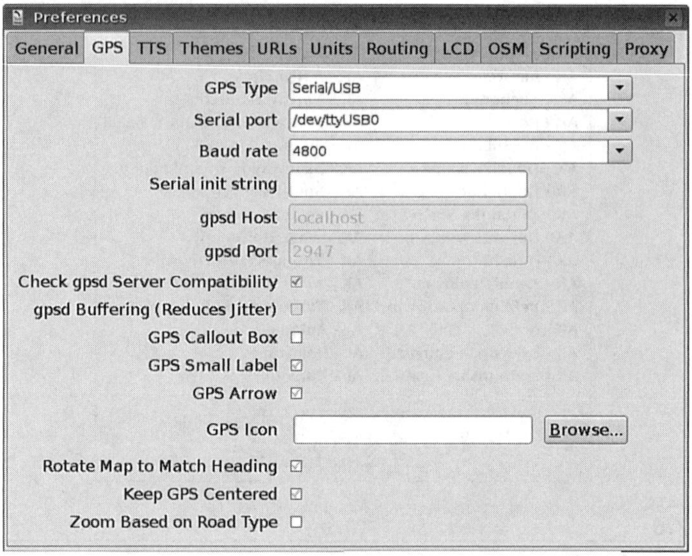

FIGURE 17.7

GPS parameters in Roadnav.

The Zoom buttons are reminiscent of web map viewers, and you can zoom in or out to any level with the TIGER maps. The detail is pretty good, including streams, rivers, county lines, states lines, and so forth.

You can try the Get Directions button if you dare. When I tried, it consistently went into an endless route recalculation loop, which, coupled with the flite voice, was a bit annoying.

While this software has some great features, it isn't very stable on the Eee PC under Xandros. There is an Ubuntu version, and it does run better under Ubuntu than under Xandros.

Using GPS in Windows: Microsoft Streets & Trips

Microsoft Streets & Trips is, for me at least, the defining application for the Eee PC. Combined with the Eee PC's tiny size and quality speakers, Microsoft Streets & Trips is a road warrior's dream come true. If you live in North America, Streets & Trips provides everything you need. If you're in the United Kingdom, Germany, Italy, or Spain, you can use the European version: AutoRoute. Either way, this will turn your Eee PC into a full-fledged navigation system.

Installing Streets & Trips

Installation is trivial, but the amount of space consumed is not. Because this is commercial software, you'll need access to a USB DVD reader. The North American version takes up just a bit over 900MB installed, which, on a 4GB SSD, is a bit daunting. Fortunately, you can install it on the MMC-SD drive

(E:), which makes this a lot more tolerable. What occupies the space is what makes it so powerful—the built-in map set. On the Linux side of things, maps are a one-at-a-time download and often originate from the U.S. Census Bureau. Although Census Bureau maps show streets, they don't show such essentials as one-way streets.

You should reboot the Eee PC after installation and before you plug in your GPS unit. Steets & Trips also installs the GPS drivers.

The version of Streets & Trips that I have came with its own Microsoft-labeled Pharos GPS receiver. Configuration was simply a matter of plug and play, and the system was up and running in seconds. I've used a lot of hand-held GPS devices, but the accuracy of the Pharos receiver was better than any of those. It was nearly in the pinpoint category.

Using Streets & Trips on the Eee PC

Frankly, my wife and I are map geeks, so navigating around the country has rarely been a problem. However, there have been times when we could have really used this combination. Like the time we were driving through rural Pennsylvania at dusk in a snow squall, and a snow-induced, multicar accident closed the road in front of us. The local police directed us to what was supposed to be an easy detour, but turned out instead to be a nerve-wracking 40-minute drive on dicey and unmarked farm roads. The Eee PC and Streets & Trips would have had us safely back on course almost at once.

To test the combination of the Eee PC and Streets & Trips, we took a family trip to a distant ice cream shop. I watched the display as my daughter drove, and it was really kind of eerie. The speed read-out on the Eee PC seemed glued to the needle on the speedometer. I know some of the elevations around our part of the world, and the altimeter seemed to be as accurate as the speed readout.

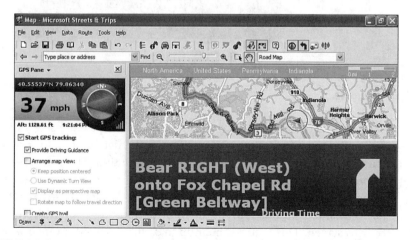

FIGURE 17.8

Typical navigational display in Streets & Trips.

The maps are really lovely and show quite a bit of detail. I tracked our progress down country roads, city streets, and a high-speed divided highway and the maps were dead on with their detail. The only unfortunate part of the trip was that we arrived at the site of what turned out to be a former ice cream shop, and we had to turn around and stop at one we had passed along the way.

Using Rerouting

I took that opportunity to map out a new course, deliberately taking back roads, and this time paying close attention to the voice instructions. Mapping the route was simply a matter of defining waypoints, which was easily done by clicking those points on the maps and then adding them into the route list.

We were off and running again, and the unit performed flawlessly. At this point, we began deliberately making wrong turns. The Eee PC speakers would announce that we were "Off route!" and then Streets & Trips would begin recalculating the route after about 0.2 miles in the wrong direction (see Figure 17.9).

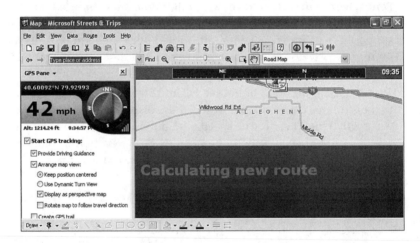

FIGURE 17.9

Recalculating route.

Over the next few days, I played with Streets & Trips extensively as I drove the 30.5 miles to or from work. On one instance, I deliberately took a much different route and ignored several attempts at rerouting. The software took only seconds to recalculate each route, even with the Eee PC's processor running in its usual underclocked mode.The native-mode display on the Eee PC 701 is just a little too cramped for all the information that's contained on the Streets & Trips screen. This reduces the map to a ribbon about an inch wide.

However, the AsTray Plus utility and the updated Intel driver, discussed in Chapter 15, give you the ability to nudge the screen resolution up just a bit and make the screen display close to perfect.

I live in a heavily forested part of the world, and I'm used to GPS devices losing contact with satellites. What surprised me with the Pharos was how rarely this happened. In several days of testing, I lost satellite contact only twice and regained it within seconds.

Frankly, if you are someone who's on the road a lot or you're planning a long trip, this one application alone makes a compelling argument for choosing a Windows-equipped Eee PC over the Linux version. If you're a travel writer or a photographer, imagine the combination of the Eee PC with either Streets & Trips or AutoRoute (the European version of Streets & Trips), Adobe Photoshop (or GIMP), and a lightweight word processor such as Microsoft Works or AbiWord. Given the wireless and video-conferencing capabilities of any of the Windows-capable Eee PC models, you'd have everything you need in a package that will fit in a large jacket pocket or a purse.

For serious car navigation, you'll need one of the car charger units currently on the market. The Eee PC's battery life will shorten your trip range to only a few hours without the charger. At last count, I had found two Eee PC chargers:

- Brando car charger for the Eee PC
- eXpansys AC Adaptor + Car Charger for ASUS Eee PC

Both eXpansys and Amazon sell the eXpansys, and a number of outlets carry the Brando unit.

The only thing that Streets & Trips lacks is topographic capabilities. Although Streets & Trips (as its name suggests) wasn't intended for this purpose, the Eee PC is small and lightweight enough that you could use it for geocaching if Streets & Trips could load topo maps. Having a topo capability would make this software and hardware combination the perfect choice for back country or field use, as well as road navigation.

Making Hardware Modifications: Internal USB Hub and Bluetooth

Everything so far in this chapter concerns things that you can do to control existing hardware or things that you can plug into the USB ports. This section is for anyone who wants to take their Eee PC to the next level of customization by tearing it apart and soldering new hardware directly to the motherboard. Risky? Oh yeah. This will definitely void your Asus warranty and, if you make a mistake, could turn your Eee PC into a paperweight. So, you are warned: neither I nor the publisher will take responsibility for anything that happens to your Eee PC if you follow these instructions. You're utterly on your own and bear the consequences of your actions.

If you're still game, here's something else to consider: All the places that you can solder to on the Eee PC to pick up USB Data+ and Data– connections are on surface-mounted device (SMD) pads or on the legs of SMD components themselves. These are really small soldering targets, and you need a precision, low-wattage soldering iron, good eyes (or a magnifier), plenty of light, and a little nerve. It's amazingly easy to bridge these small connections with a little solder, and the outcome could be very bad.

If you have never attempted soldering before, learn how to do it and practice on some old, worthless circuit boards before proceeding. The following assumes that you're comfortable with soldering and working with electronics in general. This is not a procedure for the absolute beginner.

The basic upgrade for the Eee PC is to add an internal USB hub, from which you can connect additional USB devices. For example, you can connect a Bluetooth dongle (which is the example covered in this chapter), one or more flash drives, an MMC/SD card reader, or anything else that runs on USB. The only catch is that it has to fit inside that itty-bitty case. If you think it must be cramped from looking at it on the outside, wait until you see it on the inside. There are, however, a few places where there's sufficient room for a small circuit card or something else. I found room for a hub card and the circuit card from the Bluetooth dongle. If you choose a smaller hub card, you can probably cram a few more things in there. Also, there's a little less free space inside a 900 series Eee PC than the 701.

Equipment List

The following is a list of the equipment you need to perform this modification:

- A low-power, fine-tipped soldering pencil. A temperature-controlled iron would be great, but if you don't have one, you can get by with a low-power unit. I bought one at my local Radio Shack for around $10.
- Silver solder, lead free with flux core, .032".
- 30 AWG wire. I simply cut up an old USB cable and pulled out the requisite red, green, white, and black wires.
- A solder pump or suction bulb (the pump works better). You'll need to do some desoldering in the course of this process, and you'll need to pull the excess solder away. Also, if you bridge something, you'll need to heat up that solder and suck it away from the board.
- A magnifier, with a light and "third hand." Although this is not absolutely necessary, I certainly regretted my decision to carry on without it. You should at least have some sort of magnifier to examine the solder connections.

- Unpowered USB hub, the smaller the better. Check your local big-box or discount store. You're looking for small and cheap. Mine was cheap, but could have been smaller. I had a capacitor that towered over the board like a skyscraper, and greatly limited the mounting possibilities in the Eee PC.

- Bluetooth dongle. I used a Cirago Bluetooth dongle, which was already as small as my thumbnail. Once freed from its case, it was no larger than a USB socket case.

- Wire cutters and fine gauge wire stripper.

- Small Phillips and blade head screwdrivers.

- Needle-nosed pliers (preferably magnetic).

Building the Mod

This mod requires that you complete the following:

1. Disassemble the USB hub and Bluetooth dongle cases and remove the circuit cards.

2. Solder connections from the Bluetooth dongle to the USB hub.

3. Test the hub and Bluetooth dongle.

4. Disassemble the Eee PC.

5. Solder connections from the hub to the Eee PC motherboard.

6. Mount the hub and Bluetooth dongle circuit cards in the Eee PC.

7. Reassemble the Eee PC.

8. Test the Bluetooth dongle.

Being the cautious sort, I built and tested my USB hub and Bluetooth arrangement before installing it in the Eee PC. That way, if something didn't work after the installation, at least I'd know that it wasn't in the Bluetooth or USB wiring itself and must be related to the connections on the motherboard. I picked a USB hub that was a bit too large, but it did have the advantage of having a case held together with screws. It had USB sockets that were stacked, which had both anchoring pins and connectors soldered to the board. This is where the solder pump comes in handy. To create the hub and dongle board assembly:

1. Carefully heat up the solder connections and then pull the solder away with the pump. A little solder will remain, and you may need to carefully pry the USB sockets free of the board.

2. Leave the USB cable attached to the board for now. You'll be able to plug the hub and Bluetooth dongle (or whatever peripheral you choose to install) into the Eee PC or another computer and test the whole arrangement. Also, you can use the wires in the cable to connect to the motherboard; simply snip off the end at an appropriate distance and then cut the insulating sheath and shielding off.

3. The Bluetooth dongle will probably pull apart easily with a pair of needle-nosed pliers. I just gently pried off the metal housing over the USB connection, and the circuit card pulled free of the plastic case.

USB connections use four standard wire colors:

Green: Data+

While: Data−

Black: Ground

Red: +5V

Their positions in a standard socket connector are shown in Figure 17.10, and you can use that to deduce which trace is which if you must solder directly to a connector. I was forced to do that to connect to the Bluetooth dongle board. A good practice is to double check your pin-configuration using a multi-meter.

A: +5 VDC, red
B: Data -, white
C: Data+, green
D: Ground, black

FIGURE 17.10

USB pinout.

4. Make sure that you twist and tin your wires before connecting. If you are connecting to traces on a USB connector, gently clean them with steel wool and then alcohol before soldering. Figure 17.11 shows connections solded to a Bluetooth dongle.

FIGURE 17.11

Bluetooth dongle board connections.

Disassembling the Eee PC

The Eee PC is actually not that hard to disassemble, but you must have a gentle touch and be very patient. There are many small connectors, latches, and so forth, and you must take your time to release them all. When removing the top pieces of the case, you need to be especially careful to slowly and gently flex the case plastic over the microphone and headphone jacks. When removing the motherboard, all of those USB, network, and VGA connectors must be taken into consideration when you flex the lower part of the case:

1. Unplug the Eee PC and remove the battery. Just spread the two latches on the bottom of the Eee PC and pull the battery toward the back until it's free.

2. Flip the Eee PC over and locate the three tiny metal latches at the top of the keyboard, two of which are shown in Figure 17.12.

3. Gently push the latches back toward the back of the case. They don't go very far, so push them just enough to release the keyboard.

4. Gently lift the keyboard up when the latches are disengaged. Don't pry at the keyboard. Use your fingers with a light touch. Also, don't lift the keyboard very far, because there is a ribbon cable that must be released.

FIGURE 17.12

Two of the three keyboard latches.

5. Locate the ribbon cable and, with the small blade screwdriver, gently lever the sides of the connector latches toward the keyboard recess space (see Figure 17.13). When both are unlatched, the keyboard ribbon cable will be free and you can set the keyboard aside.

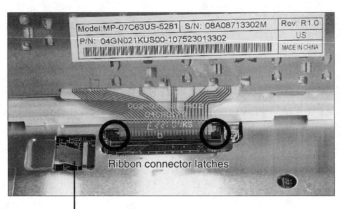

Blue pull-tab for lower ribbon connector

FIGURE 17.13

Ribbon cable connector latches.

6. Remove all eight of the small Phillips-head screws (see Figure 17.14) and set them aside. Some of them won't easily come out of their recesses, so use the needle-nosed pliers to help with this. Also, one of the screws is covered with tape that says you'll void your warranty if you break this tape. Once again, you've been warned!

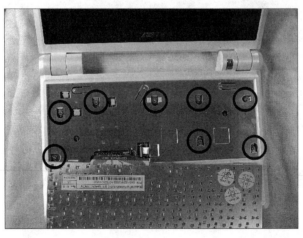

FIGURE 17.14

Remove all eight Phillips-head screws.

7. After you've removed the screws, note the blue pull tab on the ribbon connector (see Figure 17.13) that's visible in the opening. Gently pull the release tab away from the connector until it's free.

8. Flip the Eee PC on its back and remove the six screws on the bottom of the case (see Figure 17.15). Set these aside for later reassembly. All of the screws are the same size so you can just keep them together.

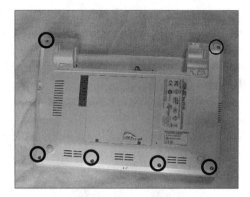

FIGURE 17.15

Remove all six Phillips-head screws on the bottom.

9. Flip the Eee PC back over and rock the display back as far as it will go. Carefully run a fingernail along the case seam starting at the back, and slowly pull the top of the case up. It will hang up on some plastic latches under the mouse button bar and around the headphone and microphone jacks. Gently pry the case over the headphone and microphone jacks. Keep going until the top pops free, and set it aside.

10. Gently free the two connectors on the top right of the motherboard. Once these connectors are loose, pull the motherboard up from the lower case while loosening the two metal latches holding the board in place. The latches are on the front (mouse button bar) side of the case. You'll need to gently flex the case to get around the various connectors. When the motherboard lifts a bit out of the case, flip the unit over so that the motherboard is lying on the display. Now you've reached your destination, and the soldering can begin.

Attaching the Hub and Dongle Assembly to the Motherboard

I picked pins 36 and 38 for the Data– and Data+ connections on the motherboard for the second PCI Express connector. The second connector is absent on my machine, which makes that a somewhat easier choice. There are lots of spots on both sides of the board to tie into for USB Data+ and Data–. A good guide to their locations is http://beta.ivancover.com/wiki/index.php/Eee_PC_Research.

That's the site I used to pick soldering points. However, there are lots of discussions of Eee PC mods on the various Eee PC forums.

If you wish to remove the mini-PCI Express card and memory, you can also do that. Just remember to reinstall them before reassembly. Seeing the Atheros wireless card lying on the table after putting the Eee PC back together is a bit of a disappointment.

If you look carefully on the Eee PC motherboard, you'll see labels for pins 20 and 50 on the PCI Express connections that will give you your bearings. Count from pin 50 back to pins 38 and 36 (see Figure 17.16). There isn't much room to spare here, so carefully tack the green wire (Data+) to pin 38 and the white wire (Data–) to pin 36.

Figures 17.17 and 17.18 indicate the positions for picking up the +5V and ground connections, respectively. These connections are a lot easier. I covered each of my connections with a little insulating tape, partly as a precaution against their moving and partly as strain relief.

FIGURE 17.16

USB Data+ (38) and Data– (36) soldering points.

FIGURE 17.17

+5 VDC connection.

FIGURE 17.18

Ground connection.

Mounting the Hub and Bluetooth Dongle

The next challenge is where to mount things. I picked the open area under the memory hatch on the bottom side of the case, which is a great choice for the Eee PC 701. However, if you have a 900 series Eee PC, you'll need to find another location. I mounted the USB hub board onto the hatch door with double-sided tape and covered the side facing the motherboard with insulating tape.

I mounted the board from the Bluetooth dongle directly to the top of a USB connector with double-sided tape (see Figure 17.19). That turns out to be a good location, because I can also see the flashing blue light around the gap in the case for the USB connection. Also, it places it near the side of the case, which should reduce interference.

FIGURE 17.19

Bluetooth dongle perched on the USB connector.

Reassembling the Eee PC

To reassemble the Eee PC:

1. Double check that your wiring is done and that your mounting is secure.

2. Reinsert the motherboard back into the base of the case and reconnect all of the connectors on the motherboard. Be especially careful to reconnect the fan connector as it's easily missed.

3. Carefully flex the case to clear the connectors, and make certain that none of your wiring is caught between the case and the motherboard.

4. Place the top half of the case back over the bottom half and carefully snap it into place.

5. Grab the blue pull tab for the ribbon cable connector through the opening, and gently push it back into the socket.

6. Install all of the screws, front and back, to secure the case.

7. Reconnect the ribbon cable for the keyboard, and when it's pushed back in its socket, carefully push the connectors back (use the small blade screwdriver) to lock it in place.

8. Gently lay the keyboard back into its recess to latch it in place.

9. Slide the battery back into position.

10. Turn on the Eee PC. If you did everything correctly, the USB peripheral you installed should be active. If you did install a Bluetooth dongle, refer to the "Enabling Bluetooth" section to activate it under Xandros. If you're running Windows, install your Bluetooth drivers.

Summary

This chapter covered ways to expand your Eee PC. Even though there are no expansion slots in the Eee PC, there's a wide range of peripherals you can add via USB connections. It also covered how to add to the expansion possibilities for the Eee PC by soldering a USB hub to the motherboard and, as an example, attaching a Bluetooth dongle to the hub.

You also learned how to overclock your Eee PC under the default Xandros operating system. Hopefully, at some point, Asus will make a BIOS update available that will let you set the processor speed from the bios, and you won't need a third-party utility.

Index

FREE Online Edition

Your purchase of **Using the Asus Eee PC** includes access to a free online edition for 45 days through the Safari Books Online subscription service. Nearly every Que book is available online through Safari Books Online, along with over 5,000 other technical books and videos from publishers such as Addison-Wesley Professional, Cisco Press, Exam Cram, IBM Press, O'Reilly, Prentice Hall, Que, and Sams.

SAFARI BOOKS ONLINE allows you to search for a specific answer, cut and paste code, download chapters, and stay current with emerging technologies.

Activate your FREE Online Edition at www.informit.com/safarifree

> **STEP 1:** Enter the coupon code: CZNA-8W1L-YWNB-QDLF-591K.

> **STEP 2:** New Safari users, complete the brief registration form.
> Safari subscribers, just login.

If you have difficulty registering on Safari or accessing the online edition, please e-mail customer-service@safaribooksonline.com